WOMEN IN JAPANESE RELIGIONS

WOMEN IN RELIGIONS

Series Editor: Catherine Wessinger

Women in Christian Traditions
Rebecca Moore

Women in New Religions
Laura Vance

Women in Japanese Religions
Barbara R. Ambros

Women in Japanese Religions

Barbara R. Ambros

NEW YORK UNIVERSITY PRESS

New York and London

NEW YORK UNIVERSITY PRESS
New York and London
www.nyupress.org

References to Internet websites (URLs) were accurate at the time of writing.
Neither the author nor New York University Press is responsible for URLs
that may have expired or changed since the manuscript was prepared.

ISBN: 978-1-4798-2762-6 (hardback)
ISBN: 978-1-4798-8406-3 (paperback)

For Library of Congress Cataloging-in-Publication date, please contact the
Library of Congress

New York University Press books are printed on acid-free paper,
and their binding materials are chosen for strength and durability.
We strive to use environmentally responsible suppliers and materials
to the greatest extent possible in publishing our books.

Manufactured in the United States of America

10 9 8 7 6 5 4 3 2 1

Also available as an ebook

For my mother, the strongest woman I know

CONTENTS

ACKNOWLEDGMENTS

It is impossible to acknowledge everyone who has supported me throughout this project. I have benefited greatly from their suggestions, and I hope that they will feel gratified by seeing this book in print. I am especially grateful to Cathy Wessinger and Helen Hardacre for urging me to take on this project. Cathy also provided much encouragement and many insightful comments as the manuscript progressed. Randall Styers, Laurie Maffly-Kipp, Sarah Shields, and several other colleagues at the University of North Carolina at Chapel Hill offered helpful suggestions on how to frame the project. I owe a special debt of gratitude to Mark McGuire, Rebecca Mendelson, Matt Mitchell, and two anonymous readers for commenting extensively on the manuscript. And I am particularly grateful to my students at UNC Chapel Hill who have explored this topic with me in the classroom. I would also like to convey my gratitude to Suzuki Kōtarō and Nogawa Yurie for their assistance in obtaining images from the Itsukushima Shrine.

As the project progressed, the North East Asia Council at the Association of Asian Studies, the Japan Foundation, the Triangle Center for Japanese Studies, and the McLester Fund in the Department of Religious Studies at UNC Chapel Hill provided essential financial support for several research trips to Japan. I would also like to thank the Institute for Religion and Culture of Nanzan University for hosting me during a trip in the summer of 2011, when conditions in the Kantō region were uncertain due to the March 11, 2011, triple disaster. The Burkhardt Fellowship of the American Council of Learned Societies and the National Humanities Center allowed me to complete this manuscript under optimal conditions. The University Research Council at the University of North Carolina at Chapel Hill, the Triangle Center for Japanese Studies, and the Japan Foundation provided seminal funding for image permissions and other production costs associated with this book.

Finally, I would like to acknowledge my friends and family: Shibasaki Hiroyo for our enlightening conversations about Japanese women and religion; Ogasawara Ryūgen and his family for generously assisting me during research in Matsumoto; Nishino Kazue for hosting me in Kanazawa; and Shinoda Kazue and Kōji, who opened their home to me during my lengthy research stays in Tokyo, and especially to Kazue for exploring the beauty of the Kumano mountains with me. Most of all, I would like to thank my husband for being so supportive throughout this project.

Introduction

Why Study Women in Japanese Religions?

In 1911, Hiratsuka Raichō (1886–1971), one of Japan's early feminists, wrote in the opening issue of the women's journal *Bluestocking*, "In the beginning, woman was the sun. An authentic person. Today she is the moon. Living through others. Reflecting the brilliance of others."[1] Hiratsuka seemed to be alluding to the female gender of the Japanese sun goddess, Amaterasu, who, according to Japanese mythology, ruled over the heavenly plain and established the imperial lineage. Hiratsuka was suggesting that during a primordial age women were once powerful and self-reliant but somehow lost their independence over the course of history. Years later she explained in her autobiography, "To be sure, the sun and the moon symbolized the objective realities of women's history—the breakdown of a matrilineal society and the rise of a patriarchal system; the tyranny of men and subjugation of women; the gradual decline of a woman's status as a human being."[2] In 1948 she amended her statement after the promulgation of the new Japanese constitution, which gave women unprecedented equal rights, saying, "Now, thirty-seven years later, I am overjoyed, and want to cry out: 'Look! The day has come! Now is the time. A big, big sun is shining out from the hearts of Japanese women!' "[3]

This book is intended as an important corrective to more common male-centered narratives of Japanese religious history. It presents a synthetic long view of Japanese religions from a distinct angle—women's history—that has typically been discounted in standard survey accounts of Japanese religions. It also provides a framework for existing works on women in Japanese religions, which are usually microhistories and lack the comprehensive perspective that only the *longue durée* can provide. Despite its focus on women, this volume resists a narrative of mythical independence that is shattered by historical oppression and then, conversely, overturned by modern liberation. Such a narrative is seductive, but ultimately it essentializes the diverse experiences of women of different social backgrounds over the vast span of Japanese history. Instead, this book explores a diverse collection of writings by and about women to investigate the ways ambivalent religious discourses in Japan have not simply subordinated women but also given them religious resources to pursue their own interests and agendas.

Scholars have widely acknowledged women's persistently ambivalent treatment within the Japanese religious traditions, including Shinto, Buddhism, Confucianism, Christianity, and new religious movements. In the case of premodern Japanese Buddhism, Bernard Faure, a scholar of religion, has eloquently surveyed and articulated this ambivalence.[4] However, while Faure has rightfully cautioned scholars against idealizing the Buddhist tradition for its egalitarian potential and removing it from the social and historical realities of its Japanese context, his work falls in line with much existing scholarship—particularly Japanese scholarship influenced by Marxist paradigms—that depicts religion as a mere means of oppression, especially for women. This raises the question of how ambivalent and even overtly misogynistic religious discourses on gender have still come to inspire devotion and emulation among women.

As the anthropologist Saba Mahmood has argued, universalized assumptions of patriarchal domination have led feminist scholars to question why women "assert their presence in . . . male-dominated [religious] spheres while . . . the very idioms they use to enter these arenas are grounded in discourses that have historically secured their subordination to male authority."[5] Mahmood contends that it is more useful to explore the matrix of concerns within which women have deployed doctrinal frameworks, networks, and institutions than to conclude that these women have merely internalized "patriarchal norms"[6]—or that they have become, in Faure's parlance, "the 'spokespersons' of a dominantly male tradition."[7] Dorothy Ko, a historian of China, has made a similar argument, showing that only when women affirm patriarchal values for their own reasons and transmit them to the next generation is their continued implementation guaranteed.[8] The Japanese sociologist Ueno Chizuko likewise has argued that in patriarchal societies, women often support the status quo in hopes of eventually gaining power as the mother of the next patriarch. Thus, "reproduction of the patriarchal system is not possible without the cooperation of women."[9]

By viewing Japanese religious history through the eyes of women, this text presents a new narrative that offers strikingly different vistas of Japan's pluralistic traditions than the received accounts foregrounding male religious figures and male-dominated institutions. For instance, many traditional versions of Japanese religious history give considerable attention to monastic or priestly lineages, which largely excluded women. Such patriarchal lineages do not play a central role in this book's narrative. It emphasizes instead issues that transcend purely sectarian concerns: female divinities as the embodiments of ideal femininity and sources of political legitimation; changing definitions of female monastic renunciation; female shamans and their links to marginality and political authority; perceptions of women as emblems of defilement and demonic power; the religious implications of the fluctuating definitions of marriage and inheritance rights; and the movement toward and contestations of gender equality in the modern era.

Comprising nine chapters organized chronologically, the survey begins with the archeological evidence of fertility cults in prehistoric Japan and ends with an examination of the influence of feminism and demographic changes on religious practices during the "lost decades" of the post-1990 era. By examining the *longue durée* of Japanese religions, this book demonstrates that key factors often cited as sources of women's oppression in Japan—for example, the taboos associated with menstrual blood, the patrilineal household, and the exclusion of women from the political sphere—have not been fully hegemonic through all periods of Japanese history, nor have they been unchanging. In order to avoid essentializing the religious experiences of women across Japanese history, it stresses that there are considerable variations across different time periods in the religious and economic roles of women based on class differences, regional idiosyncrasies, and the diversity of Japan's religious traditions.

Moreover, this text is not conceived as a narrative of oppressed, passive, weak Japanese women liberated by modern, feminist, Western thought. It not only pays attention to the agency of Japanese women who have resisted, subverted, or actively employed patriarchal ideologies to promote their own interests, but it also includes in its analysis the growing volume of Japanese feminist scholarship on women and religion that has flourished in the aftermath of second-wave feminism in 1970s Japan. As Japan has developed its own feminist movement and has shifted from a predominantly agrarian society to a highly urbanized, industrialized society, religious organizations and religious specialists have struggled to come to terms with changing roles for women—sometimes challenging patriarchal traditions and sometimes embracing traditional gender roles with nostalgia.

Finally, a brief note on Japanese names is also due. Japanese names appear in the customary Japanese order: family name followed by given name. When a person is referred to by a single name, premodern individuals are often referred to by their given name, whereas modern individuals are generally referred to by their surname. This text follows these conventions except in cases in which it is necessary to distinguish between members of the same family.

1

The Prehistorical Japanese Archipelago

Fertility Cults and Shaman Queens

We may ask ourselves when we should begin our narrative of women in the religious history of Japan. One recent survey of premodern Japanese religions begins in 500 CE, around the time when Buddhism was first introduced to the Japanese islands. The author argues that our knowledge of Japanese history prior to that date relies almost exclusively on elusive archeological material rather than textual sources; therefore, our knowledge of the concrete details of prehistorical people's lives is sharply limited.[1] To this we may add that we cannot really speak of Japan as a nation prior to 500 CE because such an entity did not exist yet. Instead, we must consider the Japanese archipelago as a geographic location and assess the evidence accordingly. Despite these reservations, we will include the period before 500 CE, even though a reconstruction of religion in women's lives in the archipelago's prehistory can only be highly speculative. In our examination of the archeological and limited textual evidence from these periods, we will address important questions and issues that are raised by the material. Here, we will single out two important facets of prehistory that speak to women and religion: female clay figures from the Jōmon period (ca. 10,000 BCE–300 BCE) and the story of Himiko, the Queen of Wa, from the Yayoi period (300 BCE–300 CE).

Female Clay Figurines in the Jōmon Period

Our knowledge of the hunter-gatherer society of the Jōmon period derives from the remains of pit dwellings, shell mounds, and burial grounds. The most significant evidence related to women is the great number of clay vessels and figurines discovered in these settlements. Many of the clay implements have clearly female characteristics such as prominent breasts, wide hips, and protruding abdomens (see figure 1.1). Some implements are vases that may have served as lamps;[2] others are figurines that seem to have been deliberately smashed into pieces and scattered about.[3]

What are we to make of these figurines and their broken condition? The human figurines may have been used in healing rituals, and could have been broken in order to effect healing from illness; the broken pieces may have had a talismanic function. Indeed, the use of ritual figurines for such healing purposes can be traced to later periods, such as the Yayoi period (300 BCE–300 CE), when figurines made of wood or straw came into use, and the Heian period (794–1185), when paper effigies were used for exorcisms.[4] While this interpretation suggests that (female?) shamans performed healing rituals—including perhaps rituals ensuring safe childbirth—it does not fully explain why so many of the figurines were female and appeared pregnant.

Another common interpretation favors the idea that the figurines were used in fertility rituals rather than in healing rituals. The figures may have been linked to human reproduction. Many clay figures depict the pregnant female form; some even contain a small clay ball inside the hollow female womb. Phallic stone rods from the same period were also discovered.[5] Therefore, the archeologist Imamura Keiji conjectures that "ceramic figurines are probably related to reproduction and fertility cults, and the prosperity of future descendants."[6] Fecundity may also have included agricultural fertility. The figures may have been linked to the cult of Mother Earth. While few such figures can be dated to the early Jōmon period, the majority date from the middle to late Jōmon period after 5500 BCE, when a hunter-gatherer society gradually began to incorporate rudimentary slash-and-burn agriculture. The figurines may have represented a female food divinity whose body needed to be broken to harness her fertility.[7]

FIGURE 1.1. *Dogū* (clay figurine). The enlarged breasts and wide hips
suggest that this figurine was a fertility symbol. Japan, final Jōmon
period (ca. 1000–300 BCE). Earthenware, H. 2 ¼ in. (5.7 cm); W. 1 ⅞
in. (4.8 cm). Gift of Mr. and Mrs. Jerome Koizim, 1978 (1978.346a-
c). The Metropolitan Museum of Art, New York, NY, U.S.A. Image
copyright © The Metropolitan Museum of Art. Image source:
Art Resource, NY.

This interpretation draws on myths from the ancient national
chronicles of Japan, the *Kojiki* (712 CE) and the *Nihon shoki* (720 CE),
which contain the earliest extant written records of Japanese mythology. According to the version in the *Kojiki*, Susanoo, the violent storm
god and brother of the sun goddess Amaterasu, visits Ōgetsuhime and

asks her to serve him food. She proceeds to take various types of nourishment out of her bodily orifices—her nose, mouth, and anus—and
serves them to Susanoo. Offended by her actions and convinced that
this food is polluted, Susanoo flies into a rage and kills her. Various
products grow out of her dismembered body: silkworms from her head,
rice from her eyes, millet from her ears, red beans from her nose, wheat
from her genitalia, and soy beans from her anus. Another deity, Kami-
musubi, collects these in order to have them planted.[8]

The *Nihon shoki* contains a similar myth. Here, the moon god Tsukiyomi, another brother of Amaterasu, is dispatched by the sun goddess to call on the goddess Ukemochi. Ukemochi faces the land and
produces boiled rice from her mouth. She then turns to the ocean and
produces fish from her mouth. Finally, she turns to the mountains and
produces wild animals from her mouth. She serves Tsukiyomi a meal
prepared from these items. Like Susanoo, he reacts with anger and kills
her. Enraged by his offense, Amaterasu banishes him from her sight and
sends another god, Amekumabito, to Ukemochi. He finds that Ukemochi's dismembered body has produced oxen and horses from her head,
two types of millet from her forehead and her eyes, silkworms from her
eyebrows, rice from her belly, and wheat and beans from her genitalia.
Amaterasu orders that these items be cultivated in order to feed and
clothe human beings.[9]

These myths might explain why the clay figurines were smashed.
Perhaps they were used in rituals that were meant to ensure the fertility of the land and the sea. However, there are also problems with
this interpretation. During the Jōmon period, agriculture and animal
husbandry were, at best, in their infancy. Yet the myths refer to the five
grains, horses and oxen, and sericulture—all of which were introduced
much later from the Asian continent. While Jōmon people would have
hunted, fished, and cultivated tubers and nut-bearing trees,[10] they
would not have grown rice or raised silkworms. While they had domesticated hunting dogs and may have begun to domesticate boars,[11] they
certainly did not keep horses and oxen. It is of course possible that as

new forms of agriculture and animal husbandry were introduced, symbols from the Asian continent were layered over an earlier myth.[12] Nevertheless, the slaying of a food goddess could hardly have had the same symbolism for people living during the Jōmon period as it did during the time when the myths were recorded in writing.

There is another important issue we might want to consider here: does the archeological and mythological evidence suggest that Jōmon people—or at least the writers of the later myths—celebrated the fecundity of women, in contrast to the later focus, as we shall see, on ritual pollution associated with women, pregnancy, and menstruation? In the two myths, the female body, though suspected of pollution by the male god, yields valuable sustenance: grains, beans, game, fish, and silkworms. In later periods, the cultivation of the five grains (and the domestication of livestock) was constructed as male labor, while the raising of silkworms was considered the domain of women, as it had been in China. For instance, the *Nihon shoki* states that in 507 CE, the Emperor Keidai proclaimed,

> We have heard that if men are of fit age and do not cultivate, the Empire may suffer famine; if women are of fit age and do not spin, the Empire may suffer cold. Therefore is it that the sovereigns cultivate with their own hands, so as to give encouragement to agriculture, while the consorts rear silkworms themselves, so as to encourage the mulberry season. How, then, shall there be prosperity if all, from the functionaries down to the ten thousand families, neglect agriculture and spinning?[13]

Thus, the fruits yielded by the female body of the goddess were supposed to be cultivated by both men and women.

Other rituals linked to female fertility have also been documented beginning in the Middle Jōmon period: the burial of placenta and umbilical-cord pots (*umegame*). This practice continued into later periods as well. In contrast to contemporaneous burial jars, which were buried with the opening facing downward in the center of abandoned pit dwellings, placenta and umbilical-cord pots were interred facing up under the threshold of dwellings. Some scholars believe that the pots may have been placed there to induce fertility in the women who crossed the threshold, but it is also possible that they had a protective function for the child. Placenta pots from the eighth century were discovered similarly buried under thresholds of houses and contained offerings for the well-being and success of the child.[14] In either case, the human tissues issued during childbirth were considered talismanic rather than polluted. They were kept close to human dwellings rather than spatially shunned.

Pollution →

Despite the positive valuation of the female body, the dismembering of the food goddess and the smashing of the figurines can still give us pause. The breaking of the female body may have symbolized the violence inherent in cultivating the soil: the burning, clearing, and tilling of the land.[15] Even if we assume that the ritual was not primarily focused on agriculture but on hunting and fishing, such practices likewise involved violence such as the killing and dismembering of prey. In the later myths, the perpetrators of such violence are male—the storm god Susanoo and the moon god Tsukiyomi, respectively. This suggests a dynamic between a female sacrificial victim and a male aggressor. From a modern perspective, this may not seem like a positive celebration of women's reproductive faculties even if the outcome benefits humanity as a whole by providing nourishment for all. In the absence of contemporaneous textual sources, the clay figurines remain highly enigmatic and open to a wide range of interpretation.

Himiko, Queen of Wa

The figure of Himiko is equally if not more enigmatic. Scholars have been debating for several centuries whether her principality, Yamatai, was located in Kyushu or in the central Kinai region of Honshu, whether she was an imposing ruler in the imperial line or only a shaman in a minor chiefdom, whether she was a powerful leader or a recluse

propped up through Chinese support, whether she illustrates matriarchal rule through female spiritual power or rule by a male-female pair
that balanced the binary opposites of *yin* and *yang*.

Himiko first appears in the *Wei zhi* (ca. 297). According to this Chinese chronicle, the country of Yamatai was ruled by a queen called
Himiko, whose investiture saved the country from constant warfare. She
was eventually succeeded by a female relative named Iyo, whose reign
also ensured political stability:

> Before that polity had a male ruler. Seventy or eighty years ago, year after
> year in the Wa polity there was chaos as they fought each other. Then
> they made a female the ruler, named Himiko. She was skilled in the Way
> of Demons, keeping all under her spell. Although well along in years,
> she remained unmarried. A younger brother assisted her in governing
> the domain. Once she became the ruler there were few people who saw
> her. One thousand maidservants waited on her and only one man. He
> served her food and drink and carried her messages in and out. She lived
> in a palace resembling a stockade, normally protected by armed guards.
> . . . Himiko died and a large mound was built more than 100 paces in
> diameter. Over 100 male and female attendants were immolated. Then a
> male ruler was installed, but in the ensuing protests within the domain
> bloodshed and killing exterminated more than 1000 people. To replace
> Himiko a 13-year-old [female] relative named Iyo was made ruler of the
> domain. Stability prevailed.[16]

In addition, the text describes Himiko's diplomatic contacts with Wei
China. This tributary relationship yielded a proclamation in 238 CE
declaring that "Himiko, queen of Wa, is designated a friend of Wei." In
return for presenting tribute consisting of male and female slaves and
cloth, Himiko's envoys were richly presented with luxurious textiles,
gold, pearls, cinnabar, two swords, and one hundred bronze mirrors.
In formal expression of their hierarchical relationship, Himiko was
awarded the title "Ruler of Wa Friendly to Wei," and was sent a gold

seal with a purple ribbon as a sign that Wa was a tributary state. Over the next ten years, Himiko remained in diplomatic contact with the Wei court, sending further tribute and receiving rhetorical support during conflict with a male ruler in a neighboring domain. Her successor, Iyo, continued this tributary relationship with Wei.[17]

The location of Himiko's chiefdom has been debated since the early eighteenth century. The debate came about because of the conflicting directions given in the *Wei zhi*. If followed literally, the text sends travelers almost due south from the Korean peninsula. The traveler would end up in the ocean. This means that the text is mistaken about either the direction of the travel or the distances traveled. If the direction of travel is shifted east rather than due south, the traveler arrives in the Kinai region. If the distances are shortened, the traveler ends up in Kyushu. Scholars have advanced archeological evidence of fortified settlements, large tombs, and discoveries of Chinese mirrors to prove the location of Yamatai, but the controversy remains unresolved to this day. Some historians have equated Himiko's Yamatai with Yamato in the Kinai region of central western Japan, which later became the power base of the Japanese imperial line. This interpretation bolsters claims concerning the antiquity of imperial rule, but it has also raised questions about the power and independence of Japan's imperial rulers, whose state was suddenly reduced to a tributary chiefdom subservient to Wei. Other scholars favored the view that Yamatai was located in northern Kyushu, where we also find a location named Yamato in the modern era. This allowed some scholars to dissociate Himiko from the imperial line. The preservation of imperial prestige was especially important to scholars during the late nineteenth and early twentieth centuries.[18]

The identity of Himiko has also been the topic of a heated debate. Scholars tend to interpret the name Himiko as a title rather than a personal name. The Chinese may have tried to transliterate a title that resembled *hime-miko, hi-miko,* or *hi-meko* in Japanese. This implies that "Himiko" could have been referring to her royal lineage, her religious function as a shaman (*miko*), and/or her link to the cult of the sun (*hi*).[19] Himiko indeed seems to have been a shaman,[20] as the Chinese text states that she practiced *gui dao* (in Japanese, *kidō*), the way of the ghosts, with which she "enchanted" the people of Wa. What exactly the writer of the *Wei zhi* meant by this term is not clear, but scholars have pointed to contemporaneous prevalent practices in China and the Korean peninsula that involved propitiatory ritual offerings and communications with divinities and the spirits of the dead as well as agricultural and healing rites that were often performed by women.[21]

Archeological evidence—consisting of Jōmon and Yayoi ceramics and Yayoi bronze bells—contains depictions of shamans, typically a human figure with both arms raised above the head, a posture that could indicate ecstasy and/or dance. The depictions on bronze bells, some of which suggest through the presence of a spindle that the shaman is female, often show agricultural and hunting rites linked to fertility. Later *haniwa*, cylindrical clay figurines recovered from burial mounds of the Kofun period (ca. 250–710 CE), link shamanic rituals with music and mirrors. Female shamans are depicted wearing curved-bead necklaces, jingle-bell mirrors, and bells on crowns (see figure 1.2). Other *haniwa* depict male figures playing instruments such as flutes or zithers, perhaps to accompany trance-inducing dances of the shaman.[22]

Such rituals were described in the *Nihon shoki*. For instance, when Empress Jingō sought a divine answer, she did the following:

> The empress, having selected a lucky day, entered the palace of worship, and discharged in person the office of the priest. She commanded Takechi no Sukune to play the zither, and the Nakatomi, Igatsu no Omi, was designated as spiritual mediator (*saniwa*). Then placing one thousand pieces of cloth, high pieces of cloth, on the top and bottom of the zither, she prayed saying: "Who is the divinity who on a former day instructed the Emperor? I pray that I may know the deity's name." After seven days and seven nights there came an answer, saying: "I am the deity who dwells in the Shrine of split-bell Isuzu in the district of hundred-transmit Watarai in the province of divine-wind Ise [i.e., Amaterasu who is enshrined at

Ise], and my name is Tsuki-sakaki idzu no mi-tama ama-zakaru Muka-tsu hime no Mikoto.[23]

In other words, Empress Jingō practiced mediated spirit possession, led by a member of the sacerdotal Nakatomi family and accompanied by the sound of the zither played by Takechi no Sukune. Spirit possession was one of the means by which a shaman, particularly a female shaman, could gain authority. Scholars have also studied the names of shamanistic figures and discovered two types: those who gained their authority through hereditary means were named *iri* ("enter" or "adopt"), and those who gained their authority through possession were named *yori* ("remain" or "possess"). Both male and female shamans could bear the name *iri*, but only female shamans were given names containing *yori*.[24]

Exactly how much political power Himiko wielded herself has also been debated. One early Japanese feminist historian, Takamure Itsue (1894–1964), argued that Himiko's rule in conjunction with her younger brother was a remnant of an earlier, matriarchal system. Himiko as the female controlled the inner quarters and the spiritual world, while her brother as the male was in charge of communicating with the outside world and politics. The folklorist Yanagita Kunio (1875–1962) depicted women like Himiko, the later Ise priestesses, female spirit mediums, and other women in the employ of the early Yamato state as evidence for the spiritual monopoly women held in protohistoric and ancient Japan. In contrast, other scholars have regarded the *hime-hiko* (female-male) system as an expression of the complementary balance between binary opposites akin to the relationship between the Chinese concepts of *yin* and *yang*. Indeed, similar pairs can be found in the national chronicles and early gazetteers. How much independent power women wielded in such a system, however, has been questioned.[25] Many modern scholars have assumed that Himiko wielded religious authority while her brother wielded political power. By contrast, the historian Yoshie Akiko argues that this notion arose only in the modern era, during a time when women were excluded from the political sphere. Thus such

FIGURE 1.2. *Haniwa* bust (hollow clay sculpture) of a shaman. Notice the beaded necklace. Japan, 5th to early 6th century CE. Earthenware with painted, incised, and applied decoration (Kantō region), H. 12 ⅞ in. (32.7 cm); W. 8 ½ in. (21.6 cm); D. 4 in. (10.2 cm). The Harry G. C. Packard Collection of Asian Art, Gift of Harry G. C. Packard, and Purchase, Fletcher, Rogers. Harris Brisbane Dick, and Louis V. Bell Funds, Joseph Pulitzer Bequest, and The Annenberg Fund Inc. Gift, 1975 (1975.268.413). The Metropolitan Museum of Art, New York, NY, U.S.A. Image copyright © The Metropolitan Museum of Art. Image source: Art Resource, NY.

an assumption was an anachronistic imposition of the modern idea that women should be excluded from the political realm and should instead be limited to the private realm of the home. Yoshie also points out that the idea that later female emperors were nothing but sacerdotal placeholders for rightful male emperors was likewise informed by modern ideas of male succession and the exclusion of women from the political realm.[26]

Scholars have also attempted to find parallels between Himiko and female figures in the national chronicles, but such claims have likewise been contested. Until the late Edo period, Himiko was traditionally identified with Empress Jingō, also known as Princess Okinaga Tarashi in the national chronicles, where she first appears as the wife of Emperor Chūai. This emperor meets an untimely end when he ignores an oracle pronounced by his wife in divine possession that he forgo a campaign against the Kumaso tribe and instead attack the country of Silla in the Korean peninsula. His pregnant wife hides his demise, and after verification through further divine possession and divination, she vanquishes local rebels and leads a successful military campaign against Silla, whose king submits to Jingō's authority. Upon her return she gives birth to the future Emperor Ōjin.[27] Even a cursory glance reveals that the description of Jingō's personality does not entirely match that of Himiko. Though both appear to have engaged in shamanic practices, Himiko was said to have remained unmarried and secluded in her stockade palace. Jingō, on the other hand, was not a virginal recluse: not only was she the wife of Emperor Chūai and pregnant with his child, but she was also said to have actively led military campaigns at home and abroad. Such discrepancies cast doubt on the identification of Himiko as Empress Jingō. One early critic of the identification with Empress Jingō suggested instead that Himiko might have been the leader of the rebellious Kumaso tribe that was later conquered by the Yamato. There is little evidence to support this claim, however.[28]

Other scholars have suggested different identities for Himiko: for example, Princess Yamato, first priestess of the Ise Shrines, sister of

Emperor Keikō and aunt of Yamato Takeru.[29] According to the *Kojiki* and the *Nihon shoki*, Princess Yamato was appointed by her father, Emperor Suinin, to serve the sun goddess Amaterasu at Ise. The appointment followed an oracle by Amaterasu in which the sun goddess expressed her wish to be enshrined at Ise rather than the imperial palace. Like her predecessor, Princess Toyosukiiri, who was said to have served the goddess for eighty-seven years, Princess Yamato remained unmarried during her ninety-plus years of service to the goddess, if we are to trust the traditional chronology. During her tenure, she transmitted pronouncements by Amaterasu that shaped military policy, particularly during the campaigns of her nephew, Yamato Takeru.[30] Princess Yamato, the priestess of Amaterasu, seems to fit the description of Himiko in many respects—she remained unmarried throughout her life, lived secluded in her sacred palace at Ise, was linked to the cult of the sun, and served in a priestly function for many decades. While her divine utterances shaped military policies, she was not the de facto ruler; however, she made most of her pronouncements during the reign of her brother, Emperor Keikō. Ultimately, it is impossible to find a conclusive match between Himiko and a figure appearing in the national chronicles.

Whether or not Himiko corresponds to a character in the national chronicles, archeological evidence has demonstrated that the *Wei zhi* is remarkably accurate in its description of late Yayoi period culture, despite small discrepancies caused by either the writer's ignorance or a sense of cultural superiority. Himiko is described as ruling a federation of twenty-two chiefdoms that faced intermittent warfare. This is supported by the discovery of fortified Yayoi settlements. Archeological finds confirm that the Yayoi cultures contemporaneous with Himiko's were shaped by wet-rice cultivation and trade in iron and bronze implements, characteristics similar to those found in the description of Himiko's chiefdom. Her death falls into the period when the first great tombs began to be constructed for chieftains during the transition from the Yayoi to the Kofun period.[31] Given the relatively high degree of accuracy, we might wonder, then, what the *Wei zhi* can tell us about the lives of women other than Himiko.

The record includes a few statements—some of which have been the cause of controversy—pertaining to the lives of women:

> [The] customs [of the Wa] are not indecent. All males have looped hair, with cotton cloth around the heads. Their wide, unsewn cloths are tied together. The women wear their hair in curved loops. The clothes are like a single cloth, worn by sticking the head through the pierced center.
>
> They plant grains, rice, flax and mulberry trees for silkworms. They spin fine threads for linen, silk and cotton fabrics. . . . The houses have rooms. Father and mother, brother and sisters sleep separately. . . .
>
> When missions cross the ocean to visit China there is always one man who does not comb his hair, does not remove the lice, lets his clothes become dirty, does not eat meat, and does not get near women. He is like a mourner and works like a diviner or an ascetic/abstainer. If there is good luck, in view of this they all give him slaves and valuable things, but if disease or injuries occur, they dispatch him because as the diviner he had not been respectful [of his vows]. . . .
>
> In their meetings, [whether] sitting or standing, there is no distinction between father and sons or between men and women by sex. . . . The custom is for all aristocrats to have four or five wives, commoners perhaps two or three. Women are not morally loose or jealous.
>
> There is no thievery and litigations are few. If a crime is committed, for a minor offense the person's wife and children are enslaved, and for a major offense members of the person's household together with his relatives are eradicated.[32]

According to the records, Wa women wore poncho-like dresses, in contrast to men, who tied their robes together. Women wore their hair in loops, a hairstyle that has been confirmed by the hairstyles of cylindrical clay figurines placed on tombs during the Kofun period and by the discovery of hair on female remains from the seventh century.[33] The Wa engaged in agriculture and sericulture, the latter of which, as already mentioned, was usually considered women's labor, as were spinning and the weaving of cloth. It is likely then that linen, silk, and cotton— apparently highly valued commodities—were produced by women. Wa society had both male and female slaves.

The record also suggests elements in the social and kinship structures of the Wa. Society was polygynous, and the number of wives depended on, and possibly expressed, the status of the husband: the lower his status, the fewer his wives. A later Chinese record, the *Hou Han shu*, further states that women outnumbered men. The practice of polygyny may have been motivated by high infant mortality rates; however, some scholars have questioned whether universal polygyny, even among commoners, would have been demographically sustainable.[34] To the Chinese observers, Wa women seemed to be "not morally loose or jealous." From a Confucian perspective, chastity and lack of jealousy were prized in women, but what this exactly meant in the context of Wa is difficult to assess.

Scholars have also questioned whether the writer of the *Wei zhi* was actually referring to an egalitarian society that did not make age or gender distinctions. This observation might have been relative. Compared to the complex Confucian hierarchies of China, the interactions among kinship or status groups in Wa may have seemed less hierarchical. Burial practices seem to indicate that at least in some places in the Japanese islands people were buried in age cohorts, suggesting clear age differentiation but not necessarily gender boundaries.[35] The observation that males and females of different generations did not share sleeping quarters also needs further explanation. Scholars have suggested that this may refer to the practice of maintaining separate residences rather than merely separate rooms or beds. This in turn may support the argument that Wa kinship structures were bilateral rather than patrilineal or matrilineal. Again, compared to the complex kinship relations of China, where paternal and maternal relatives were distinguished linguistically by specific nomenclature, the Japanese language did not draw such boundaries. Such bilateral relations could have had concrete advantages for women. The historian William Wayne Farris has argued that "bilateral kinship grants power to women, often allowing them to live separately from their husbands and hold their own property."[36] Yet despite their potential economic independence, women were held collectively responsible for their husbands' actions and could be punished, along with their offspring, by enslavement or even death.

Of great interest is the observation that the abstinence keeper employed during voyages kept his distance from women. In the sacerdotal bureaucracy of early Japan, the keeping of abstinences combined with divination was the domain of members of the Inbe family, who competed with another sacerdotal family, the Nakatomi.[37] The abstinence keeper behaved like a mourner, who—as mentioned in the *Wei zhi*—abstained from eating meat. In addition, the abstinence keeper refrained from sexual intercourse. Similar taboos were also observed during much later periods at times of abstinence, in order to maintain or restore ritual purity in preparation for court rituals and pilgrimages to sacred sites, or during periods of mourning. This seems to suggest that the act of sexual intercourse, or perhaps even women themselves, may have been linked to ritual pollution.

Conclusion

In prehistory, women emerged as powerful symbols of fertility and as politico-sacerdotal figures. Ultimately, many enigmas remain about these periods. As we try to understand these materials, we must be careful not to let our modern assumptions of normative gender roles color our reading of these sources. Modern Japanese folklorists have sometimes been quick to assume that prehistoric women were exclusively associated with spiritual power and fertility while men took charge of the political sphere, but this view is based on biological determinism. There is convincing evidence that spiritual power was not understood in ancient Japan to be unique to women but, rather, that women and men usually conducted rituals jointly. Similarly, divisions between religious and political, private and public spheres did not exist in the modern sense. Therefore, we should be cautious about presuming that women did not serve as full-fledged political leaders but were limited to sacerdotal functions.[38] Furthermore, while some scholars have tried to elucidate the archeological record by seeking parallels and explanations in Japan's ancient myths, such a methodology has its own problems and often unveils as many contradictions as parallels between the myths and the archeological record. In the following chapter we will examine the myths in the *Kojiki* and *Nihon shoki* in greater detail by placing them in the historical context in which they were compiled.

Ancient Japanese Mythology

Female Divinities and Immortals

We have already encountered the first extant national chronicles of Japan, the *Kojiki* and the *Nihon shoki*. Both texts are important sources for our knowledge about ancient Japan, not only as historical chronicles but also as the earliest extant sources for Japanese mythology. Therefore, the myths, especially those in the *Kojiki*, have often been constructed as reflections of native beliefs and the deepest and most immutable values of Japanese culture. For this reason, they are regarded by some as the core sources of the Shinto tradition, the supposed "indigenous tradition of Japan." However, as a concept Shinto was first used after the introduction of Buddhism in the mid-sixth century. Even though it has often been constructed as Japan's original and native tradition, it incorporated numerous continental features that are also apparent in these ancient myths. Ideal images of women in the myths have also therefore been influenced by continental concepts, such as *yin* and *yang*, immortality cults, and sericulture.

Furthermore, the chronicles, including the chapters on mythology, need to be read with caution. While the texts are illuminating from the perspective of folklore and literature, they also must be understood in the context of the culture from which they emerged. Both texts were commissioned by the imperial court in the seventh century and completed in the early eighth century. It is not surprising, then, that they strongly reflect the court's interests, in particular in their emphasis on creating orthodox accounts of the imperial lineage. Both were written during a time when continental culture was pouring into Japan: Buddhism had been introduced about a century and a half earlier, continental models of rulership and ritual had been adopted, and continental cults of divinities and immortality flourished. Therefore, while these chronicles might teach us about early Japanese conceptions of female divinities, female ritualists, and gendered kinship practices, they invariably reflect continental influences and the ideological agendas of the ruling elites. The influence of the imperial line is particularly evident in their descriptions of the heavenly pantheon, cultural heroes, and courtly rituals. In this chapter, we will examine two important female divinities, Izanami and Amaterasu, and correlate them with contemporaneous ritual practices involving women at the court.

The Introduction of Patriarchal Legal Structures and Actual Japanese Practice

Before we examine the myths in the *Kojiki* and the *Nihon shoki*, we will take a brief look at what family structures might have looked like in early eighth-century Japan around the time of completion of the two chronicles. Unfortunately, reliable evidence from this era is very limited. In the early eighth century, the Japanese court promulgated a series of legal codes (*ritsuryō*), the Taihō Code (702) and the Yōrō Code (718), which were inspired by codes of the Chinese Tang dynasty (618–907). Since the Former Han dynasty (206 BCE–9 CE), Confucian theories of statecraft had largely been normative and had also saturated the Tang dynasty legal codes that served as models for the emerging Japanese state. Confucian thought assumed that society was based on five basic, mostly hierarchical relationships, including that between husband and wife, supposedly based on chaste conduct between the spouses and the wife's obedience to the husband. Such hierarchical conceptualizations are already apparent in the *Seventeen-Article Constitution*, whose compilation is traditionally attributed to Prince Shōtoku (572–622) in 604 but likely occurred a number of decades later. Other Confucian concepts also gradually found their way into Japan. For instance, in one of his poems included in the *Manyōshū* (ca. 759), Yamanoue Okura (660–ca.

733) invokes the idea that a woman was supposed to obey the three major male figures in her life: her father before marriage, her husband after marriage, and her son after being widowed. He also alludes to the concept of the four womanly virtues, mentioned in the Confucian classic the *Book of Rites*, and discussed at length by the female Confucian scholar Ban Zhao (45–116) in her primer *Precepts for Women* (*Nü jie*): feminine virtue, feminine speech, feminine countenance, and feminine conduct. Most importantly, Confucian ideas informed the laws regarding the family promulgated in the eighth-century legal codes. The codes constructed the family as a virilocal, patrilineal unit and encouraged filial piety as the foundation of the national social order. Penal law took gender differences for granted, making a wife's offense against the husband's parents a graver infraction than the husband's offense against her parents. A husband's physical violence against his wife was not punishable as long as he did not kill her, but if he assaulted her parents, this was ground for divorce. A husband had various reasons to divorce his wife: for example, if she spoke ill of her in-laws or attempted to harm them, or if he wished to divorce her based on seven conditions (failure to bear a son, adultery, failure to serve her in-laws, loquaciousness, jealousy, and severe illness). The wife, however, had no corresponding rights. A wife's adultery was punishable, but no corresponding offense existed for the husband.[1]

However, while these legal codes were meant to govern familial relations, evidence from contemporaneous census records raises doubts whether the Japanese actually practiced virilocal marriage, in which the wives resided with their husbands' family, during this period or whether visiting, duolocal marriages, in which the husband visited his wife and both continued to reside with their natal families, were more prevalent. Clearly, Japanese kinship practices seem to have been quite different from those in China, as already indicated in Chinese records about residential practices in Himiko's time. Similarly, evidence from the very early Heian period (794–1185) suggests that Japanese women also seem to have held property individually, a practice contrasting with those prescribed by Chinese-style legal codes, which made property ownership the prerogative of the patriarchal household. Husband and wife in Japan held property individually rather than jointly, and when the marriage ended, both partners held on to their respective properties. Eighth-century texts such as regional gazetteers, the *Kojiki*, and the *Manyōshū* further suggest that women had considerable freedom to choose or reject their partners. Thus female chastity and adultery were not important concepts in actual practice until the emergence of virilocal marriage practices in the late medieval period. The Confucian concept of the Three Obediences (to father, husband, and son) likewise seems to have become a prevalent concept only by the late medieval period.[2]

One clear indication of how important maternal connections were during this period is the practice of moving the imperial palace after the death of the sovereign. Rather than establishing a permanent capital, the ancient Japanese court moved its location frequently during this time period. Even when the court established the first permanent capital in Nara (710–784), there was still an interlude in the 740s in which the capital was briefly moved elsewhere. A move enabled the successor not only to avoid the ritual pollution associated with the death of his predecessor but also to cement his political power vis-à-vis any rival contenders for the throne. Usually the palace was moved to a geomantically auspicious place that was associated with the lineage of the reigning monarch and where the maternal relatives of a sovereign had a power base. Since royal and aristocratic children were raised by their maternal relatives, their connections were stronger with their mother's clan. Therefore, when the Emperor Kanmu (737–806, r. 781–806) decided to move the capital away from Nara, a region strongly associated with Emperor Tenmu's line, to which Kanmu did not belong, he chose Yamashiro Province, where Paekche immigrants like his mother's family were strongly represented. Kanmu first settled in Nagaoka (784–794) and in 794 moved again to nearby Heiankyō, which became the imperial capital for more than a thousand years.[3]

Izanami and Izanagi

The *Kojiki* and the *Nihon shoki* were compiled in this cultural context. Both begin with accounts of the creation of the world in the age of the gods. These myths feature strong female characters, including Izanami, a creator goddess, and Amaterasu, the sun goddess. As the archetypal husband-wife pair, Izanami and Izanagi, her spouse, have been venerated at, among other places, the Taga Grand Shrine in Shiga Prefecture. From the late Edo period (1600–1868) to the present, they have often been upheld as role models for conjugal relations. Amaterasu has been worshipped at the Inner Ise Shrine and is known as the progenitor of the royal line.

The deities Izanami and Izanagi appear near the beginning of the two chronicles as the last of five sets of divinities that came into existence as brother-sister or husband-wife pairs, unlike their predecessors, who appear as single, unpaired divinities. Of the first five divine husband-wife pairs in the national chronicles of the early eighth century, Izanami and Izanagi play the most important role as creator divinities who produce the Japanese islands. Izanami and Izanagi stand on a bridge that connects heaven and earth, and they churn the sea beneath with a jeweled spear—which has often been interpreted as a phallic symbol. The brine that drips from the tip of the spear solidifies into an island where Izanami and Izanagi then proceed to make their home. In their new abode, the two divinities discover their complementary sexuality and decide to procreate. According to the *Kojiki*, Izanagi asks his wife, "How is thy body formed?" She answers, "My body, formed though it be formed, has one place which is formed insufficiently." Izanagi rejoins, "My body, formed though it be formed, has one place which is formed to excess. Therefore, I would like to take that place in my body which is formed to excess and insert it into that place in your body which is formed insufficiently, and [thus] give birth to the land. How would this be?"[4] Izanami agrees. The two divinities pledge their troth by walking around a heavenly pillar. On the first try, Izanami accosts Izanagi first, which dooms their union and produces a malformed "leech child," whom they set afloat in the ocean. On the second try, Izanagi speaks first. The two divinities subsequently create multiple islands and divinities that will populate the land as natural phenomena—mountains, rivers, and plant life. Izanami eventually dies after giving birth to the fire god. In his insightful reading of gender constructions in this myth as it appears in the *Kojiki*, the scholar of religion Allan Grapard argues that Izanami's female body is viewed as deficient in contrast to the excess of Izanagi's male body. Despite being a woman, Izanami usurps the male role of initiating speech and intercourse. This transgression leads to the production of misshapen offspring.[5] This story has often been interpreted in this way, but it is also important to note the variants that appear in the *Nihon shoki* and to place them within the wider context of East Asian constructions of gender.

The *Nihon shoki* lists several variants that contain many of the same elements, though not always in the same order. In some cases, the changes in order are quite significant. For example, in the primary *Nihon shoki* version, Izanami's blunder of speaking first has no major consequences except that Izanagi declares this act inauspicious and insists on repeating the nuptials, this time speaking first himself. Their union eventually produces the leech child at a later time for no apparent reason, after they have created various islands. Another important difference is the explicit way the *Nihon shoki* casts Izanami and Izanagi as the archetypal male and female, as *yin* and *yang*. When Izanami and Izanagi decide to procreate, the text refers to Izanami as the *yin*, or female, divinity and to Izanagi as the *yang*, or male, divinity. As they examine their bodies, they do not speak of being formed in excess or insufficiently but of "the source of masculinity" and "the source of femininity." Their union is described as follows: "Hereupon the male [*yang*] and female [*yin*] first became husband and wife."[6] The complementary relationship between Izanami and Izanagi, derived from Chinese models of masculinity and femininity, is only hinted at in the *Kojiki*, but here it is highlighted as fundamental. Clearly, Izanami and Izanagi embody the principles of *yin and yang*—the female is dark, yielding, and destructive, whereas the male is bright, forceful, and constructive, notions that appear in the early Chinese classics such as the *Yijing*.[7]

This gendered complementarity also plays an important role in the story of Izanami's death. After giving birth to the fire divinity, Izanami dies. According to the *Nihon shoki*, the bodily discharges produced as she dies—vomit, urine, and feces—transform into additional divinities: a fire goddess, an earth goddess, and a water goddess. This visceral reproduction is not limited to Izanami's female body. Weeping in grief, Izanagi crawls around her head and feet, his tears producing more divinities in the process. Up to this point, we do not sense any implication that Izanami's female body has been polluted either through childbirth or through bodily functions. Instead, her excretions are fecund, but this apparent positive valuation soon changes. After killing the fire god in anger to avenge his wife's death and creating yet more divinities, Izanagi follows Izanami to the land of darkness, *yomi no kuni*, to which both the *Kojiki* and the *Nihon shoki* refer to with the characters "the land of the Yellow Springs," hinting at Chinese conceptualizations of the afterlife, according to which the *yin* parts of the human spirit descended to the Yellow Springs while the *yang* parts of the spirit were thought to travel to heavenly realms. Izanagi implores his wife to return with him to the world of the living, an implicit reference to ancient spirit-calling rites that have their origin in China and were conducted in ancient Japan for ailing rulers in order to prevent the spirit from straying.[8] However, Izanami tells him that she has already consumed food prepared at the stove of *yomi*. She makes him promise not to look at her while she goes off to seek special permission from the divinities ruling *yomi*. When curiosity gets the better of Izanagi, he breaks a piece of his comb and lights it. In horror, he sees Izanami's decaying body, squirming with maggots. According to the *Kojiki* version, Izanami's body (her head, chest, stomach, genitals, and four extremities) generates eight snake-like thunder divinities. Filled with fear, Izanagi flees while Izanami—shamed and enraged by his broken promise—sends after him in pursuit a squadron of hags, eight thunder divinities, and a whole army of *yomi* warriors. When they fail to capture him, she confronts him herself. At the border of *yomi*, Izanagi seals off the path with a large boulder, and they end their marriage. Izanami vows henceforth to take 1,000 lives daily, whereas Izanagi counters that he will ensure the birth of 1,500 daily.[9]

To rid himself of the pollution he encountered in *yomi*, Izanagi purifies himself in a river, creating twenty-six divinities as he undresses and washes himself. According to the *Kojiki*, the ritual washing produces from his eyes and nose Amaterasu (the sun goddess), Tsukiyomi (the moon god), and Susanoo (the storm god), respectively.[10] We may be reminded of the *Wei zhi*'s account of Japanese funerary rites, which resembled Chinese ritual bathing practices: "After interment [of the dead body] the family assembles to go in water for purification, just like ablutions."[11] As Michael Como, a scholar of religion, has shown, Chinese texts that predate the Japanese chronicles attest to the link between spirit-calling/propitiation rituals and ritual bathing.[12]

Many scholars regard Izanami as an archetypal figure that exemplifies the association of the female body with pollution. For example, according to Grapard, the rite of purification is the central ritual act in the Izanami and Izanagi story. It sets up a division between female and male that associates the former with impurity and the latter with purity. In an extension of Sherry Ortner's argument in her classic "Is Female to Male as Nature Is to Culture?" (1972), Grapard pushes this point even further by asserting that the myth associates the male with cultural production: the male divinity Izanagi creates the imperial ancestors Amaterasu and Susanoo. By contrast, the female divinity Izanami is associated with nature and decay.[13]

However, we should note that according to the *Nihon shoki*, Izanami and Izanagi jointly produce these three divinities before Izanami dies in childbirth;[14] therefore, the alignment of female with nature and male with cultural production is perhaps not as categorical. Even the *Kojiki* later refers to Izanami as Susanoo's (and by implication also Amaterasu's) mother and thus a royal ancestor. We must also be careful about imposing the nature-culture dichotomy too readily onto the Japanese myth. According to the anthropologist Arne Kalland, the nature-culture divide is less emphasized in Japan, where cultured, domesticated nature is often prized more than nature in the raw. This valuation of cultured nature over wild nature applies also to gender and sexuality. In later periods, women were constructed as cultured and virtuous if they respected the social order, but they became threatening if they disrupted conventions.[15] Thus the opposition between order and chaos may be the more prominent dichotomy than the one between nature and culture.

While simple dichotomies may never yield an entirely satisfying framework, shifting the emphasis from nature-culture to chaos-order alters our interpretation significantly. The myths suggest that in an ideal state, the two sexes are balanced and complementary, with the male being dominant and the female being submissive. In a balanced state, male and female are fertile and productive: they create various natural phenomena together. Izanagi, as the male representative, enforces this order. Izanami, as the female representative, repeatedly challenges this order. Each time the feminine, or *yin*, force becomes overbearing, it leads to chaos, deformity, death, and decay. Perhaps Izanami's unruliness and her supposed audacity to speak first also suggest that the imperial court was at pains to inscribe Chinese-style gender relations onto its official myths at a time when the court was promulgating similarly patriarchal legislation but when contemporaneous women were not really following these new prescriptions on feminine virtue. Be that as it may, as we will see, nativist scholars of the Edo period (1600–1868) often upheld the nuptial rites between Izanami and Izanagi as foundational for the ideal relationship between male and female. Another completely different paragon of female virtue singled out by these scholars was Amaterasu, the sun goddess.

Amaterasu and Susanoo

In the myth of Amaterasu and Susanoo, it is the male divinity who causes chaos and whose body is linked to pollution. Susanoo desires to join his mother in the netherworld but wishes first to bid his sister Amaterasu farewell. Unsure about the violent storm divinity's intentions, Amaterasu dresses herself in armor to defend her realm. Susanoo convinces her to conduct a divination ritual to see whether his intentions are pure. They make a pact to procreate children from each other's insignia. Susanoo hands Amaterasu his sword, which she breaks into three pieces, chews up and spits out, producing three girls. Amaterasu then hands Susanoo her beads, which he chews up and spits out, producing five male children (see figure 2.1). The *Kojiki* and the *Nihon shoki*

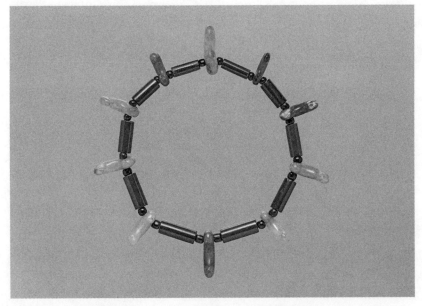

FIGURE 2.1. Necklace with claw-shaped beads (*magatama*). Curved beads were considered one of the three imperial regalia of ancient Japan. Japan, ca. 7th century CE. Chalcedony and green jasper, L. 11 ½ in. (29.2 cm). Rogers Fund, 1912 (12.37.84). The Metropolitan Museum of Art, New York, NY, U.S.A. Image copyright © The Metropolitan Museum of Art. Image source: Art Resource, NY.

each interpret the result of the divination differently. In the *Kojiki,* the female children produced from Susanoo's sword are counted as his children. Susanoo claims that his pure intentions are proven by the fact that he produced girls.[16] In the *Nihon shoki,* Susanoo states that if the children he produces are female, his intentions arc dishonest, and if they are male, his intentions are honest. Since Susanoo produces male children (albeit from Amaterasu's beads), these count as his children, but Amaterasu accepts his male offspring as her own children. In either case, his intentions are proven to be honest. Since the two accounts interpret the generation of female children as auspicious in one case and as inauspicious in the other, we cannot universally say that female offspring were necessarily seen as inauspicious. It is significant, however, that premenstrual, young maidens can serve, as in the *Kojiki* account, as symbols of purity—an important trope that we will encounter again later.

It has been suggested that the myth incorporates a conflict over royal succession, a persistent problem in the early Japanese state. The stories of Izanami's death and of Amaterasu and Susanoo's encounter not only illustrate ritual practices observed at the ancient Japanese court—for example, double burial and the sovereign's authority over the annual Harvest Festival—but also dramatize the political strife that could follow a royal death: Susanoo grieves violently for his mother, confronts Amaterasu, and produces children with her.[17] Conflicts over succession were generated because the Japanese royal house did not rely on strict patrilineal succession, thus allowing for the proliferation of viable contenders. In order to stem conflict, the Japanese royal line practiced endogamy (marriage between close kin), occasionally allowing even half-siblings to marry, thus strengthening the royal blood in the lineage and the claims of potential bilineal contenders. If a suitable male heir was unavailable, too young, or unable to muster enough support, a female princess of the blood (often the previous monarch's wife— potentially also his half-sister) was chosen instead. This practice combined the earlier *hime-hiko* system with the Chinese practice in which the queen consort served as the regent for a royal heir who was too young to rule.[18] Thus the struggle between Amaterasu and Susanoo bears echoes of the conflict inherent in royal succession.

The struggle between Amaterasu and Susanoo continues despite, or perhaps because of, Susanoo's apparent victory. Violating sacred boundaries, he destroys the heavenly rice fields and irrigation systems and pollutes through defecation the ritual space in which the Harvest Festival is held. Amaterasu, though initially lenient, is shocked when he skins a piebald pony backwards and drops it through the roof of the hall where she has been weaving garments in preparation for the Harvest Festival. Depending on the versions in the *Kojiki* and the *Nihon shoki*, either an attending weaving maiden or Amaterasu herself is killed in the incident when she impales her genitals on the shuttle of the loom. In either case, Amaterasu withdraws into a cave, plunging the realm of the heavenly plain into complete darkness. The other gods lure her out of the cave through another spirit-calling rite. Unlike Izanagi's attempts to lure the deceased Izanami back to the world of the living, the gods' ritual succeeds in the case of Amaterasu. The female goddess Ame no Uzume, also known as Ama no Uzume, performs a revealing striptease dance, which makes the gods roar with laughter. This piques Amaterasu's curiosity, luring her out of seclusion. The other gods thrust a mirror into her face. Dazzled by her own brightness and cut off from the cave by a sacred rope, Amaterasu is forced out of the cave, thus restoring light to the world. The other gods punish Susanoo by cutting his beard and nails to purify him, sentencing him to pay a heavy fine, and banishing him from the heavenly plain.

One important aspect of the myth is the role of Ame no Uzume. The *Nihon shoki* states,

> Moreover, Ama no Uzume no Mikoto, ancestress of the Sarume no Kimi, took in her hand a spear wreathed with Eulalia grass, and standing before the door of the Rock-cave of Heaven, skillfully performed a mimic dance. She took, moreover, the true Sakaki tree of the Heavenly Mount Kagu, and made of it a head-dress, she took club-moss and made of it braces,

she kindled fires, she placed a tub bottom upwards, and gave forth a divinely-inspired utterance.[19]

Ame no Uzume is not the only one taking an active role in summoning Amaterasu, as the divine ancestors of the sacerdotal Nakatomi and the Inbe clans also participate significantly by preparing the ritual space and closing it off to prevent Amaterasu's retreat. However, Ame no Uzume is noteworthy because she takes on the role of a shaman who enters a trance and becomes possessed by means of a dance performance. During this performance, she carries a spear, wears a headdress of *sakaki* branches,[20] and ties back her sleeves. She lights fires and turns a bucket upside down, in order—as the *Kojiki* explains—to stomp on it. The *Kojiki* also states that she exposes her breasts and genitals as she becomes divinely possessed. Ame no Uzume appears again later in the *Nihon shoki*, when she confronts Sarutabiko, a divinity who is blocking the heavenly descent of Amaterasu's grandson and heir. Again, she exposes her genitals before communicating with the unruly divinity, indicating that the exposure of female genitalia is a powerful gesture. As a matter of fact, Ame no Uzume is described as the only one among the myriad heavenly deities who is capable of subduing Sarutabiko, supposedly because she was so captivating to the eye. Ame no Uzume becomes the wife of Sarutabiko and receives his name as her new title. Together they become the ancestors of the Sarume clan.[21] Apparently, Amaterasu is not the only female divinity in this myth who has a sacerdotal function and serves as a divine ancestor of a sacerdotal lineage.

To return to Amaterasu and the heavenly rock-cave myth, the story has often been understood as a nature myth illustrating a solar eclipse or the annual solar cycle. Indeed, the rituals described in the story reflect court rituals conducted around the winter solstice.[22] There is yet another cultural layer embedded in this myth. As Como has argued, the myth of Amaterasu hiding in the heavenly grotto is layered with references to sericulture and the cult of immortality, both heavily influenced by practices from the Asian continent, particularly China. Amaterasu is engaged in proverbial women's labor, the weaving for the gods of silk garments to be used in the Harvest Festival. In the myth of Ōgetsuhime (also known as Ukemochi), the agricultural food divinity—a story that either immediately precedes (*Nihon shoki*) or follows (*Kojiki*) Amaterasu's encounter with Susanoo—Amaterasu emerges as the one who not just orders the proliferation of agriculture but also begins the practice of sericulture by placing silkworm cocoons in her mouth to pull off the silk thread. She is thus taking on the role of a food and sericulture goddess. In her seclusion, she behaves like a silkworm herself. The silkworm spins silk, retreats into a cocoon, and emerges as a moth. Likewise Amaterasu spins and weaves, then retreats into her cave and emerges radiantly after being ritually lured out of seclusion. Like a Daoist immortal, she has escaped physical death. In other tales of female immortals, the immortal's powers are often linked to a magic silk cloth that the immortal needs or leaves behind to travel to the realm of the immortals. As in other East Asian tales of weaver maidens, the myth of Amaterasu includes male violence perpetrated against the maiden.[23] We may remind ourselves that like agriculture and hunting, sericulture also involves violence: preserving the integrity of the silk thread requires that the cocoon be placed in boiling water, which prevents the insect from hatching and destroying the cocoon; in the process, however, the silkworm is killed. The myth thus links women to a form of labor that was considered their special domain, in addition to reflecting related immortality practices. This suggests that the female body was considered not only potentially polluted and linked to decay but also potentially transcendent.

The myth of Amaterasu is particularly important because she was given preeminent status as the royal ancestor in the seventh century, and for over a millennium the sun goddess has been considered the divine ancestor of the imperial line and has been worshipped at the Inner Ise Shrine. Throughout the ancient period she was considered a powerful, dangerous divinity who could help subdue enemies and mete out terrible punishments to those who offended her.[24] The worship of sun divinities was originally not the special privilege of the Japanese royal line, as there were multiple sun cults, including some linked to immigrant lineages from the Korean peninsula. In fact, several immigrant groups who came to Japan from the Asian continent worshiped sun divinities linked to sericulture. Furthermore, Amaterasu may not always have been the focus of the royal cult. Several scholars have suggested that the divinity Takami Musubi was the cult's first object and was later replaced by Amaterasu.[25]

The elevation of Amaterasu was closely linked to the solidification of power of the royal line under Emperor Tenmu (631–686; r. 672–686) and the female Emperor Jitō (645–703; r. 686–697), who succeeded Tenmu. Whereas an earlier monarch, the female Emperor Suiko (554–628; r. 593–628), had likened her position to that of the Heavenly Polestar based on Chinese models, poets at the court of Jitō emphasized the divine descent of the ruling monarch by calling her Heavenly Sovereign (*tennō*), which has become the appellation of Japanese emperors ever since. It was under Jitō's predecessor Tenmu that records concerning the royal and other aristocratic lineages were first compiled, presumably in order to create a centralized orthodoxy. It was also under Tenmu that the Department of Divinity (*jingikan*) was instituted in order to control diverse local cults. It has been argued that the Ise Shrines themselves were established as late as the reign of Tenmu. Under Tenmu, the office of the royal princess serving as the high priestess (*saigū*) of Amaterasu, which had been revived under Tenmu's predecessor after a hiatus of about fifty years, also became a regular institution.[26]

The Royal High Priestess at Ise

Not only was Amaterasu said to be the royal ancestress, she was also served by a royal princess who served as a symbolic liaison with the court. According to legend, the office of the royal high priestess at Ise was established during the reigns of Sujin and Suinin. According to the *Nihon shoki*, the daughters of the royal sovereign had been sporadically appointed to the office from the reign of Emperor Keikō (71?–130?) to that of Emperor Yōmei (518–587; r. 585–587). The office became standardized under Tenmu as the Ise Shrines began to play a greater ceremonial role in the government.[27] The priestess—either a young, unmarried daughter of the emperor or, if he had none, one of his nieces—was supposed to serve as the royal liaison between the emperor and his divine ancestor on whom his sacral authority was based. With the decline and fragmentation of imperial power in the fourteenth century, the office of the priestess was no longer filled.[28]

According to the *Engishiki* (927), during the priestess's tenure, which typically corresponded with the reign of the monarch who assigned her through divination, the royal high priestess had to observe various taboos to avoid ritual pollution. Once she was chosen, she had to reside in seclusion for one year at the imperial palace and for another year at a residence in the southwestern section of the capital before taking ceremonial leave of the emperor and moving in a grand procession to Ise, where she would then serve as priestess during important annual rites. Once her service was complete (on average after eleven years), she would perform one last purification in Naniwa Bay during her return to the capital. If she was still young enough, she might then take a husband. During her time in office, however, the mandatory taboos affected not only her actions—performing purifications and avoiding sexuality and contact with death—but also her language:[29]

> At all times, certain words are taboo for the Princess. The inner seven words are: the Buddha is the "Central One," the sutras are "dyed paper," a pagoda is a "yew tree," a temple is a "tiled roof," a monk is a "long hair," a nun is a "female long-hair," a Buddhist meal is "short rations." Besides these there are the outer seven words: death is called "getting well," illness is "slumber," weeping is "shedding brine," blood is "sweat," to strike is to "caress," meat is "mushrooms," a tomb is a "clod of earth." There are also other taboo words: a Buddhist Hall is called "incense burner" and an upāsaka [Buddhist layman] is called "bow notch."[30]

The language taboos of the priestess remind us that Buddhism had already become a major cultural force in Japan by the time that the Japanese myths were committed to writing. We will learn more about the introduction of Buddhism and its effects on the lives of women in the next chapter. Despite these taboos against Buddhism, even the cult of Amaterasu came to be recast in the medieval period as that of a deity associated with several Buddhist divinities. According to one theory, Amaterasu was a divinity in a Buddhist underworld and distributed reward and punishment based on the Buddhist principle of karma. According to another, Amaterasu was identified with Mahāvairocana Buddha, and the rock-cave myth was read allegorically as a tale of enlightenment. It was only during this period that Amaterasu became important outside the royal line, which had previously held the monopoly on worshipping the divinity.[31]

Conclusion

The myths of Izanami-Izanagi and Amaterasu-Susanoo give us clues about ambivalent and sometimes contradictory constructions of femininity and masculinity in ancient Japan. Women can cause chaos, pollution, and destruction, but they can also be symbols of purity, sovereignty, immortality, and fertility. Izanami is a creator goddess associated with the realm of the dead and death itself. Amaterasu is ambivalent as well. On the one hand, she was constructed as a powerful (and sometimes irascible) ancestor of the royal line. On the other hand, she is described as a vulnerable weaver maiden. There is also evidence that Amaterasu was not always the progenitor of the royal line. Multiple sun cults existed in ancient Japan, several of which were tied to immigrant clans and centered on both male and female divinities.[32] The pluralism of the early Japanese mythological landscape is also evidenced by the tensions between the versions of myths contained in the *Nihon shoki*, a text that prized encyclopedic diversity, and the versions in the *Kojiki*, a text that claimed exclusive authoritativeness in order to bolster the legitimacy of the royal lineage. As a result of these variations, scholars have reached no definitive consensus on how to define gender relations based on these myths. Perhaps the safest interpretation is that these tales reveal considerable diversity between regions and lineages that can possibly be extended to the estimation of and roles given to women.

3

The Introduction of Buddhism

Nuns, Lay Patrons, and Popular Devotion

Buddhism was introduced to Japan in the mid-sixth century CE, radically altering the religious landscape of Japan. As we shall see, women played significant roles in the introduction and spread of Buddhism from the sixth through the eighth centuries as Buddhism evolved into a state religion. At the same time, however, we are also faced with important questions concerning this period of Japanese religious history: How did the introduction of Buddhism affect women's lives? Did it influence the lives of women beyond the upper elites in any significant way? How did Buddhism, a highly patriarchal tradition, incorporate Japanese women who had played significant roles as shamans and priestesses in local cults? In order to address these questions, we will examine the introduction of the nuns' order to Japan and its early development, the roles of female monarchs as great patrons of Buddhism, and the spread of Buddhism beyond the confines of court society.

The Introduction of the Buddhist Nuns' Order

Buddhism had been introduced from the Korean peninsula to Japan during the reign of Emperor Kinmei (r. 509–571) but did not begin to take firm root until the reigns of Emperors Bidatsu (r. 572–585), Yōmei (r. 585–587), and Sushun (r. 587–592). There are actually two alternative dates for the official introduction of Buddhism to Japan. The *Nihon shoki* gives the date as 552, while the *Founding Legend of Gangōji* (*Gangōji engi*; 747) gives 538. According to the *Nihon shoki*, the southwestern Korean kingdom of Paekche twice sent Buddhist images and scriptures to Japan, in 552 and 577. Soga no Iname is said to have installed and worshiped the first Buddhist image (received in 552) in his residence, which he turned into a temple. Following an epidemic that was attributed to the wrath of the local deities, however, he was said to have abandoned the experiment. The second time, Paekche sent Buddhist images and scriptures that were accompanied by four monastics (including one nun), a Buddhist sculptor, and a temple architect, leading to the establishment of a temple staffed by these monastics. While Buddhist icons and monastics continued to trickle into Japan from the Korean kingdoms of Paekche, Silla, and Koguryŏ, no one had yet become ordained as a monk or a nun in Japan. This would change in 584, however, after Soga no Umako (Iname's son) received two Buddhist images from Paekche. He sent two of his men, one of whom was a Chinese immigrant called Shiba Tattō, in search of qualified Buddhist clergy. They found a former Buddhist monk from Koguryŏ named Hyepyŏn, who had since become laicized. Hyepyŏn was appointed as the teacher, and three women—Shima, the daughter of Shiba Tattō; Toyome, the daughter of Ayabito no Yaho; and Ishime, the daughter of Nishikori Tsubu—became nuns under his tutelage, taking the Buddhist names Zenshin, Zenzō, and Ezen. The nuns were installed at Soga no Umako's mansion, which had been converted into a Buddhist temple for an image of Maitreya Buddha. Soga no Umako sponsored a vegetarian feast for the nuns, during which Shiba Tattō discovered a Buddhist relic in his vegetarian food. He offered it to Soga no Umako, who subsequently tried to destroy the relic by force but failed. As a result, Soga no Umako and Shiba Tattō were strengthened in their faith in Buddhism. Soga no Umako erected a temple at his residence and a pagoda on Mount Ōno for the Buddhist relic.[1]

The passage is revealing in several ways. According to the *Nihon shoki,* the introduction of Buddhism appears to have been supported by a male patron, the Grand Minister Soga no Umako. Umako had the help of several male associates, the most significant of whom was Shiba Tattō, a Chinese immigrant presumably from Southern Liang and a member of the Kurabe, a clan of saddle makers. Not only did one of Tattō's daughters, Shima, become ordained as a nun, but also his grandson, Kuratsukuri no Tori, would later become a significant sculptor to whom many of the masterpieces of early Japanese Buddhism have been attributed.

Moreover, at the vegetarian feast for the nuns, Tattō, the head nun's father, was credited with discovering a Buddhist relic. The veneration of relics (in Sanskrit, *śarīra*; in Japanese, *shari*) has a long history in Buddhism. Soon after the Buddha's passing, his followers began to venerate his remains as a means to maintain physical contact with their departed teacher. Bone fragments, flesh, teeth, and hair rumored to have come from the historical Buddha's body, and even objects he had purportedly touched, were treated with great reverence and enshrined in reliquaries across Asia. The remains of Buddhist saints—usually men—were treated with similar reverence. Such relics often took the shape of stone, pearl, glass, or crystal fragments that were said to form during the cremation of a spiritually advanced person.[2] As we shall see in the following chapters, in Japan the miraculous discovery and guardianship of Buddhist relics was frequently linked to women. The relic discovered at the vegetarian feast for Japan's first nuns is thus the first recorded incident of this sort in Japan.

What are we to make of the young women who were ordained as Japan's first nuns? On the one hand, it is significant that the first monastics ordained in Japan were women. Their pioneering role in introducing Buddhism mirrored the powerful position that female shamans held in ancient Japan.[3] On the other hand, the nuns appear to have only limited personal agency in their ordination, and this ordination did not follow the Buddhist monastic tradition's orthodox guidelines. Zenshin was only twelve years old at her initial ordination, not likely old enough to make such an important decision on her own. As a matter of fact, she and the two other women appear to have become ordained at the command of Soga no Umako, who may have supported Buddhism to gain an advantage over his political rivals. This means that the nuns' ordination was not a matter of personal choice. Two of the women, Zenshin and Zenzō, were from Chinese immigrant families, which may have been a factor in their selection. Their religious lives were determined by clan politics:[4] when Soga no Umako's rival, Mononobe Moriya of the sacerdotal Mononobe clan, convinced Emperor Bidatsu to suppress Buddhism, Umako's temple and pagoda were burned to the ground. The three women were defrocked, jailed, and whipped as a punishment. Flogging the nuns was likely considered particularly humiliating: an eighth-century code governing monks and nuns specified that monastics were usually punished by hard labor rather than by flagellation. Later, when the emperor and Mononobe Moriya fell ill, the nuns were reinstated and the temple rebuilt.[5] The nuns' lack of agency was not simply a result of their female gender. As we know from later events in Japanese history, boys often also became Buddhist novices at a young age at the decision of their families—because they were orphaned, were second or third sons, were supposed to fulfill a parent's vow, or lacked a powerful political supporter. Ordinations, particularly novice ordinations, thus were not always undertaken by personal choice. Hyepyŏn, the laicized monk from Koguryŏ, is another case in point: his agency in the nuns' ordination is also not clear, as he was made teacher and ordered to take the three nuns as his students.

Another striking detail is that the nuns' initial ordination was likely a novice ordination performed by a laicized monk. According to orthodox monastic regulations, the Vinaya, a quorum of ten monks and ten nuns was required for full female ordinations. By orthodox standards, the nuns were not fully ordained, especially because the person who ordained them had been previously defrocked. However, this hardly appears to have been a concern for the participants here. As a matter of fact, when the nuns' order was introduced to China, it apparently took over a hundred years for full ordinations to take place. Prior to 433, nuns' ordinations appear to have relied on an abbreviated set of ten precepts used for novice ordinations.[6] In Japan, orthodox ordinations for monks did not occur until the mid-eighth century, but orthodox ordinations for women were never introduced from China to Japan, even for nuns who served in state-supported temples.[7] It was only during the medieval period that full ordinations became available within a precept revival movement.[8]

Furthermore, the fact that Zenshin and the other two girls began their service as nuns immediately after their ordinations—just as a shrine priestess would have served at a shrine—is equally revealing. In order to perform the necessary ritual duties, they apparently needed little training in the Buddhist teachings. However, the nuns later asked to receive further training in Paekche. In 587, Zenshin, who was then fifteen years old, requested Soga no Umako to let them travel to Paekche for further instruction in the precepts. The three were eventually sent there with a returning Paekche envoy in 588. After the three nuns returned to Japan in 590, three other women, two of Korean heritage, and seven men of Chinese heritage (including Shiba Tattō's son Tasuna) were ordained.[9] While we do not know for certain whether the *Nihon shoki*'s representation is accurate, the text seems to suggest that Zenshin did make the decision to pursue further training herself. If this is indeed the case, then we must assume that she had some agency in the matter. Furthermore, the return of the nuns seems to have led others, including Zenshin's brother Shiba Tasuna, to take religious vows. So perhaps Buddhist ordination and devotion were viewed as resembling the *kami* worship rites (that is, rites for divinities) conducted by sacerdotal lineages, activities that were likewise transmitted within families.

Another intriguing point is that the *Founding Legend of Gangōji* attributes far greater agency to the nuns than the account in the *Nihon shoki*:

> At the time in the province of Harima there was an old monk from Ko[gu]ryŏ named Hyepyŏn who had given up the priestly robes and returned to lay life, as well as an old nun named Pópmyóng. The three girls—Shimame, the seventeen-year-old daughter of Tatto, the head of the saddle-makers; Tokome, a daughter of Ayahito Hōshi; and Ishime, daughter of Nishigori no Tsuho—together had attached themselves to Pópmyóng and were currently receiving instruction in the Buddhist Law.

They all said, "We wish to leave home [as nuns] and be taught the Buddhist Law." The Grand Minister was overjoyed and arranged for them to be ordained. (The Buddhist name of Shimame was Zenshin; that of Tokome was Zenzō, and that of Ishime was Ezen.)[10]

According to this version, the women initiated their entry into the Buddhist clergy of their own volition. They were not randomly assigned to Hyepyŏn but had already been the students of a Korean nun called Pŏpmyŏng. They also appear to have been old enough to make this decision on their own—Shimame was seventeen rather than twelve years old. Moreover, in this version the nuns were supported not only by Soga no Umako and his male associates but also by a powerful female patron, the future female Emperor Suiko (554–628).[11]

Female Monarchs as Buddhist Patrons

During the first two centuries of Japanese Buddhism, women played important roles in spreading the teachings. One significant factor was that during these two centuries there were six female monarchs, beginning with the female Emperor Suiko (r. 593–628) and ending with the female Emperor Shōtoku (718–770; r. 764–770), who had previously reigned as Emperor Kōken (r. 749–758). Several of these female monarchs, as well as the consorts of male monarchs, served as Buddhist patrons. Let us examine the roles of the female Emperor Suiko, Emperor Shōmu's wife Queen Consort Kōmyō (701–760), and the female Emperor Kōken-Shōtoku, as the most prominent examples.

Scholars have debated the role of early female rulers in the sponsorship of Buddhism. Posterity has largely credited Suiko's nephew Prince Shōtoku (574–622) as one of the great early patrons of Buddhism. By contrast, Suiko's direct patronage is difficult to prove. Many historians assume that the compilers of the *Nihon shoki* retroactively credited early Japanese monarchs before 645, from the female Emperor Suiko to the female Emperor Kōgyoku (594–661; r. 642–645), with Buddhist patronage when they may have been more actively involved in *kami* worship.[12] Citing the *Founding Legend of Gangōji*, others have argued that Suiko may have played a vital role alongside her nephew Prince Shōtoku in the establishment of Buddhism. Through her mother's line, Suiko was related to the Soga clan, whose members were strong patrons of Buddhism at the time. Even before ascending the throne, Suiko and her brother, who later ruled as Emperor Yōmei, may have had an important role in defending Buddhist icons and texts when the Soga clan's rivals tried to eliminate them. Once Suiko ascended the throne, she appears to have supported Soga no Umako generously in the founding of the Buddhist temple Hōkōji (also known as Asukadera) by providing the funds for its central image, a sixteen-foot-tall image of Śākyamuni Buddha cast from a vast amount of precious metals. After its completion, the temple was staffed by male and female monastics of immigrant background. Suiko not only replicated the monarch's central role in the *kami* cult but also took as her example the monarchs on the Asian continent, who also sponsored and regulated the Buddhist clergy. Therefore, based on southern Chinese models, Suiko instituted the office of the Buddhist prelate in 624 in order to oversee the growing Buddhist clergy. By this time, the aristocrats in Suiko's court had funded the construction of forty-six temples, staffed by 816 monks and 596 nuns.[13]

Suiko may have been particularly attracted to Buddhist texts that bolstered her legitimacy as a universal female monarch: the *Queen Śrīmālā Sutra* and the *Lotus Sutra*, to which we may also add the *Vimalakīrti Sutra*. Suiko's nephew Prince Shōtoku is said to have written (or at least sponsored) commentaries on all three. All three texts contained important teachings about the ideal roles of women in Buddhism. The *Queen Śrīmālā Sutra*'s depiction of a woman as a wise and capable leader may have held particular appeal to Suiko.[14] Even though the contemporaneous commentary attributed to Prince Shōtoku nods in the preface to the Confucian concept of the women's Three Obediences (to their fathers, husbands, and sons), this reference may be due to direct copying from a Chinese commentary and should not be interpreted as evidence for the pervasiveness of the notion in early seventh-century Japan. Moreover, the commentary accepts that Queen Śrīmālā will achieve Buddhahood without special restrictions based on her female gender.[15] Likewise, the *Vimalakīrti Sutra* denied the essential gender differences between men and women. The scripture contains a passage in which a female goddess upstages Śāriputra, one of the Buddha's chief monastic disciples. In order to teach Śāriputra that gender distinctions are ultimately empty, she transforms herself into a man and him into a woman.[16]

The *Lotus Sutra* could also have appealed to Suiko for its relatively inclusive, though still ambivalent, attitude toward women,[17] but not because of the Dragon King's daughter's story in the Devadatta chapter. The story in which the Dragon King's daughter attains Buddhahood presents a case for the salvation of women by means of transformation into male bodies. Even though the Dragon Girl's transformation became in the Heian period (794–1185) a prevalent paradigm for women's salvation, pre-Nara texts of the *Lotus Sutra* did not include the Devadatta chapter.[18] Nevertheless, the *Lotus Sutra* contains other, similarly ambivalent passages about women's potential for salvation and Buddhahood, in addition to the Devadatta chapter. Some passages suggest a misogynistic attitude that rejects the female body. Promises that women devoted to the *Lotus Sutra* will have their last rebirth as women and assertions that women are absent from various celestial Buddha lands are cases in point. And most of the major characters in the scripture are male—suggesting that the ideal practitioner was assumed to be male. Other passages stress inclusion: women (nuns and laywomen) are included in the audience of the Buddha while he is preaching the *Lotus Sutra*. Most importantly, in the chapter on "Encouraging Devotion," which now follows the Devadatta chapter, the Buddha promises the nun Mahāprajāpatī, his maternal aunt and foster mother, and the nun Yasodharā, the Buddha's former wife, that they will become great teachers and eventually achieve Buddhahood—thus repudiating allegations of women's spiritual inferiority. Still, Mahāprajāpatī and Yasodharā are the last of the Buddha's major disciples to be given a prophesy of future

Buddhahood, indicating that the other disciples are accorded greater importance.[19] Ultimately, the *Lotus Sutra* did assure women of their potential for Buddhahood despite recognizing the physical limitations of their bodies. That teaching could have made the text an important conceptual tool for Suiko.

While we do not know for sure whether Suiko was a patron of Buddhism or whether later texts—written when imperial patronage of Buddhism became more commonplace—merely portrayed her as such, there are more evident examples of great female patrons from the Nara period (710–784). Empress Kōmyō, the wife of Emperor Shōmu, was influenced by her parents' dedication to Buddhism and became a vital patron of the tradition. Kōmyō's father, Fujiwara no Fuhito (659–720), had been involved in the compilation of the "Regulations for Monks and Nuns" (*Sōniryō*) section of the Yōrō Code (718), which regulated the Buddhist clergy while giving them a special legal status. More importantly, Kōmyō's mother, Agatainukai Tachibana no Michiyo (665?–733), had served at the courts of Emperors Monmu, Genmei (female), and Genshō (female). When Genmei fell ill in 721, her successor and daughter Genshō had one hundred men and women ordained to pray for the retired monarch. Michiyo, who had been widowed a year earlier, also took the tonsure at this time—perhaps to pray for her deceased husband or for the recovery of Genmei. Her daughter Kōmyō was given the title empress in 729.[20]

Empress Kōmyō's household included offices for craftsmen trained in the construction of temples and the sculpting of Buddhist images, as well as for scribes employed to copy Buddhist scriptures (see figure 3.1). She engaged in charitable works, such as dispensing medicine to the destitute, that were inspired by the ideals of the *Vimalakirtī Sutra*. Kōmyō is also credited with the establishment of the nunnery Hokkeji at the site of her father's mansion. Most importantly, Kōmyō is thought to have played a vital role in the founding of Tōdaiji, the "Eastern Great Temple" in Nara, and the provincial temple system that included both monasteries and nunneries. These monasteries, formally called "Temples of

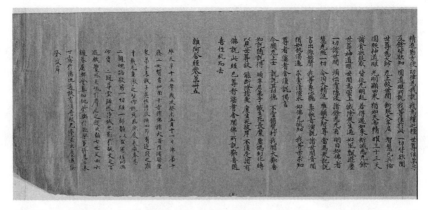

FIGURE 3.1. Detail of Fascicle 45 of the *Saṃyuktāgama Sutra* (in Japanese, *Zōagonkyō*) offered by Empress Kōmyō. Japan, 743 CE. Important Art Object. Gift of the Ogura Foundation. Tokyo National Museum, Tokyo, Japan. Image copyright © Tokyo National Museum. Image Source: DNP Art Communications, Tokyo.

the Golden Light and the Four Heavenly Kings of the Nation," and nunneries, formally called "Temples of the Lotus Atonement for Sin," were to perform prayers for the protection of the state. They were both named after important Mahāyāna Buddhist scriptures that claimed to offer protection to those who venerated them—the *Golden Light Sutra* in the case of the monasteries and the *Lotus Sutra* in the case of the nunneries. Some scholars have suggested that the official name of the nunneries with its reference to "atonement for sin" indicated that women were already seen as spiritually inferior by being linked to a sinful state inherent to being female. Most scholars believe, however, that "sin" here refers not to the sinful *female* nature of the nuns but to the sins accrued by all humans, male or female, over the course of their lives or to the sins accrued by the state. Be that as it may, Kōmyō seems to have been personally involved in the founding of the system in 741 because the invocations that accompanied its establishment included not only prayers for the state but also requests for the salvation of Kōmyō and her relatives, living and dead. In fact, Kōmyō may have been responsible for raising the funds for the massive project. She was likely motivated by her link to the Buddhist monk Genbō, who had studied in China from 716 to 735 and had resided in a temple within the precinct of Empress Kōmyō's palace upon his return to Japan.[21]

Empress Kōmyō was not the only strong Buddhist patron of the Nara period. Her daughter, who ruled twice as Emperor Kōken and as Emperor Shōtoku, was chastised by later historians for her excessive support of Buddhism, in particular of the monk Dōkyō (700–772). Born as Princess Abe, she was designated by Emperor Shōmu during a time of political and social turmoil as the heir apparent. After Shōmu retired, she ascended the throne as Emperor Kōken. Temporarily outmaneuvered by her mother, Kōmyō, after Shōmu's death in 756, she abdicated and took the tonsure. After her mother's death she displaced her successor, Emperor Junnin, and ascended a second time as Emperor Shōtoku. She immediately began the construction of a new Buddhist temple, Saidaiji ("Western Great Temple"), meant as a counterpart to her father and Kōmyō's Tōdaiji. She also ordered the dedication of one million pagodas, each about five and a half inches high and containing a printed amulet with a protective magic formula, and had them distributed at various temples in her realm. Furthermore, Shōtoku gave positions in the Council of State to monks from the monastic prelate's office. She especially singled out the monk Dōkyō, her personal preceptor, whom she appointed as a joint minister of state and meditation master and eventually named "Dharma King." Scholars have argued that Dōkyō sought to succeed Shōtoku and end the imperial line; but Shōtoku's actions could also have meant that she took complete control over the monastic orders. As was the case with her mother, Kōmyō, who emulated the Chinese Empress Wu Zetian (624–705) in her establishment of the provincial temple system, Shōtoku may likewise have patterned herself after Empress Wu in her patronage of the Buddhist orders in exchange for legitimization. Ultimately, both Empress Wu Zetian and Shōtoku were reviled as bad rulers by later Confucian historians who resented both their patronage of Buddhism and the fact that they were female rulers. In the end, Dōkyō did not succeed Shōtoku. After Shōtoku's death in 770, he was demoted and exiled.[22]

The Influence of Buddhism beyond the Court

While we have some evidence for the influence of Buddhism at the court and among the high nobility, it is difficult to assess its effect beyond courtly circles. Among the few possible sources available are government regulations suppressing popular, subversive activities and the stories contained in the *Nihon ryōiki*, a didactic tale collection compiled by the Buddhist monk Kyōkai between 787 and 824. Buddhism was spreading not just among the aristocracy but also among common people. As early as 717, the court issued an edict prohibiting public preaching, fundraising, and forming devotional associations, as these activities were considered subversive, in part because they eroded the state's tax base as adherents sought unauthorized ordinations.[23] The "Regulations for Monks and Nuns," promulgated in 718, specifically prohibited male and female monastics from taking orders or proselytizing outside recognized state-approved institutions. They were also forbidden to engage in prognostication, fortune-telling, and healing illness by means of exorcisms or magic. Such activities were punishable by expulsion from the monastic order or hard labor, depending on the offense.[24] The regulations did not single out women in particular, encompassing both monks and nuns. As in medieval China, the Japanese state was wary of unauthorized monastics reducing the tax base and corvée-labor pool and unduly influencing the populace through magic rites of healing.[25] In any case, it is unclear whether the state was able to enforce these rules broadly. Perhaps we should understand them as an indication of what kinds of activities were actually common among the populace.

Indeed, the Council of State issued the following declaration in 722, portraying public preaching and unauthorized ordinations as violating Confucian values of loyalty, fidelity, and filiality:

Recently, the priests and nuns of the capital, being shallow in knowledge and weak in intelligence, have been wandering around the capital
expounding the doctrine of karma and not abiding by the laws, thereby
leading the populace astray. On the one hand, they defy the teaching of
the sages. On the other, they disregard the decrees of the emperor. As a
result, people's wives and children are running to them and having their
heads shaven. Too often it happens that people hastily abandon their families in the name of Buddhist doctrine, utterly disregarding the rules of
social order, not giving a second thought to their husbands and parents.[26]

The text is couched in Confucian tropes according to which those
illegally flocking to Buddhist preachers are disrespecting important
Confucian relationships (husband-wife, parent-child, and so on). The
decree also targets devotees of both genders, understood to be in violation of Confucian expectations about public decency and gender roles.

As a matter of fact, the "Regulations for Monks and Nuns" demanded
a strict separation of the two genders in their accommodations in order
to preserve public order. Monks were allowed to employ a young male
relative under the age of seventeen as an attendant, while nuns could
retain a female attendant regardless of her age. Monks and nuns were
prohibited from spending the night in the residence of a monastic
belonging to the opposite sex. They also were not supposed to enter
each other's monasteries or convents unless they were formally visiting
the abbot or abbess, summoned due to the death or illness of a monastic, attending a ritual, or seeking or receiving instruction in the Buddhist
teachings.[27] The popular itinerant monk Gyōki (670?–749) responded
both to these regulations and to the Council of State's condemnation of
gender mixing by building forty-nine practice halls in the Kinai region.
These halls seem to have been segregated by gender and thus served as
the prototypes for the provincial monasteries and nunneries established
by Emperor Shōmu and Empress Kōmyō.[28]

The *Nihon ryōiki* is another source that may give us insight into how
and why Buddhism spread among women outside courtly circles. The

text was compiled by Kyōkai, a low-ranking monk at Yakushiji, one of the great temples in Nara, from the late eighth to the early ninth centuries, although it includes material dating mostly from the seventh and eighth centuries. Close to a third of the 116 stories deal with women, some of whom are identified as followers of Gyōki. The collection describes women from all walks of life, including laywomen and nuns. The compiler upholds many women as paragons of devotion and compassion instead of describing women as spiritually inferior. In some cases, the compiler even elides the misogynistic messages of Buddhist scriptures in favor of a more egalitarian view. This is also reflected in the story of the nun Sari, who is awarded the title Bodhisattva and dazzles her erstwhile male detractors with her erudition.[29] The *Nihon ryōiki* provides further evidence that during the Nara period the Buddhist idea of women's Five Obstructions (the inability of a woman to become Brahma, Indra, King Mara, a Cakravartin king, or Buddha) and the Confucian concept of a woman's Three Obediences (to father, husband, and son) were not widely established and became stock concepts only centuries later. Similarly, the *Nihon ryōiki* does not depict women as inherently polluted, a concept that would have precluded the existence of female emperors and the well-documented presence of nuns and court ladies in close proximity to the emperor, whose person was supposed to be ritually pure.[30] Thus the *Nihon ryōiki* contains stories of a variety of women, both good and bad, but not inherently sinful or defiled.

Despite its relatively positive attitude toward women and their salvation, the collection reflects a conflicted attitude toward female sexuality and motherhood. The above-mentioned girl Sari is born without fully formed genitalia, implying that she can never be reproductive like most women and thus is more likely to succeed on a spiritual plane. Other women who were reproductive are either praised for their maternal love or upbraided for their lack of it. As Nakamura Kyōko notes, "After the arrival of Buddhism, women became symbols of Buddha's boundless compassion, and motherly love was idealized. . . . Motherhood was the major reason for deferring to women, whose status was low in society."[31] However, in addition to these stock roles for women, there are other stories that praise women for putting their faith in the Buddhist teachings before their relationships with their parents, husbands, or children, and that criticize a woman's excessive attachment to her son. A few stories depict women whose superhuman strength is understood as a karmic reward for their actions in past lives. Other stories show nuns and laywomen being rewarded physically and materially for their religious fervor. Several stories involving women especially advocate for the compassionate release of animals, who were said to shower the sponsor with material and spiritual blessings. A number of stories encouraged faith in the *Lotus Sutra*, without mentioning the female-to-male transformation of the Dragon Girl described in the Devadatta chapter. As noted above, the transformation from female to male had yet to become a dominant religious ideal. Even though the Devadatta chapter was introduced during the Nara period, Nara commentaries generally did not emphasize it.[32] Instead, in one of the stories, a mother of seven children is shown as extraordinarily preoccupied with rituals of purification, herbal knowledge, and spiritual and physical discipline, all of which allows her to communicate with heavenly beings and ascend into heaven herself like a Daoist immortal.[33] Bernard Faure has remarked, "the motifs of stupidity, malice, and guilt of women are practically absent from the [*Nihon ryōiki*]," even though they later came to be pervasive in similar collections of the late Heian period, when such prejudices had become ingrained.[34] This suggests that in Kyōkai's time, expectations of women's conduct had not been completely subjected to Confucian norms or later Buddhist notions of female pollution.

Conclusion

From its introduction in the sixth century until the end of the Nara period, the Buddhist tradition was relatively inclusive of women in Japan. Female monastics were included in the state-sponsored temple system and fulfilled priestly functions similar to those of their male peers. That the full ordination tradition had not been transmitted to Japan seems to have been of little consequence for these female monastics during this early period. On a popular level, a positive and inclusive attitude toward women prevailed as well. Many of the negative concepts that would become more important in the Heian and medieval periods—such as those relating to women's Five Obstructions and Three Obediences, the need for female-to-male transformation in order to achieve Buddhahood, and the pollution associated with female reproductive functions—were not widespread during this period. As a result, women participated in the Buddhist tradition in multiple ways: as nuns, patrons, devotees, and even venerated exemplars of Buddhist virtues. On a social level, Buddhist renunciation provided new social options for women, including celibacy and communal living segregated by gender. In the Heian period, the state-sponsored network of Buddhist convents declined, but women continued to enjoy close integration into their natal families and chances to inherit property. In the meantime, particularly misogynistic concepts derived from Confucianism and Buddhism had not become popularly accepted, even though they existed in the writings of scholar monks.

4

The Heian Period

Women in Buddhism and Court Ritual

From the sixth through the eighth centuries, Buddhism was marked by a relative inclusiveness toward women. This was to change in the Heian period (794–1185). The imperial court moved the capital first in 784 to Nagaoka and then in 794 to Heiankyō, after which the new period has been named. Heiankyō, now known as Kyoto, remained the imperial capital until 1868. It is from the Heian period onward that we gradually have more information about individual women's lives and religious practices, particularly among the aristocracy. Despite the inequities of polygyny, the prevailing marriage system allowed elite women to remain integrated into their natal families, and they could inherit property freely. Women could also hold some kinds of government offices: they could serve as palace attendants or, to a limited extent, as priestesses at state-sponsored shrines as the power of female shamans waned. Furthermore, even though the system of state-sponsored Buddhist convents declined with the result that nuns no longer officiated in state rituals, elite women engaged in devotional practices as nuns, pilgrims, and patrons.

Marriage and Inheritance

Heian marriage and inheritance patterns shaped women's religious choices and opportunities. In premodern Japan, polygyny was an accepted practice among social elites. The Yōrō Code of the early eighth century technically allowed a man to have one principal wife while having as many concubines as he pleased. This practice was based on

Chinese models. Heian-period evidence suggests that the Japanese made no rigid distinctions between wives and concubines. There was a sense, however, that the principal wife had a privileged status compared to the secondary wives: she had special titles unique to her position, the husband was more likely to reside with her, and her sons would receive higher official appointments. The position of principal wife often fell to the woman whom a man married first, but in certain cases the principal wife was determined upon the selection of the wife's son as the principal heir. If the relationship with the principal wife ended in divorce or death, another wife might take her place. While the number of secondary wives was not legally restricted, in practice the number of wives in simultaneous relationships with a husband was usually limited to two or three, if not one. In addition to marriage, aristocrats would also engage in casual relationships with women serving as ladies-in-waiting at the imperial court, or they could take temporary wives while on an official appointment in the provinces.[1]

While marriage to the primary wife was usually based on political alliances between families, relationships with secondary wives and casual liaisons were romanticized in Heian fiction and poetry, in which the practice of *kaimami,* the male discovery of a beautiful woman by spying on her without her realizing that she has been exposed to view, was likened to the hunter's discovery of prey. To some scholars, this seems to suggest an undercurrent of symbolic male violence toward women.[2] This violence is sometimes graphically expressed in tales of male demons literally cannibalizing a female victim.[3] Actual rape was considered a punishable offense according to eighth-century legal codes following Chinese models: forcible sexual violation, meaning rape, was listed along with consensual sexual violation, meaning adultery. In both cases, the violation was not of the victim's body but of patrilineal authority. In the absence of virilocal marriage, however, premarital violations of female chastity and virginity were not problematized in Heian Japan. Forcible and consensual violations were actually often romanticized in Heian literature such as *The Tale of Genji.*[4]

As mentioned in the previous chapter, even though the Yōrō Code of the early eighth century and other contemporaneous government documents reflect a virilocal family structure similar to that of China, poetry of the time suggests that duolocal marriage was in fact commonly practiced in Japan in the Nara period. During the Heian period, marriages among the elites were usually not virilocal (the wife residing with the husband's family) but uxorilocal (the husband residing with the wife's family) or duolocal (husband and wife residing in separate households). In both cases, the wife resided with her parents. This meant that women remained closely tied into their birth families rather than being brought into their husbands' family, possibly along with other consorts. Duolocal marriage seems to have been more common for secondary wives, while primary wives were more likely to be in an uxorilocal marriage, particularly if the wife was of equal or higher status than her husband. An uxorilocal marriage might eventually evolve into a neolocal marriage (husband and wife residing in a joint residence but separate from their parents), as the wife's parents might relocate to another residence. Toward the end of the period, marriages were often neolocal, but in such cases the wife's parents provided the residence unless the wife was of significantly lower status than the husband or lacked her family's backing. In Heian literature, neolocal marriages in which the husband provided the residence were portrayed as representative of romance, functioning as Cinderella stories of sorts. By the end of the twelfth century, uxorilocal marriages had become very uncommon.[5]

The households of the courtly elites were populated not only with wives and daughters, but also with a variety of female attendants, many of them married to other men. For instance, the inner palace of the imperial court housed empresses, grand empresses, and senior grand empresses, junior consorts, and concubines, who were all imperial consorts of varying ranks. In addition, there were female attendants (*nyōbō*) and female officials (*nyokan*), who ranked lower than female attendants. These attendants and officials were based upon female officials whose offices were established by the Chinese-inspired law codes of the eighth century. They served the imperial consorts, the emperor, and the crown prince, and they were assisted by female servants such as maids and servant girls, who acted as the menial support staff. Similar to the imperial court, the households of the aristocracy and imperial princes likewise employed female attendants, wet nurses, and servants. Wet nurses and their husbands, who might serve the family as stewards and tutors for male children, enjoyed particularly privileged positions.[6]

Women could legally inherit wealth during the Heian period. Before the Heian period, the Taihō Code, enacted in 702, closely followed Chinese examples and allowed only for inheritance by sons, privileging the eldest, but this may not have reflected actual Japanese practice. The Yōrō Code seems to have incorporated Japanese customs by making some allowance for the male heir's mother and sisters: the mother stood to inherit nearly as much as the principal heir, while the other sons received half and daughters a quarter. The codes allowed the adoption of heirs, who by the Heian period also included women. Actual inheritance documents from the Heian period indicate that women freely inherited property and were also adopted into other families for this purpose. Not only did daughters inherit property from their mothers or fathers, but wives also inherited from their husbands with the understanding that the property transfer was in perpetuity and did not revert to male heirs with the woman's death.[7]

According to Jeffrey Mass, "women were daughters and sisters before they were wives, mothers, and widows."[8] Marriage was not generally believed to involve joint property, but each of the spouses had his or her own. Therefore, daughters with close relationships to either parent supersede a more distant male relative and inherit property; furthermore, such inheritances were conveyed in perpetuity, meaning that the daughters could do with the property as they pleased. Women's inheritance was limited only insofar as it involved only private property but not public offices, which women could not hold or inherit. Aristocratic women in the capital owned or became custodians of large estates

(*shōen*), but women in the provinces could not hold offices oversee-
ing estate land. Ultimately, these restrictions limited women's political
power and meant that sons rather than daughters received a larger share
of the inheritance from both parents.[9] Yet their economic assets gave
women some freedom to pursue their religious goals.

Demons, Spirit Possession, and Polygyny

In the highly aestheticized society of Heian Japan, polygyny posed problems for elite women even though they were economically privileged.
Social etiquette among the nobility prohibited the open expression of raw emotions in romantic relationships. Emotions had to be
carefully packaged in poetic expression. Repressed tensions within
polygynous relationships, such as overt female sexuality, jealousy, and
resentment, were expressed metaphorically by likening women to
demons—potentially demonizing women themselves. In courtly poetry
and prose, sexual desires were playfully likened to demonic emotions,
whether felt by men or by women. In didactic tales that were more
strongly reflective of Buddhist doctrine than was the courtly literature,
such metaphors were expressed more literally, with actual demons (*oni*)
taking human form to gratify their sexual desires and engage in cannibalistic violence. While demons in earlier tales generally took male
form, we see the emergence of demons in female form—both young
and old women—from the latter half of the Heian period onward. In the
case of demons in the form of young, attractive women, the demons are
motivated by jealousy and rage at having been spurned.[10]

We sense here a didactic lesson that cautions women against expressing rage and jealousy (lest they turn into demons) and men against
pursuing affairs with an unknown woman (lest she turn out to be a
cannibalistic demon). Such stories seem to carry similar messages as
contemporaneous tales about men being lured into relationships with
foxes who had taken female human form. While the foxes—at most,
causing mental confusion, and at best bringing good fortune to the

men—are generally more benign than the demons, such liaisons are equally doomed to failure upon discovery. This again suggests that relationships with unknown partners, though ostensibly romantic, were considered potentially dangerous.[11]

There were also stories about old women turning into demons. In some tales, demons in the form of elderly women lull unsuspecting travelers into trusting them in order to cannibalistically consume them later. In many such stories, the demons are discovered and the plot is foiled. Another tale features an elderly mother who turns into a voracious demon that attacks her own sons. We sense here resistance against the ideals of filial piety and respect for the elderly, as there seems to be a tendency to express through metaphor intergenerational strife, the mental deterioration caused by senility, and the conflicted feelings younger family members might have caring for elderly relatives. Paradoxically, however, the tales seem to encourage readers to engage in filial piety and to take good care of children as well. In one tale, for instance, a young woman seeks shelter at an old woman's residence in order to give birth to her unwanted child; once she realizes that the old woman plans to devour the child, she decides to escape and care for her baby after all. The mother's plans to abandon her child are transformed into motherly care when she is confronted with the even greater horror of cannibalism.[12] The image of the female demon persisted and further evolved throughout the medieval period, sometimes imbuing women with mysterious and erotic but terribly violent powers, sometimes marginalizing and ultimately disempowering them.[13] While it is impossible to give a consistent, universal interpretation to these demon tales, it is undeniable that the tales simultaneously were influenced by and contributed to the growing demonization of women and their bodies from the Heian period through the medieval period.

A similarly complex argument can be made about spirit possession. Heian literature depicts women as particularly (but not exclusively) susceptible to spirit possession. Spirit possession was one of several causes commonly believed to be at the root of physical or mental ailments.

Women were thought to be especially vulnerable during childbirth, which was very dangerous and often fatal before the advent of modern medicine. During childbirth, Buddhist monks and *yin-yang* diviners were commissioned to conduct esoteric rituals and chant spells and incantations in order to transfer the possessing spirits into female mediums, where they then could be identified and expelled. Spirit possession, especially as described in *The Tale of Genji* by the female author Murasaki Shikibu (ca. 973–ca. 1020), may not simply have signified that women were the passive, weaker sex (because they were more likely to be affected by possessing spirits), but may also have served as a means by which women in polygynous relationships could find empowerment. Raw emotions such as jealousy and resentment, which otherwise had to be repressed, could be voiced and acted out in spirit possession because the "victim" was not considered culpable. While from the male perspective the relationship with the possessing spirit was antagonistic, from the female perspective the possessed and the possessing spirit could enter an alliance to articulate in an oblique way their grievances in polygynous settings.[14]

Female Shamans and the Kamo Priestess

Scholars have noted that the status and influence of independent female shamans and shrine priestesses who received patronage from the court declined during the Heian period. Scattered records in court diaries and national histories also attest that women continued to serve as shamans and spirit mediums elsewhere in Heian society, often merging Buddhist practices with local cults. However, the court often regarded the shamans' activities with suspicion if their predictions led to social unrest or interfered with the affairs of the court. As early as the mid-seventh century, the court sought to limit the activities of spirit mediums among the populace. Restrictive legislation was also enacted with the eighth-century Yōrō Code, which prohibited leading people astray with magic. As a result of the legislation, female shamans found in violation were sentenced to exile. The Yōrō Code allowed female shamans to practice only at official shrines, but unlike their male counterparts, they held no formal office at these institutions. The *Engishiki* of 927 further curtailed the practices of female shamans who acted outside the official shrine system by incorporating into the official shrine system the cult of vengeful spirits (*goryō*), which had been the specialty of independent shamans. The *Engishiki* did create positions for shamans at the shrines, but they were largely given domestic tasks such as making clothing for the divinities and cleaning the sacred precinct. Furthermore, female shamans were increasingly viewed as divinities' consorts who had to entertain their divine spouses.[15]

The example of the priestess at the Upper Kamo Shrines illustrates how female shamans were increasingly integrated into the official bureaucracy. The office of the Kamo Shrine priestess, who came from imperial stock like her Ise counterpart, was instituted during the early Heian period and persisted until the early Kamakura period. The office of the Kamo priestess as documented in the *Engishiki* shared many features with the office of the Ise priestess in terms of her legal status, selection process, installation, and term of office. However, while the office of the Ise priestess was established before the Heian period, the first Kamo priestess was appointed under Emperor Saga (785–842, r. 809–823) in the early ninth century. This priestess was Princess Uchiko, who was the daughter of Emperor Saga and Queen Consort Kōno. In this role, she was followed by thirty-three imperial princesses, the last of whom was appointed in 1204.[16]

It appears that the Kamo Shrine Festival included a ritual in which a consecrated maiden became the Upper Kamo Shrine divinity's bride for one night. Before the appointment of an imperial princess for this role at the Upper Kamo Shrine, a maiden from one of the sacerdotal families serving the shrines may have been chosen to perform this role. When the capital was moved closer to the shrines, the importance of the shrine increased and the Kamo Festival became an important event in the court's ritual calendar. Consequently, an imperial princess was appointed to serve the Upper Kamo Shrine. The divine marriage rites involving the Kamo priestess were attended only by appointed officials, but the processions associated with the festival became elaborate public spectacles.[17] Sei Shōnagon (966–1017) records in her *Pillow Book* (ca. 1002) how she enjoyed the splendor of the processions and beauty of the scenery. She was also in awe of the priestess's ritual purity. As she sat waiting for the priestess's procession to arrive, she registered her dismay that the priestess's purity may have been violated:

> While we sat in our carriage waiting impatiently for the procession, we saw a group of men in red coming from the Upper Shrine . . . , carrying the High Priestess's empty palanquins. It impressed me deeply that the High Priestess herself had traveled in one of these palanquins; but I was rather disturbed at the thought that low fellows like these could have come close to her sacred presence.[18]

Once chosen for office, the Kamo priestess resided in a special apartment within the imperial palace until the following year, when she proceeded to her residence near the Kamo Shrines. There she remained for the rest of her appointment, served by a large retinue of male and female officials and attendants. While in office, the Kamo priestess had to observe periods of fasting, purifications, ablutions, offerings, and festival celebrations, the most important of which was the Kamo Festival. She also observed linguistic taboos similar to those of the Ise priestess, avoiding words associated with ritual pollution and with Buddhism.[19]

In fact, the case of the priestess who served at the Upper Kamo Shrine illustrates the complex presence of Buddhism at an official shrine. The taboos did not prevent several Kamo priestesses from developing an interest in Buddhism that culminated in taking the tonsure after their tenure as priestess ended. The most fascinating example is the Kamo priestess Senshi (964–1035), the daughter of Emperor Murakami (926–967), who held this office for fifty-seven years. Senshi was an accomplished poet and wrote a large number of poems on Buddhist themes that were collected along with poems composed by her immediate female attendants in the *Hosshin wakashū* (A collection of Japanese poems for the awakening of faith).[20] Her poetry gives voice to the tension between her Buddhist faith and the strictures of her office. She writes, for instance,

> Though I think about it, it is taboo, a thing not to be said,
>   and so all that I can do is turn in that direction and weep.[21]

One twelfth-century editor explained that the Kamo priestess wrote this poem while facing west, suggesting that she was yearning for Amitābha Buddha's Pure Land. A careful reading of the *Hosshin wakashū* suggests that Senshi had considerable familiarity with and insightful comprehension of Buddhist scriptures popular during her day, including first and foremost the *Lotus Sutra*, but also the *Heart Sutra*, the *Flower Garland Sutra*, the *Great Wisdom Sutra*, the *Benevolent King's Sutra*, the *Nirvana Sutra*, and others.[22] Buddhism clearly had retained its appeal for elite women during this period, even though the system of state-sponsored convents had declined by the Heian period.

The Decline of State-Sponsored Buddhist Convents

Scholars have debated the reasons for the decline in state-sponsored Buddhist convents. With the passing of the last female emperor of the Nara period, Emperor Shōtoku, no female emperor would ascend the throne until 1629. Some scholars have credited the absence of a ruling female monarch with the decline in state support for provincial nunneries. Additionally, with the arrival of the precept master Ganjin (688–763) in 754, orthodox ordinations for male monastics (who staffed the provincial monasteries) had been established without equivalent for female monastics. This may have led to the perception that the nuns were incapable of conducting valid state rites. Furthermore, the decline of the state-sponsored nunneries can also be attributed to the overall decline of the state's power based on the imperial legal codes of the eighth century, which were gradually eroded by private interests and court nobles' private estates.[23]

Moreover, the institutional hierarchy of Shingon and Tendai, two new Buddhist lineages introduced in the early Heian period, showed little interest in training nuns. Both excluded women from their respective mountain centers (Mount Kōya and Mount Hiei), a practice that was eventually adopted at some temples belonging to the older Nara lineages. Even though the Tendai master Ennin (794–864) promoted the establishment of an ordination platform for women, his attempt remained isolated and was ultimately unsuccessful. Nunneries that managed to survive often lost their autonomy and were placed under the authority of a monastery, relegating them to a state of dependency and secondary status. Simultaneously, belief in blood pollution (through menstruation and childbirth) slowly began to gain currency among the nobility and in monastic circles alongside the Confucian concept of women's Three Obediences and the Buddhist notion of women's Five Obstructions. Given the proliferation of such beliefs, the notion that women were innately flawed and sinful spread. It remains unclear which of these factors caused the disappearance of state-sponsored convents; the end result, however, was that nuns were excluded from participating in state-sponsored assemblies.[24]

Buddhist Theories of Salvation

It is also from this time that the story of the Dragon King's daughter's transformation into a male before attaining Buddhahood—in the Devadatta chapter of the *Lotus Sutra*—became more widely known. The spread of Tendai Buddhism increased the popularity of the *Lotus Sutra*. With the growing prominence of the scripture as a whole, the Devadatta chapter also received greater exposure (see figure 4.1). From the Heian period onward, scholarly monks stressed that a woman needed to transform into a man first before becoming a Buddha. Among the nobility,

FIGURE 4.1. Frontispiece of the Devadatta chapter of the *Lotus Sutra*. The Dragon Girl offers her jewel to the Buddha. *Heike nōkyō*. Japan, 1164. National Treasure. Ink, colors, gold and silver on paper. Itsukushima Shrine, Hiroshima Prefecture, Japan. Image copyright © Itsukushima Shrine. Image Source: Benridō.

the practices of sponsoring elaborate assemblies for eight expositions of the scripture and copying the text spread knowledge of the *Lotus Sutra* beyond elite scholar monks. Ideas regarding the transformation from male to female are reflected in devotional poetry and prose literature attributed to women.[25] This gives credence to Bernard Faure's argument that Buddhism contributed actively to women's loss of status. Ironically, Buddhist teachings that stressed special salvation for women reinforced the notion that men were spiritually superior.[26] In the *Miraculous Tales of the Lotus Sutra* (*Dainihonkoku hokke genki*; ca. 1040), compiled by the monk Chingen, the nun Gansei, for instance, is said to have excelled in her devotion to the Buddhist precepts and abhorrence of evil. According to Chingen, "Although she had a female appearance, she had the faith of a male novice."[27] She transcends the limitations of her female gender and adheres to a male ideal—which appears to a modern reader to be a backhanded compliment.[28]

Similarly, the scriptures of Pure Land Buddhism, which also became an important force within Tendai (and within other forms of medieval Buddhism), held that women would not be reborn as women in Amitābha's Western Pure Land, again mandating a female-to-male transformation at the moment of rebirth. Religious vows accompanying funerals (often composed by men on behalf of women) reiterated the trope of the Five Obstructions, suggesting that a woman would benefit from transforming into a man upon rebirth.[29] In some cases, the aristocratic families, including the Fujiwara, had the remains of female family members interred within temple precincts, such as on Mount Hiei and Mount Kōya, that were closed to women while they were alive. Prayers recited upon their deaths suggest that these women were thought to have transcended their female form and joined the male ancestors in guaranteeing prosperity for the family line.[30]

However, such prayers may give us only limited indications as to how women (or their families) actually imagined their rebirth (see figure 4.2). Contemporaneous grave goods such as combs and mirrors suggest that both women and their families continued to think of their reborn selves as women.[31] Hagiographical accounts from the Heian period of women's rebirth in the Pure Land are remarkably silent on the matter of transformation and merely describe the physical signs in this world upon the women's passing: beautiful fragrances, music, mist, or purple clouds at the moment of death.[32] Despite Pure Land doctrines about female transformation, devotees would envision rebirth in their own female bodies and reunion with previously deceased relatives, male or female.[33]

Likewise, Chingen's *Miraculous Tales of the Lotus Sutra* is silent on the matter of female-to-male transformation. It contains no reference to the Devadatta chapter in particular, but depicts devout nuns and laywomen venerating the scripture as a whole or perhaps the chapter on the bodhisattva Avalokiteśvara. As in the miracle tales about rebirth in Amitābha Buddha's Pure Land, at death these women are said to have

FIGURE 4.2. Frontispiece of the Medicine King chapter of the *Lotus Sutra*. A woman faces Amitābha Buddha. The image is inscribed with the words "if," "this," "there is," "at the end of this life," "immediately," "world of peace and delight," "born." These verbal fragments refer to a passage in the Medicine King chapter that reads, "If . . . there is a woman who hears this sutra and carries out its practices as the sutra directs, when her life here on earth comes to an end she will immediately go to the world of Peace and Delight where the Buddha Amitayus dwells surrounded by the assembly of great bodhisattvas and there will be born seated on a jeweled seat in the center of a lotus blossom" (translation in Watson, *The Lotus Sutra*, 287). *Heike nōkyō*. Japan, 1164. National Treasure. Ink, colors, gold and silver on paper. Itsukushima Shrine, Hiroshima Prefecture, Japan. Image copyright © Itsukushima Shrine. Image Source: Benridō.

experienced miraculous signs: bright lights, pleasant fragrances, and reawakening from the dead. In all accounts, the women maintain their female bodies as they are transported to the world beyond. For example, a pious laywoman belonging to the Fujiwara clan transforms into a celestial lady after refusing defiled, this-worldly food and subsequently flies off toward the east (implying that she has gone to the paradise of the Buddha of Jeweled Dignity, who according to the twenty-eighth chapter of the *Lotus Sutra*, resides in this direction). Another pious laywoman appears to an attendant in a dream, in which she "ascended into the air, wearing a beautifully decorated celestial robe and having a jeweled crown on her head, her body radiating light as she went to the Tosotsu Heaven [i.e., Maitreya's Tuṣita Heaven]."[34] At the death of a third woman, the monk Kōdō dreams that the woman is picked up by a procession of monks with three jeweled vehicles. She herself is "dressed in the robes of a heavenly lady and wearing a jeweled crown and necklace."[35] And finally, the father of a fourth woman dreams "that his daughter, dressed in beautiful clothes, pressed her palms together and said, 'Thanks to the power and assistance of Kannon, I have left the hell of Tachiyama, and have been reborn in the Tōri Heaven [i.e., Trāyastriṃśa, ruled by Indra].'"[36] These dream visions suggest that the women were thought to have transformed into female celestial beings (*tennyo*) rather than into men. Rebirth as a celestial lady presented an appealing alternative to transformation into a male body. It also suggests that during this period there were many different soteriological possibilities for women, including rebirth in Maitreya's Tuṣita Heaven, Indra's Trāyastriṃśa Heaven, the Buddha of Jeweled Dignity's Eastern Paradise, and Amitābha's Western Pure Land.

Family members remained deeply concerned with the posthumous well-being of their female relatives. In one case of the high aristocracy, both male and female members of the Fujiwara clan took an active role in the spiritual care of the family matriarch, the nun Ichijō (1024–1103), as she was dying, particularly during the months of illness preceding her death. They eventually moved her to the worship hall in the family residence. Ten days after her death, her grandson dreamed that she had been reborn in the Pure Land due to her devotion to Amitābha, Avalokiteśvara, and the Buddhist scriptures, particularly the Medicine King chapter of the *Lotus Sutra*. After the death of another female member of the family, Lady Nishi, the women of the family offered copies of sutras and Buddhist images at seven-day intervals during the first forty-nine days after Lady Nishi's death. These seven-day intervals were considered particularly significant for effecting a good rebirth for the deceased.[37]

Private Ordinations, Patronage, and Pilgrimage

Despite the decline of official nunneries, ordinations remained an important factor in women's lives; they became linked, however, to specific times in the female life cycle and did not always imply permanent withdrawal to a convent. While full, state-sponsored ordinations were not an option for women, they could commit to varying numbers of basic Buddhist precepts (generally five to ten), through either self-ordination or private ordinations from a male preceptor. While Buddhist ordinations were often referred to as "leaving home" (*shukke*), many women continued living with their families after taking the tonsure rather than forsaking all elements of their lay lives. Therefore, some scholars call such ordinations "lay ordinations." Men also had similar ordinations, but they technically also had the option of obtaining state-sponsored, official ordinations. Lay ordinations among the aristocratic elites were elaborate affairs with their own ordination traditions, as recorded in ordination manuals.[38]

In the Heian period, such ordinations were thought to generate karmic merit for the ordinant, thus alleviating illness and securing divine protection. Furthermore, ordinants hoped to attain a good rebirth for themselves through such generation of merit. For instance, ordination was one way people endeavored to secure birth in the Western Pure Land of Amitābha Buddha, devotion to whom became popular during this period. During this time, the elites spent considerable effort preparing for death in order to be reborn into the Pure Land. Once having taken lay ordinations, men and women could retire from their household obligations and devote themselves to devotional practices such as Amitābha worship. For women, ordination also signaled an end to their sexual activity, which meant that it was similar to a divorce from their husbands, who might or might not stay sexually active with other, perhaps younger, wives. Occasionally, women took the tonsure because of the death of a child (particularly in the early Heian period) or of their husband (particularly in the mid- to late Heian period), presumably to

FIGURE 4.3. Frontispiece of the Encouragement of Devotion chapter of the *Lotus Sutra*. Two Buddhist nuns praying in front of a Buddhist altar. One has a partial tonsure, the other a full tonsure. *Heike nōkyō*. Japan, 1164. National Treasure. Ink, colors, gold and silver on paper. Itsukushima Shrine, Hiroshima Prefecture, Japan. Image copyright © Itsukushima Shrine. Image Source: Benridō.

pray for salvation of their deceased child's or husband's spirit along with their own. The tendency to take vows after a husband's death became stronger from the Kamakura period (1185–1333), when renunciation became a way for women to demonstrate their chastity and loyalty to their husbands' households by not remarrying.[39]

The extent of the women's commitment to the precepts was expressed in the tonsure style. Women's long hair was eroticized in Heian literature; thus, even a moderate cropping could indicate a religious commitment (see figure 4.3). A woman could choose to cut her bangs or cut all of her hair shoulder-length. If she wanted to show the deepest commitment, she could choose a full tonsure. Since long hair was a prominent sign of feminine beauty, tonsure implied casting off one's femininity. Therefore, full tonsure for women implied an end to courtship and marriage. Cutting one's hair to intermediate length may have been related to probationary nunhood, whether as one step in the orthodox ordination of nuns, who, according to monastic codes, first had to pass two years of intermediate renunciation to ensure that they were not pregnant before being fully admitted to the community of nuns, or in the sense that the ordination was considered provisional and thus reversible. Similarly, these nuns' clothing, ranging from colorful lay robes to simple monastic robes, indicated their level of monastic pledge, removing them in varying degrees from sexualized femininity. Interestingly, the withdrawal from an overt sexual identity and the adoption of an androgynous monastic name entailed legal and political privileges for the nuns. Through this monastic masculinization, women were occasionally able to act legally on a par with men in the public sphere.[40]

Like their Nara predecessors, female members of the highest levels of courtly elites also became Buddhist patrons. Tachibana no Kachiko (786–850), Emperor Saga's queen consort, was inspired by a nun from Hokkeji, a temple founded by Empress Kōmyō. Kachiko subsequently sponsored a Japanese monk on his journey to China and later built a large temple for a Chinese monk, where she eventually retired after taking the tonsure following her husband's death. Her daughter, Seishi (809–879), who was Emperor Junna's queen consort, eventually also became a nun, either because of her husband's death or because her son was deposed as the crown prince. She withdrew to her deceased husband's retirement palace, the Junna'in, which she turned into a family convent. There she sponsored lectures on the *Lotus Sutra* and engaged in providing assistance to abandoned and orphaned children.[41] According to the *Sanbō ekotoba*, a Buddhist primer composed by Minamoto no Tamenori for Sonshi (ca. 965–985), an imperial princess who had taken the tonsure, the nuns at Junna'in celebrated a biannual service honoring the memory of Ānanda. A close disciple of the Buddha, Ānanda had convinced the Buddha to admit his aunt and adoptive mother Mahāprajāpatī and other women to the Buddhist order.[42]

In the late Heian period, aristocratic women were also engaged in sponsoring services to honor Buddhist relics. In the tradition of the court, women had long been associated with Buddhist relics and jewels, whether through scripture (e.g., the Dragon Girl's giving her jewel to the Buddha), through legend (e.g., the tale of the nun Sari, literally "relic," in the *Nihon ryōiki*), or through practice (e.g., female Emperors Suiko and Shōtoku engaged in relic worship and stupa construction). In the twelfth century, imperial consorts of Fujiwara descent sponsored large relic assemblies at Buddhist temples. They also gave their patronage for stupa veneration and rites of relic worship. Such rituals were probably meant to assure the propitious afterlife of familial ancestors. Not only did these women engage in relic worship, but they were also responsible for the storage, maintenance, and protection of their families' relic collections. In this way they helped maintain the familial lineage, particularly the Fujiwara Kujō line.[43]

Whether or not they had taken the tonsure, noblewomen living in the capital engaged in pilgrimages to Buddhist temples in the foothills surrounding Kyoto and Nara. Pilgrims prepared themselves spiritually by observing a fast before and during the pilgrimage. They were usually accompanied by attendants on their journeys, and the size of their retinue and means of travel were reflective of their status. Female pilgrims appear to have undertaken these journeys for gender-specific concerns: to pray for wealth and success including successful marital relations; healing (especially gender-specific illnesses related to spirit possession and pregnancy); and the conception of a child.[44] Like spirit possession, pilgrimages may also have afforded women an opportunity to voice their discontent and gain liberation from the emotional distress caused by the institution of polygyny.[45] For instance, the poet Izumi Shikibu (b. 978) records in her diary that when her husband failed to visit her, she decided to set off on a seven-day pilgrimage to Ishiyamadera in order to dispel her boredom. Her absence immediately sparked interest from her husband, who sent her a message leaving her satisfied with his renewed attention.[46]

Conclusion

During the Heian period, elite women were not yet subjected to the strictures of the virilocal, patrilineal household, nor had spiritual concepts such as the Five Obstructions, the Three Obediences, the transformation from female to male, and the notion that the female body was exceptionally polluted become widely prevalent. While polygyny did have its negative aspects and led to the demonization of female jealousy, prevailing marriage and inheritance practices still gave women considerable privileges and freedoms. Even though women were largely excluded from holding political and religious offices—with the exception of courtly attendants and high priestesses—they were not prevented from seeking private ordinations, engaging in personal devotion, and even becoming great patrons of Buddhism. However, as we shall see in the subsequent chapter, the virilocal, patrilineal household became the norm and women were increasingly associated with defilement over the course of the medieval period. At the same time, they were reintegrated more fully into the monastic order.

5

The Medieval Period

Buddhist Reform Movements and the Demonization of Femininity

Japan's medieval period (1185–1600) was marked by political and military instability and multiple power centers, including warrior governments and an imperial court split into two competing lineages for nearly sixty years during the fourteenth century. A single imperial lineage was reestablished in 1392, but peace was short-lived. The Onin War (1467–1477) marked the beginning of a period of protracted warfare between rival regional warlords that lasted into the late sixteenth century. Among the most important legal developments for women were changes in marriage and inheritance patterns spurred on by political and military instability. While women retained a fair amount of autonomy until the end of the Kamakura period (1185–1333), they became increasingly integrated into their husbands' households during the fourteenth century. The rise in virilocal marriages was accompanied by a loss of women's inheritance rights. Additionally, remarriage gradually became less acceptable for widows, due primarily to the spread of Confucian ideas about marriage and feminine ideals such as the Three Obediences (to father, husband, and son). These changes had far-reaching repercussions for female renunciation, the increasing demonization of female jealousy and sexuality, the association of women's bodies with pollution and defilement, and the exclusion of women from some religious spaces. At the same time, women found new opportunities for participation in religious practices in Buddhist revival movements, the emergence of new forms of Buddhism, and the growth of devotional and pilgrimage cults, as well as the introduction of Christianity toward the end of the period.

The Emergence of the Patrilineal Household

In contrast to the uxorilocal and neolocal practices of the Heian (794–1185) and Kamakura periods, virilocal marriage, in which the wife moved into the husband's household, became the norm in the fourteenth century. Takamure Itsue (1894–1964), a pioneering Japanese feminist historian, interpreted this shift as a gradual development toward the disempowerment of women. Women were severed from their birth families at marriage and needed to integrate into their husbands' household. The new system constructed women's bodies as means to produce offspring for the patriarchal lineage of the husband's household and unilaterally imposed ideals of chastity on women. Since the new bride now needed to be formally integrated into the husband's household, wedding rituals, which during the Heian period had been a relatively simple acknowledgment by the bride's parents and exchange of food and drink between the couple at the wife's residence, became more elaborate public affairs. The bride had to be gradually integrated to overcome the so-called hearth taboo, occurring when women of two different lineages (those of the mother-in-law and the daughter-in-law) shared the same kitchen. To achieve such integration, the bride was brought to the husband's residence in a grand procession and installed in a separate residential section before formally moving into the main household.[1]

Yet the growing affirmation of the patrilineal household did not necessarily disempower women. Rather, it strengthened the authority of the primary wife as a manager in the husband's household. Additionally, the primary wife often acted as the head of the household after her husband's death. Furthermore, whereas the parent-child bond had previously been most important, the relationship between husband and wife became far more central during this period, even though motherhood retained its importance because it was essential for the continuation of the patriarchal lineage.[2] To put it another way, before the fourteenth century, a woman's primary identity was derived from being her father's daughter, but from the fourteenth century on, it was derived from being her husband's wife. Naturally, not every woman in an elite household was a primary wife and household manager. These households also included concubines and a variety of servants.[3]

These marriage patterns and the above-mentioned roles accessible to elite women should not, however, be generalized to nonelite women, about whose lives much less is known. It is unlikely that polygynous, virilocal marriages and multigenerational households with a large staff of attendants extended beyond the socioeconomic elites (including wealthy commoner townspeople). Archeological evidence suggests that nonelite urban households likely consisted of nuclear families (husband, wife, and children) rather than extended households comprising multiple generations, servants, and concubines. Among townspeople such marriages were not supported by the husband's wealth alone, but rather relied upon the labor of both husband and wife.[4]

Among the elites, the shift from uxorilocal to virilocal marriage had important consequences for inheritance patterns. While Heian women were full-fledged members of their fathers' households with complete inheritance rights and continued to inherit property throughout the Kamakura period, by the fourteenth century, virilocal marriage had made women temporary members of their natal families. They were therefore less likely to inherit property from the paternal line of their natal household.[5] During the Kamakura period, women of warrior families retained the right to inherit property, and overall they held more political power and influence than in previous and later periods. However, women's inheritance rights began to shift from those held in perpetuity to those held only for one generation. An early trigger for the shift in inheritance rights was military threat from abroad. When Japan faced the threat of a Mongol invasion in the 1280s, the military government issued legislation to curtail female inheritances to safeguard the funds to maintain regional military guard posts. Shortly thereafter, other kinds of restrictions against female heirs were practiced widely. Such restrictions included limitations to lifetime inheritance, inheritances that daughters could pass on only if they bore sons, or inheritances in which daughters received much less land than sons.[6]

However, women were not entirely left without property of their own. Even as fathers gradually became reluctant in the late Kamakura period to bequeath property to their daughters, mothers continued to bequeath property to their daughters and found backing from the shogunate in legal disputes.[7] Luis Frois (1532?–1597), a Jesuit missionary who spent more than three decades in Japan in the late sixteenth century, observed, "In Europe, property is held in common by the married couple; in Japan, each has his or her property separately, and sometimes the wife lends hers to the husband at interest."[8] Some women were able to accumulate a great deal of wealth independent of the men in their families, and some even became wealthy moneylenders. Moreover, while women had largely lost the right to own land as the Muromachi period (1336–1573) progressed, they retained the right into the Edo period (1600–1868) to own movable property.[9] Women could bring such property into their husbands' household upon marriage and retained their property rights even if the marriage ended in divorce.[10]

These changes in marriage and inheritance patterns had direct consequences on religious practices. The new patriarchal values permeated associations that managed and supported local shrines in medieval Japan. Initially, membership in such associations mostly comprised local elite males—excluding outsiders, tenant farmers, and other poor village members. Women could play limited roles due to their status as daughters and wives of male members. In some cases, women even had their own shrine associations. As virilocal marriage became more widespread, daughters were increasingly seen as outsiders because they would eventually move outside their natal villages after marriage. This meant that from the mid- to late fourteenth century, they were often barred from taking ceremonial roles in the shrine associations of their natal villages. By contrast, wives could occasionally form adjunct associations linked to their husbands' associations. This shift also had economic reasons.

From the mid-fourteenth century, many villages owned communal land that was tied to membership in the shrine guild. Even though membership eventually expanded beyond elites to include all peasants in the village, outsiders (including daughters who had married out of the village) were excluded. In contrast to daughters, wives were valued not just for their labor but also for their role in the continuation of the patriarchal line by bearing children. As a result, even though there were some exceptions, women were relatively unlikely to donate land directly and independently of male family members to village shrines. This contributed to further gender discrepancies in political status, since male members of the community used such donations to affirm their political status in the community and in the patriarchal organization.[11]

The Revival of Female Renunciation

Changes in marriage and inheritance practices also affected women's motivations for choosing monastic renunciation. The warfare that accompanied the transition from the Heian to the Kamakura period left many widows, many of whom chose to become nuns. For instance, several aristocratic and warrior women whose husbands were on the losing side of the Jōkyū Disturbance (1221) became the disciples of the monk Myōe (1173–1232), who was instrumental in helping the widow of Nakamikado Muneyuki (1174–1221) establish Zenmyōji, a Kegon convent, in Hiraoka, Yamashiro Province, in 1223. Like Zenmyōji, other convents were founded to support widows and orphans left behind in the aftermath of military conflicts. The convent Keiaiji in Kyoto, for example, was founded by the nun Mugai Nyodai (1223–1298), a prominent disciple of the Chinese Zen master Wuxue Zuyuan (1226–1286), after her father died and her husband was exiled.[12] During the medieval period, renunciation was no longer chosen only to signify retirement from a sexually active life. Now renunciation, and refusal to remarry, became a way for widows to demonstrate loyalty to their husbands' household. Over the course of the medieval period, widows came to be expected to seek Buddhist renunciation, regardless of whether they were very young or of advanced age. Widows also now had an additional reason for choosing renunciation. Since they were less likely to inherit property from their natal household, they needed to rely on their late husbands' household for support. By becoming nuns, they could simultaneously continue to lay claim to support from their husbands' household and maintain a certain level of independence from their parents-in-law. During this period, then, elite practices in Japan signaled a renewed embrace of Chinese values, including the Confucian virtues of loyalty and female chastity.[13]

At the same time, the introduction of Zen Buddhism and precept revival movements led to growth in elite convents for women. The largest number of medieval convents was affiliated with the Zen sects, particularly Rinzai Zen. These Rinzai convents were mostly founded in the Muromachi period and located in the Kyoto and Kamakura areas. Eventually, the Rinzai sect identified major convents as "five mountain" (*gozan*) convents, which were the structural equivalent of the elite *gozan* temples for Rinzai monks. Sōtō Zen had a much smaller number of convents, most of which were founded in the late Kamakura period and several of which belonged to the lineage of the monk Keizan Jōkin (1268–1325). The Ritsu precept revival movement of Eison (1201–1290) also led to the founding or revitalization of a significant number of convents, including the elite convents Hokkeji and Chūgūji in Yamato Province. Eison emphasized observance of the orthodox monastic precepts for both male and female renunciants. As a result, his lineage established full ordinations for women, beginning with ordinations as novices (in Japanese, *shamini*; in Sanskrit, *srāmaṇerika*) and postulants (in Japanese, *shikishamana*; in Sanskrit, *sikṣamaṇā*) and culminating in fully ordained nuns (in Japanese, *bikuni*; in Sanskrit, *bhikṣuṇi*). In addition to Zen and Ritsu convents, there were also a few Pure Land convents belonging to the Jōdo and Ji sects, such as Daihongan at Zenkōji in Shinano Province and Mantokuji in Kōzuke Province, respectively. However, there is evidence that some of these Pure Land convents may have originally belonged to the Zen or Ritsu sects and switched affiliation beginning in the sixteenth century.[14]

New interest in women's ordination and the establishment of convents may have been spurred on by the introduction of Zen lineages from China, where female monastic orders had much greater presence than in Japan. Chinese Zen masters who came to Japan and Japanese Zen masters who had traveled to China had been exposed to the prominent presence of nuns in Chinese Buddhism and thus may have understood the female monastic order as integral to Buddhist monasticism as a whole. The influx of Zen Buddhism was one of the motivating factors for the older Buddhist sects in Japan to form revival movements. Zen monks and other monks who had contact with Zen were the first to take an interest in women's ordination and train female disciples. However, these prominent advocates—such as Myōe and Eison—radically re-envisioned women's roles vis-à-vis their male teachers: female adherents were supposed to act not as privileged patrons (who ultimately controlled valuable assets and thus acted as de facto employers of the monks) but rather as supplicant disciples to a male teacher even if the women were of higher social status.[15]

Whether these elite women entirely accepted this new hierarchy is questionable. Even though several Japanese scholars have argued that the community of nuns associated with Eison was closely monitored and managed by the male clergy, Lori Meeks, a scholar of Japanese Buddhism, has shown that the nuns had relative autonomy in their daily lives. Eison visited their temples relatively infrequently, and there is no evidence of male administrators for the convents. Ultimately, the nuns probably did not internalize the more androcentric aspects of Eison's movement based at Saidaiji, reflecting perhaps a gendered difference in doctrinal focus.[16] According to Meeks,

> Unlike Saidaiji texts, which emphasize both women's weak position in the Buddhist cosmos and their reliance upon the mercy of the male priests, the texts associated with the women's order do not treat gender

as a problem. They also downplay men's roles in the restoration of Hok-keji and other convents, focusing instead on the contributions of nuns—women whom they portray as self-reliant and confident.[17]

Meeks also dismisses the theory that the nuns affiliated with Eison regu-larly served as laundry women—this theory is particularly unlikely in the case of nuns of elite background at Hokkeji. Instead, nuns occasion-ally provided the monks in Eison's movement with monastic robes that they had sewn. These robes were regarded as prestigious, valuable items that generated income for the nuns. The nuns also served as the purvey-ors of Buddhist relics, which were very important to Eison's community and thus gave the nuns a seminal role in the popularization of the reform movement.[18] The relics were a means of empowerment that linked the nuns symbolically with the court, where the keeping of relics had fallen to elite women. Additionally, the relics legitimized the nuns as members of the Buddhist lineage traceable to Śākyamuni Buddha himself.[19]

Even though the Pure Land and Nichiren sects did not found as many convents as did the Zen and Ritsu sects, this does not mean that their founders, Hōnen (1133–1212), Shinran (1173–1262), and Nichi-ren (1222–1282), took no interest in women's salvation. Certain schol-ars have argued that these monks belonging to the "New Kamakura" sects were actually more interested in the salvation of women than were their contemporaries in the older Buddhist sects. Some scholars have even asserted that these founding monks were proto-feminists of sorts. We do indeed find evidence of Hōnen and Nichiren welcoming women as lay devotees and patrons and rejecting certain discrimina-tory ideas, such as notions that women should be excluded from sacred sites and that menstruation was ritually polluting. Yet they also tacitly accepted stereotypical characterizations of women, as did many of the above-mentioned male reformers in the Zen and Ritsu sects. Hōnen, the founder of the Pure Land sect, welcomed women to the commu-nity of his devotees but mentioned them in the same breath as evildo-ers, a frequent pairing in medieval Japanese Buddhist texts.[20] Similarly,

Hōnen stressed Amitābha's fifty-third vow that promised salvation to women despite their being afflicted with the Five Obstructions. This emphasis implies that Hōnen took for granted that women were subject to the Five Obstructions. Likewise, Nichiren, after whom the Nichiren sect is named, counseled one of his female devotees that even though menstruation should not represent an obstacle against recitation of the *Lotus Sutra*, she should still refrain from reciting more than the title of the scripture out of respect for social convention and in recognition that menstruation is reflective of her female condition, which is ultimately sinful.[21]

Unlike Hōnen and Nichiren, Shinran, the founder of the True Pure Land sect, left no writings specifically addressed to women. He did, however, openly choose to renounce his vows of celibacy and marry. His wife, Eshin-ni (1182–1268), and his daughter, Kakushin-ni (1224–1283), played important roles in the devotee community. Kakushin-ni was in charge of managing her father's mausoleum, and Shinran's lineage, which has since become hereditary, was transmitted to Kakushin-ni's son, Kakunyo (1270–1351). While Shinran did consider men and women equal beneficiaries of Amitābha's salvific grace, his extant writings suggest that he accepted the concept of the Five Obstructions and the necessity of female-to-male transformation to attain salvation. Extant correspondence between Eshin-ni and Kakushin-ni after Shinran's death, however, does not contain any evidence that they similarly embraced these concepts or that such notions were central to Shinran's thought.[22]

Female Pollution, Karmic Hindrances, and Jealous Demons

During the medieval period, concepts of female pollution and karmic hindrances became widespread. While these ideas had existed in Buddhist scholar monks' writings even earlier, they seem not to have been common knowledge in lay circles until the medieval period. Androcentric concepts such as the Five Obstructions, the Three Obediences, and the transformation into a male—concepts that were quite common in the scholar monks' writings—were largely ignored by laywomen into the Kamakura period, when they recorded at temples their spiritual petitions and prayers for health and rebirth in the Pure Land.[23] By the late medieval period, references to these androcentric teachings appeared frequently in medieval literature such as Buddhist didactic tales. For instance, in *The Tale of the Brazier* from the Muromachi period, an angry husband upbraids his wife: "Your sins are grave indeed, even the gods, buddhas, and the Three Treasures must deplore you. Even if you were virtuous, though, it is no easy matter for a woman to aspire to Buddhahood, as the Five Hindrances and the Three Duties attest."[24] Similarly, in the farcical late medieval tale *Lazy Tarō*, an aristocratic woman frets at the prospect of having been guilty of causing somebody's death: "As a woman, my sins are already deep enough, what with the Five Hindrances and Three Duties."[25] By the medieval period the concept of the Five Obstructions had evolved to imply not simply an external hindrance suffered by women but an inherent moral flaw. From the late medieval to the early modern period, allusions to the Five Obstructions and Three Obediences were usually paired, rather than occurring individually.[26]

By the late medieval period, belief in women's karmic hindrances and pollution had become widely accepted. Another striking example is the cult of the *Blood Pool Sutra*. According to this scripture, which originated in China around the turn of the thirteenth century and was probably introduced into Japan in the early fifteenth century, the Buddha's disciple Maudgalyāyana journeys into hell to save his mother. He discovers her in a pool of menstrual and parturitive blood, which she and the other women in the pond are forced by the guardians of hell to imbibe. This is their punishment for polluting the soil and thus antagonizing the earth gods as well as sullying the drinking water of holy men. In Japan, recitation of the text was initially sponsored by descendants who wanted to ensure the salvation of their female relatives. Eventually the text served as a preventive talisman to ensure one's own salvation in the afterlife and to nullify the negative karma incurred in this

FIGURE 5.1. Itinerant nun preaching from the *Kumano kanshin jikkai mandara* to an audience of women. Detail from a folding screen depicting a festival at the Sumiyoshi Shrine. Japan, early seventeenth century. Color and gold on paper. Image copyright © Smithsonian Freer and Sackler Galleries. Image Source: Smithsonian Freer and Sackler Galleries.

life by menstrual pollution. In the sixteenth and seventeenth centuries, female itinerant preachers, such as Kumano *bikuni*, actively promoted the scripture through sermons on their fund-raising campaigns (see figure 5.1).[27] During the Edo period, Sōtō Zen clerics incorporated the scripture into the ritual repertoire for conducting funerals for female parishioners, and women gathered in consororities to promote the salvific teachings of this scripture.[28]

There is definitely a tension between the sutra's salvific message and its inherent misogyny that condemns women based on their natural reproductive functions. It is tempting to assume that the text was a prime example of Buddhist misogyny that took advantage of vulnerable women aware of the ever-present risks of childbirth.[29] But not all women who propagated the text were vulnerable victims of sexist propaganda. For female itinerant preachers, the *Blood Pool Sutra* was perhaps a graphic and gripping tool for proselytization and a means to encourage women to take their posthumous salvation into their own hands through devotion to the sutra. What exactly Kumano *bikuni* preached about the blood pool hell is unknown, but the *Kumano kanshin jikkai mandara* (Kumano mandala for the contemplation of the ten worlds), a visual aid used by the Kumano *bikuni* in their preaching, provides us with some clues. Several women are depicted seated on lotus leaves raised above the bloody pool, an indication that they have already been saved. Another woman kneels in front of the bodhisattva Avalokiteśvara, who is shown handing her a scripture—presumably the *Blood Pool Sutra*. Unlike the memorial scene at the center of the painting or several scenes depicting the monk Maudgalyāyana, this scene does not feature a young child or a Buddhist monk intervening on behalf of the women. The woman is approaching Avalokiteśvara directly without an intermediary. Kumano *bikuni* (see figure 5.2) certainly helped spread misogynistic belief in the pollution of uterine blood, but at the same time, the version that they preached perhaps gave women greater personal agency than those promoted by their male contemporaries because women could take control of their own posthumous salvation.

For members of early modern consororities, gatherings may have provided companionship, and devotion to the *Blood Pool Sutra* may have been a way to demand special posthumous care when posthumous rites had become very focused on the patriarchal lineage. In medieval China, where concubinage was far more common than in Japan, a birth mother could use the teachings of the blood pool hell to exact filial posthumous care from her son, who may have been raised by her husband's primary wife and would have honored his stepmother in ancestral rites rather than his birth mother. Thus the birth mother had much to gain from promoting the *Blood Pool Sutra* even if its teachings were misogynistic.[30] Similarly, a Japanese hymn dedicated to the *Blood Pool*

FIGURE 5.2. Itinerant Buddhist nun speaking to two little girls who are following her. Kondō Katsunobu (active 1716–1736). Japan, ca. 1730. Polychrome woodblock print (*urushi-e*); ink and color on paper, H. 11 ¾ in. (29.8 cm); W. 5 ⅞ in. (14.9 cm). Rogers Fund, 1022 (JP1311). The Metropolitan Museum of Art, New York, NY, U.S.A. Image copyright © The Metropolitan Museum of Art. Image source: Art Resource, NY.

Sutra states, after a long litany describing the horrors of the blood pool hell, "One must therefore have gratitude for one's mother and perform services in memory of her, which will without doubt take away her suffering and give her ease."[31]

It must be remembered, however, that notions about female pollution and sinfulness were not confined simply to authors of Buddhist didactic tales, male monastics, and female itinerant preachers; rather, medieval society at large became preoccupied with such notions. This is particularly apparent in medieval literature. One such example is the story—and its multiple variants—of the woman, typically named Toran, who attempts to transgress the boundary marking the prohibition against women on sacred mountains and is, alternately, chased away or turned to stone. The narrative transpires at sacred mountains that were the sites of religious practice for male ascetics. In many versions, Toran is described as an accomplished shaman who claims exemption from the female pollution that afflicts ordinary women, yet is confounded despite all her magical powers. Early variants of the story do not attribute her expulsion to menstruation but, rather, to her urinating in deliberate violation of the mountain's ritual purity. In later versions of the tale, however, Toran's transgression is menstruation. For instance, one Toran-like figure is the mother of the Buddhist monk Kūkai (774–835), the founder of Shingon Buddhism in Japan, who established Mount Kōya as a monastic center. According to late medieval legend, Kūkai's mother seeks to persuade Kūkai to allow her access to the monastic precinct on Mount Kōya, which is off-limits to women. She argues that she, in her eighties, is postmenopausal and thus exempt from menstrual pollution. Kūkai takes off his monastic surplice and makes her tread on it. At this moment, she suddenly begins menstruating and is swept away by the burning surplice. She ultimately gains salvation by means of Kūkai's filial posthumous care for her. A memorial hall for Kūkai's mother outside the border of the monastic complex on the mountaintop of Mount Kōya became known as a site where women could gain salvation in Maitreya's Tuṣita Heaven, despite being barred from the summit of Mount Kōya.[32]

Not only were women associated with pollution, but they were also said to be particularly sinful. The monk Yoshida Kenkō (1283–1350) explained in *Essays in Idleness* (1330–1332) that women were selfish, covetous, irrational, superstitious, evasive, loquacious, deceitful, and foolish.[33] In *Mirror for Women* (1300), the monk Mujū Ichien (1227–1312) elaborated on the seven sins stereotypically associated with women by citing the Chinese precept master Daoxuan (596–667): (1) women awaken sexual lust in men; (2) they are jealous, malicious, and selfish; (3) they are deceitful and envious; (4) they neglect religious practice and are vain and lustful; (5) they are dishonest and vengeful; (6) they are shameless; and (7) they are ritually unclean, being stained by menstruation and by the effluvia of childbirth, thus attracting evil spirits and dispelling benevolent divinities.[34] Similarly, *The Tale of Fuji Cave*, a popular didactic tale originating in the early sixteenth century, expounded, "It's true that both men and women fall into hell, but many more women do than men. Women's thoughts are all evil. Still, women are forbidden to approach men on only eighty-four days a year [while they are menstruating]. Women don't know their own transgressions, which is why they fail to plant good karmic roots."[35] The tale gives specific examples of women suffering in hell because they are faulted for failing to bear children and being lustful, vain, envious, stingy, cruel, and jealous in previous lives.[36]

Women's jealousy became a common trope in medieval literature. In didactic tales and Noh plays, jealous women were described as transforming into vicious, sometimes cannibalistic demons. While the pining wife served as an aesthetic poetic trope during the Heian period, the figure of the jealous demon Hashihime (literally, the lady of the bridge) marginalized the woman who was jilted in a polygynous relationship. When abandoned by her lover, Hashihime resolves to turn herself into a demon by forming her hair into horns with resin. By means of this willful transformation, she becomes a demon that begins to prey on people at random. Particularly in the context of war epics, which as a means of spirit pacification glorified the violent conflicts of the medieval period,

Hashihime reemerged as a powerful, violent demon that wreaks vengeance. Hashihime-like jealous demons also figured frequently in late-medieval Noh plays, in which they are shown to be defeated and pacified by Buddhist ascetics through exorcism. The image of the jealous demon emerged out of the polygynous context of the time. Jealousy was regarded as an exclusively female emotion. Once jealousy is attributed to a demon, the powerful and threatening force can be quelled through exorcism; conversely, however, such depictions render the jealous woman as a powerful being, victimizing men in a reversal of expected power relations.[37]

A woman's demonic vengeance arising from unrequited lust is the focus of the story of Dōjōji, which also exists in multiple versions across various genres, from didactic tales to Noh plays. In an early version appearing in *Tales of Times Now Past* (ca. twelfth century), a woman tries to seduce a traveling monk on a pilgrimage to Kumano. To escape her sexual advances, he promises her gratification on his return journey. When he does not fulfill his promise, she dies in chagrin and transforms into a demonic serpent. She pursues him to a temple, where fellow monks hide him under a bell. In her serpentine form, she coils around the bell and incinerates the monk inside. Both the monk, now also reincarnated as a serpent, and his serpentine pursuer are saved by a Buddhist monk who recites the *Lotus Sutra* on their behalf.[38] As the literary scholar Susan Klein argues, the portrayal of women in earlier didactic tales that feature this story is misogynistic: "Women are psychologically and biologically determined to a weakness of will that keeps them from being able to control their passions; women by their very existence are an inevitable obstacle to men's spiritual progress."[39] Nevertheless, the story promises salvation to both the monk and the woman. In later Noh theater versions, however, the woman is no longer granted salvation in the end.[40]

In the Noh play attributed to the playwright Nobumitsu (1435–1516), the Dōjōji story is retold within another story that features a female dancer (*shirabyōshi*), who gains admittance to a bell consecration at a temple even though women have been specifically barred from attending the ritual. The dancer convinces the gatekeeper to allow her entry because she is dressed in male garb, as was typical for women of her profession in the late Heian to early Kamakura period, and because she has come to perform a dance to purify the bell. Thus she claimed exemption to the exclusion of women by virtue of being a religious professional. After enchanting with her dancing all those in attendance, the dancer attacks the bell, jumping inside it and bringing it down with a loud crash. The head monk retells the Dōjōji story and then leads an exorcism against the dancer, who has turned into a serpent, chasing her into a nearby river as she is incinerated by the flames of her own passion. The Noh play does not answer the question of whether the dancer actually was the serpent or whether the dancer was an innocent performer who became possessed by the serpent's vengeful spirit.[41] This story about the dancer turned serpent not only illustrates the demonization of women. The presence of the dancer in the play and her ritual role in the consecration of the bell also hint at the existence of female religious professionals other than nuns in medieval Japan.

Shamans, Religious Performers, and Marginality

As suggested by the presence of the dancer in the Noh play, a wide variety of female religious professionals served as shamans and dancers combining sacred functions with entertainment, even prostitution: female shamans (*miko*), itinerant fund-raising nuns (*bikuni*), dancers (*shirabyōshi*) and puppeteers (*kugutsu*). Scholars have widely debated the status of such female performers/religious specialists, many of whom led itinerant existences. Given the paucity of historical documents about them, let alone documents composed by them, we may never come to any definite conclusions. Some of the early scholars working on the history of prostitution hypothesized that these performers' roles could be traced back to those of female shamans serving local divinities. They also speculated that initially, such entertainers were highly regarded by

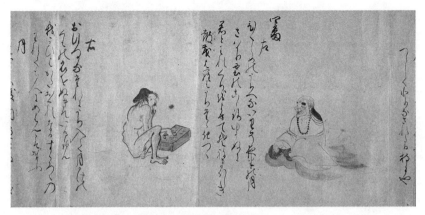

FIGURE 5.3. Female shaman (*miko*) portrayed in the *Tōhokuin shokunin utaawase emaki* (Picture scroll of the Tōhokuin poetry contest among persons of various occupations). The shaman holds a drum and wears a rosary, both distinctive accoutrements of her trade. Japan, fourteenth century. Important Cultural Property. Light color on paper. Tokyo National Museum, Tokyo, Japan. Image copyright © Tokyo National Museum. Image Source: DNP Art Communications, Tokyo.

society, and that only later their status declined. Other early scholars suggested that these women were social marginals whose profession was ultimately foreign to Japan. Later scholars, however, reasserted the former theory and argued that the entertainers' roles were derived from those of female court entertainers serving a quasi-sacred function who formed their own hereditary lineage of performers. Most scholars assume that such entertainers, including courtesans (*asobi*), dancers, and puppeteers, were once highly respected professional performers in pre-Heian Japan whose status—like that of other marginal groups—declined over the course of the medieval period.[42]

However, this narrative of marginalization and decline is not without problems: not all female shamans were marginal figures. There were various types of female shamans; some settled like other townspeople and others were peripatetic. Focus on the latter, also known as itinerant shamans (*aruki miko*), has led scholars to overemphasize the marginal status of female shamans in general (see figure 5.3). According to another common narrative of decline, female shamans lost their power in the seventh and eighth centuries as the Yamato state was introducing new governmental and ritual structures inspired by Chinese models. At state-sponsored shrines, female shamans were displaced from their official positions in the ritual bureaucracy and were relegated to performing less prestigious tasks, such as sewing robes for the gods and serving as consorts and entertainers to the gods, rather than serving as powerful mouthpieces of the spirits. Female shamans who continued to serve as oracles outside the structure of state-sponsored shrines were censored, particularly if they proclaimed divine messages of a political nature. Nevertheless, some female shamans associated with shrines led lives that were far from marginal and maintained cordial relations with the Buddhist clergy. By the Kamakura period, some female shamans who were responsible for providing dance performances at shrines formed professional guilds. By contrast, itinerant shamans often served as professional fund-raisers and as spirit mediums for hire by private clients. Visually, the two types of female shamans, though not always completely exclusive, were distinctive: shrine shamans were often depicted with zithers, bells, and drums, indicating their role as musical performers, while itinerant shamans were shown only with drums and rosaries, which they used to contact the spirits and perform prayers.[43]

The Introduction of Christianity

In the mid-sixteenth century, a period of great political instability, Jesuit missionaries introduced Christianity to Japan. Despite linguistic and cultural challenges, the mission was quite successful in western Japan, where the Jesuits were able to make converts among the warrior class and general population in their domains until Christianity was outlawed in the early to mid-seventeenth century. These converts of course also included women. Portraits of their lives emerge in the records of the Jesuit mission, but their actual personalities are filtered through European Christian tropes, casting them as chaste virgins, obedient wives, or faithful martyrs when they were supportive of the mission, or demonic witches if they were antagonistic and supported the local religions. For instance, the wife of Ōtomo Sōrin (1530–1587) and daughter of Nata Akimoto, the head priest at the Nata Hachiman Shrine, staunchly resisted the encroachment of Christianity into her husband's domain of Bungo and remained a dedicated devotee of Hachiman and patron of Buddhist monks and mountain ascetics. The Jesuit missionaries therefore regarded her as a witch inspired by the devil and dubbed her "Izaberu," in reference to King Ahab's wife Jezebel, who was a fervent supporter of the cult of Baal.[44]

In spite of the Jesuit-filtered rhetoric that implied a gulf between Christianity and local religions, these records suggest that Christianity offered similar opportunities to women as did Buddhism. Some Christian women became lay nuns who took vows of chastity at home. One former Buddhist nun even founded a nuns' order called *miyako bikuni*, literally meaning "nuns of the imperial capital." Still others were active in consororities dedicated to charitable activities or devotion to Mary. For some women of Pure Land background, Christianity's teaching of salvation in paradise through divine grace was comfortingly familiar, while others familiar with Buddhist forms of disputation used their background to become successful Christian catechists. Fucan Fabian (1565–1621), a Japanese Christian convert who had been a Zen monk by the name of Enshun prior to his conversion, wrote *Myōtei mondō* (1605), a fictional question-answer debate between the Buddhist nun Myōshū and the Christian convert nun Yūtei, ending in Myōshū's conversion. Most likely, the protagonists were modeled on members of the *miyako bikuni* order, and the text was meant to assist the nuns in their role as catechists in the conversion of elite women. Ironically, Fucan Fabian, who had served as a spiritual advisor to the *miyako bikuni*, renounced his affiliation with the Jesuit order in 1608, began to live with a former *miyako bikuni*, and authored several anti-Christian tracts. In contrast, Naitō Julia (ca. 1530?–1627), the foundress of the *miyako bikuni* order, was exiled to the Philippines in 1614 with the rest of her order; there, they lived out the rest of their days as members of a cloistered order.[45]

Conclusion

Throughout the medieval period, women were active as various types of religious professionals—nuns, shamans, dancers, and Christian catechists. Despite facing increased emphasis on the notions of female pollution and spiritual inferiority, women derived meaning from the religious teachings of their time, becoming devoted adherents of Pure Land or Nichiren Buddhism, Zen adepts, orthodox Ritsu nuns, and itinerant preachers. Women continued to flock to important temples and shrines that did not exclude them, such as Kumano and Zenkōji, and organized themselves in devotional consororities. Despite the development of the virilocal, patrilineal household, women continued to enjoy a limited measure of independence through their right to transmit and inherit property, at least through their maternal lineage. It was in the following centuries, during the Edo period, that women's independence was further curtailed through the full development of the virilocal, patrilineal household.

6

The Edo Period

Confucianism, Nativism, and Popular Religion

In contrast to the turbulent medieval period, the Edo period (1600–1868) was marked by relative political stability. Edo society was profoundly hierarchical and status-conscious. Officially, society comprised four main hereditary status groups: warriors, peasants, tradesmen, and merchants. Social groups outside the official status system included aristocrats, Buddhist clerics, other religious professionals, performers, and outcasts. The period has often been described as a low point in the status of Japanese women. As we shall see in this chapter, the solidification of the patrilineal household, the emergence of a hierarchical, stratified status system, and the spread of Confucian values during the period strongly supported patriarchal values. The development of an extensive print culture together with widespread basic literacy among women further facilitated the diffusion of these patriarchal ideas. A large number of primers infused with patriarchal values instructed women on acceptable social conduct, health, and practical knowledge. Nevertheless, women in the upper strata of society enjoyed access to education and relative stability through their positions within the patrilineal household. Women beyond the social elites were not nearly as constricted by patriarchal limitations as were elite women.

The Early Modern Patrilineal Household and Its Fissures

In her introduction to *Women and Religion in Japan*, the feminist historian Okuda Akiko states, "In Japan . . . it was the patriarchal community structure of samurai society and the concomitant *ie* system of the military community with its resultant ideology, which played a main part in the perpetuation of patriarchy."[1] According to Okuda, Japanese women were not fully oppressed until the emergence of the patrilineal household (*ie*) with its emphasis on the power of the head of the household and the subordination of individual needs to the interests of the household.[2] The patrilineal, virilocal household emerged in the warrior society of the Muromachi period (1336–1573) and served to ensure patrilineal inheritance patterns during periods of political and military instability from the late fifteenth to the early seventeenth centuries. Over the course of the subsequent Edo period, the institution of the patrilineal household became one of the cornerstones of society. By the middle of the Edo period, the patrilineal-household system had spread beyond the warrior elite to wealthy, landed peasants and merchants who were equally concerned about transmitting their assets through patrilineal inheritance. The patrilineal-household system disenfranchised elite women because it diminished their inheritance rights and circumscribed their marriage and childbearing patterns.[3] It is important to note that the patriarchal structures did not apply to everyone in every class equally. As the historian Anne Walthall points out,

> What we might call marriage in Japan's early modern period varied according to region, class, and status, and the relations between husband and wife also exhibited considerable differences. Generally speaking it can be said that a large gap existed between marriages in the ruling class—everyone from court noble to warrior, village official, and rural entrepreneur—that took the patrilineal household's continuity over generations as the chief concern versus commoner marriages that placed the most emphasis on harmony between husband and wife.[4]

While the patrilineal household was established across different social classes in the Edo period, local variations continued. This can be illustrated by the development of temple parishes. By the seventeenth century, the temple parishioner household (*danka*) system emerged that eventually became a standard feature of Edo Buddhism. Most commonly, all household members belonged to the temple of the patriline, and persons entering into the household would switch their affiliation upon marriage. In some regions, however, it was quite common that husbands, wives, and children were listed as parishioners of different temples based on their gender. Colloquially, this was known as a "half-parish household" (*handanka*), meaning that each half of the household belonged to a different temple. However, single household affiliation in the patriline became much more common as the period continued.[5] This seems to suggest that the hegemonic patrilineal household, which placed all members under the authority of the (male) household head, did not fully develop until fairly late in the period.

Another example of the malleability of the Edo household system was divorce. Divorce was pervasive among both warriors and commoners, even though the former needed to secure their superiors' permission to marry or divorce. By contrast, commoners divorced with relative ease without needing local officials' consent. Generally, divorces (and remarriage) occurred more frequently in urban areas than in rural areas and among poorer families engaged in wage labor than among wealthier families. Divorce rates were also higher in eastern Japan than in western Japan.[6] Officially only the husband could initiate the divorce, by issuing a simple letter of divorce. While women technically could not initiate the divorce, they could solicit the help of their natal families and through them, seek the additional assistance of local officials, village heads, or the initial matchmaker to negotiate the divorce if the husband did not give his consent.[7]

In procuring a divorce, women in the Kantō region could resort to one more device: seeking refuge in one of two Buddhist convents, Tōkeiji in Kamakura or Mantokuji in Kōzuke Province. In earlier periods, there may have been more temples that offered sanctuary, but in the Edo period, these two seem to have been the only ones that could grant sanctuary to women while other temples were officially prohibited from doing so. In effect, a woman seeking to procure a divorce entered the convent to become a servant of the abbess for a period of two to three years. The temple then helped the woman negotiate a divorce. In this process the abbess might additionally seek the intercession of the magistrate of temples and shrines. This service came at a substantial cost; therefore, only relatively midlevel and well-to-do peasants and merchants could afford the service. In return, the stay at the temple might not only lead to a divorce for the women but would also, like other forms of service in elite households, serve as a finishing school that would make her more marriageable upon the completion of her stay.[8]

However, not all women during this period were wives. As in the medieval period, some women became nuns either before marriage or, more commonly, after being widowed. While many nuns may have had a relatively low social status,[9] women of elite background were able to live cultured lifestyles in convents such as the above-mentioned Tōkeiji and Mantokuji, as well as in other aristocratic and imperial convents known as bikuni gosho. For women with imperial connections, life in such a convent was a viable option until the early Meiji period, when the identification of the imperial house with Shinto forced existing nuns to return to lay life until the government relaxed its policy later in the Meiji period.[10]

Moreover, there were women who remained outside the patrilineal-household system by becoming prostitutes. During the Edo period, the popular imagination distinguished between two types of sexually active women: wives, who were supposed to ensure the continuity of the patrilineal household, and prostitutes, who were supposed to provide sexual pleasure to men. The two spheres were portrayed as diametrically opposed in the contemporaneous literature. Concubines, even though they often provided heirs for polygynous households, were sometimes seen as similar to prostitutes in that they also served to provide pleasure.[11] Prostitutes were not unduly stigmatized by early modern society, especially in the first half of the period. Young women working in the sex trade were portrayed as filial daughters who sacrificed themselves for the sake of their families. Only in the second half of the period, when prostitution had become ubiquitous throughout Japan, were prostitutes constructed as selfish women who sought profit outside the patrilineal household. However, most sex workers did not *choose* the life of a prostitute but were *indentured* by their families. This means that these women did not necessarily reject the patrilineal household as much as it had failed them.[12] A prostitute might dream of entering a household as a bride of a devoted customer, even though such hopes were largely unrealistic in the vast majority of cases.[13] Therefore, the plight of prostitutes reminds us that being a wife in a patrilineal household did have its advantages for women even while being oppressive, and that many women, including those to whom this status was denied (such as prostitutes), considered being a wife desirable.

Acceptance of the patrilineal-household system, and other patriarchal systems modeled on it, could assure women privileges not only as wives but also as religious professionals. For instance, since the mid-Edo period, many artistic professions relied on the *iemoto* (family-foundation) system, which was modeled on kinship relations within the patrilineal household. In this system, a patriarchal grand master bestowed licenses on his affiliates that permitted them to gain access to trade secrets and special techniques in exchange for membership fees.[14] Similar licensing systems also became prevalent among religious performers, including female shamans. In the Kantō area, female shamans received licenses from Tamura Hachidayū, who was associated with the Sanja Gongen Shrine at Asakusa Kannon Temple in Edo. In the eighteenth century, Tamura oversaw a regional network of male dance masters and female catalpa-bow shamans (*azusa miko*), who were usually married to each other. While not all female shamans in the area were part of his network, a license from Tamura offered female shamans a means to defend their territory from competitors (such as *yin-yang* diviners, mendicant monks, and mountain ascetics) and claim exclusive rights to perform certain services therein. Such services included distributing hearth talismans and New Year's talismans, invoking the divinities and the spirits of the dead, performing rites of exorcism, and offering prayers transmitted in Tamura's combinative Shinto lineage. In exchange for the license, female shamans paid Tamura a yearly fee of six hundred coppers. Such licensing was a common feature of Edo period religion as different religious professionals vied for a stable client base.[15] The licensing body for female shamans was usually determined by their husbands' affiliation: the wives of shrine priests licensed by the Yoshida or Shirakawa houses likewise received Yoshida or Shirakawa licenses, while the wives of mountain ascetics affiliated with Tōzan or Honzan Shugendō lineages received licenses from Tōzan or Honzan lineages. The same principle applied to the wives of *yin-yang* diviners and dance masters.[16]

Neo-Confucian Values for Women

During the Edo period, Neo-Confucianism became an important socio-political ideology for the ruling regime. Confucianism as a whole took for granted that human beings, including women, existed in a hierarchical society and should follow the rules of proper etiquette. The Confucian classics championed a submissive role for women, expecting them to yield to the demands of their natal families and in-laws. While such ideals had been part of the Confucian tradition since its inception, such teachings gained more societal force in China during the Ming dynasty (1368–1644). At this time the *Four Books for Women* (in Chinese, *Nü sishu*), modeled on the *Four Books* that were at the center of the Neo-Confucian canon advocated by the Song scholar Zhu Xi (1130–1200), became the standard canon for women's education. The *Four Books for Women* were all authored by women who belonged to the Chinese literati elite. These texts stressed that women needed to strive to acquire virtue, consisting primarily of purity, chastity, obedience, and filial piety. Male and female spheres were ideally separated into distinct domains, with women occupying the inner, domestic sphere. Women were encouraged to be industrious and conduct themselves with proper decorum and dignity. Upon marriage they should serve their parents-in-law and husband diligently. They were responsible for managing the affairs of the household with frugality and educating their children, especially their daughters. Jealousy, laziness, and licentiousness were to be avoided, especially because these behaviors were seen as common womanly flaws.[17]

We might wonder what motivated educated women to propagate such patriarchal values. It is likely that they appropriated such accepted paradigms in order to stress the necessity of providing an education—albeit a conservative one—for young women.[18] Furthermore, Confucian primers for women were ultimately meant to help young women navigate through life without engaging in scandalous behavior so that they could eventually become powerful matriarchs.[19] And women were given responsibility for the morality of the entire household: as a paragon of virtue, a wife should influence her husband for the better, which gave her justification to resist her husband's will if morality demanded it.[20] Only when women affirmed patriarchal values for their own reasons and transmitted them to the next generation was their continued implementation guaranteed.[21]

Educated Japanese elites in the Edo period had access to the Neo-Confucian primers and also compiled their own texts. The best-known Japanese primer for women is the *Great Learning for Women* (early eighteenth century), which has traditionally been attributed to the Neo-Confucian scholar Kaibara Ekken (1630–1714). Like the Chinese *Four Books for Women*, the Japanese *Great Learning for Women* emphasized that girls should be given an education so that they could better serve their future husband and in-laws. Women were told to avoid anger, harsh speech, arrogance, envy, and pride—supposedly innate to all women but most apparent in those who lack proper cultivation, such as the lower classes. Instead, women should cultivate virtues such as obedience, chastity, gentleness, and calmness. Before marriage, a girl should be filial to her parents. In marriage, a woman should submit completely to her husband's household, serving him and his parents with obedience, filial piety, and diligence, even if treated with hostility by them. She should be respectful to her siblings-in-law and chaste in her dealings with male family members and kinsmen. She should never express jealousy toward her husband even if he engages in reproachable behavior. At all times must she conduct herself in order to maintain familial harmony. She should dedicate herself to the domestic sphere, contributing her labor—such as sewing, weaving, and spinning—for the greater good of her husband's family. She should not engage in personal religious pursuits such as pilgrimages—which would take her outside the home—until the age of forty (when she might turn her duties over to her daughter-in-law) and should at all times avoid religious rituals, such as those performed by female mediums and shamans, that might lead her toward licentious behavior.[22]

Japanese Confucian scholars initially tried to promote such values for women beginning in the mid-seventeenth century because they felt considerable anxiety over the political influence that women in the Inner Quarters of the shogun and the daimyo houses wielded over their husbands. Confucian scholars compared influential women in the Inner Quarters to famous *femmes fatales* in Chinese history who were said to have brought ruin to ruling dynasties. Other scholars, such as Ogyū Sorai (1666–1728), upbraided daimyo wives as decadent, unproductive profligates who failed to engage in feminine labor such as needlework and instead wasted their time on idle pursuits. He also strongly criticized the marriages between warrior or aristocratic women and lower-ranking men of the warrior class—marriages that upset the ideal gender hierarchy because the wives had higher status than their husbands. As a matter of fact, such marriages were common among the highest-level daimyo houses because marriages with such women garnered the male cultural prestige and helped to cement political relationships.[23]

Over all, the status system was also not quite as rigid in practice as it may first seem, particularly for women. Not only did some elite women marry into families of slightly lower status, women of lower status were also able to manipulate the status system in order to become upwardly mobile. Women from the peasant and merchant class achieved this by entering service in warrior households, which taught them cultural and social skills that allowed them to become more eligible brides by the end of their service. While many then married into their own status group, some eventually entered into the warrior class by means of adoption and marriage. However, as the women surmounted the strictures of their status group, they also contributed to the spread of warrior values throughout other status groups. By the late eighteenth century, such elite values began to curtail the ease with which peasant women had mingled with the opposite sex previously.[24]

The ruling elites advocated chastity and filial piety for all women in order to encourage social order. In the late eighteenth century, the shogunate collected the *Official Records of Filial Piety* to promote Neo-Confucian values among the populace. The record documented monetary rewards issued by the shogunate and the daimyo to low-ranking warriors and commoners who had shown exemplary virtuous conduct and could thus serve as role models for their fellow commoners. Nearly a quarter of the over 8,500 cases were awarded to women. Women's distinctive virtue was chastity, although many were also lauded for filial piety, loyalty, and diligence in agriculture. Similar to men, virtuous women were praised for their dedication to their households. They were also commended for making decisions about marriage based on the needs of their families—either their natal or their husbands' families.[25]

The effect of Confucianism on women in Edo Japan was double-edged. While primers such as the *Great Learning for Women* promoted dedication to patriarchal values among the socioeconomic elites, they also promoted education for women and served as instructional manuals to teach women literacy skills. Educated women had opportunities to serve as teachers, initially within their households and by the nineteenth century even in private academies. Such an education also gave women an opportunity to move up the social ladder by marrying into households of slightly higher status than that of their natal families. An education allowed women from urban and village elites even beyond the warrior class to fulfill important managerial functions within the household that were predicated on literacy. Paradoxically, the same texts that instilled patriarchal values in women thus also created opportunities for them.[26]

This is illustrated by the Shingaku (Study of the Mind) movement, founded by Ishida Baigan (1685–1744). With its focus on self-cultivation and contemplation, Shingaku incorporated Confucian, Daoist, Buddhist, and Shinto elements. Baigan, a Kyoto townsman of peasant stock, started as a popular Shinto street preacher and eventually founded a school in which he taught a practical morality that stressed frugality, benevolence, and knowledge of human nature. Baigan's teachings appealed first and foremost to townspeople but also found a following among peasants and warriors. Baigan held that human desires and selfishness had to be overcome through meditation, self-restraint, and dedication to one's vocation and social responsibilities. After Baigan's death, Shingaku spread throughout Japan through the efforts of his disciples, including Tejima Toan (1718–1786), who took great interest in educating women.[27]

Toan's lectures and seminars were intended to prevent young men and women from engaging in scandalous behavior and rehabilitating women who had strayed from a virtuous path. Toan based his lectures on canonical Neo-Confucian works, including Chinese primers for women, as well as Japanese classical literature and the *Nihon shoki*. Toan exhorted women to "discover their original heart" in order to master the "six virtues for women": obedience, purity, kindness, frugality, modesty, and diligence. He thought that women could best accomplish this ideal through marriage because it would teach them how to reduce their egotism. Wives were told to cultivate four feminine virtues: wifely words, wifely virtue, wifely accomplishment, and wifely etiquette. Once married, they should break their bonds with their natal families and devote themselves completely to their husbands' household. As wives and mothers, women were encouraged to contribute to the household through their labor—spinning, weaving, sewing, and cooking. Echoing the Chinese Confucian classic, the *Book of Rites*, Toan told women above the age of ten to restrict themselves to the inner, domestic sphere and to leave public business to their husbands. Applied to merchants and artisans, this meant that women were supposed to leave sales and business trips to the men of the household. Such separation of male and female domains was also maintained at Shingaku academies, where men and women were carefully divided into separate rooms or areas partitioned by bamboo blinds.[28]

The Shingaku movement did not just rely on male preachers to spread its message, but also had several female preachers who were active in Edo and Hiroshima, one of whom even lectured to female servants at Edo Castle. One particularly prominent female preacher was Jion-ni Kenka (1716–1778), who had become a Buddhist nun as a young woman in order to pray for her deceased mother. After a strict regimen of ascetic practices had diminished her health, she decided to convalesce in Kyoto. It was here that she encountered Ishida Baigan and became his disciple. Kenka's tale of her fall and redemption suited Shingaku's teachings for women, and her autobiography was published as a primer for the movement in 1756. Around this time, Kenka moved to Edo, where she opened a Shingaku academy. At the height of her popularity, her lectures seem to have drawn an audience of hundreds, if not more than a thousand listeners twice daily. Her lectures were based on eclectic materials, including not only Baigan's teachings but also Buddhist sutras, Yoshida Kenkō's *Essays in Idleness*, and excerpts from Noh plays. Like her male counterparts, Kenka took a conservative stance that echoed Confucian ideals, such as the idea that a woman should accept the Three Obediences to her father, husband, and son.[29]

Nativist Women

The nativist movement, with its rejection of Confucian rationalism and elevation of the "indigenous" Japanese past, might have presented a liberating alternative for educated women. However, even though the nativist scholar Hirata Atsutane (1776–1843) emphasized fertility, procreation, and sexual desire in his writings, he did not specifically address women. Nor did he accommodate his writing style to an audience that included women, who were less likely to be able to read Sino-Japanese (*kanbun*). As Walthall notes, "Unlike some of his predecessors in the nativist tradition, Atsutane thoroughly approved of Confucius, if not later scholars in Chinese intellectual history, and he believed that the inequality between husband and wife reflected the natural order."[30]

Despite the patriarchal and unwelcoming attitude of the Hirata school, some women were attracted to nativist teachings. For instance, Matsuo Taseko (1811–1894), the daughter and wife of a village headman in the Ina valley of Shinano Province, joined the Hirata school and read several of Atsutane's and Motoori Norinaga's (1730–1801) works. One of Atsutane's essays that Taseko read was *The Biography of the Goddess Miyabi*, a text about the goddess Ame no Uzume. Rather than condemning Ame no Uzume for exposing her breasts and engaging in a lewd dance, Atsutane praised her loyal service to Amaterasu and recommended that she be worshiped as a goddess of business success, longevity, and harmonious relationships. Another text that Taseko read and even helped publish was a chapter from *Lectures on Ancient History*, in which Atsutane discussed the story of Izanami and Izanagi's first sexual encounter. He used the story to illustrate that ideal male-female relations should be hierarchical, placing women in a submissive position. In addition to Taseko helping to publish this text, her own poetic response to the Izanami-Izanagi story of the leech child is revealing. In 1864 she composed a poem in which she likened her existence as a weak, dependent woman to that of the leech child produced by the botched sexual union of Izanami and Izanagi. In order to express her sense of helplessness as a woman, which prevents her from fighting for the cause of the imperial restoration, she apologizes that she is "like the leech child / unable to stand on its own" and expresses her "regrets at having / the weak body of a woman." She feels profoundly "useless" despite the (masculine) ardor in her heart.[31]

Similarly, Tadano Makuzu (1763–1825) found herself inspired by nativist writers such as Motoori Norinaga and Kamo no Mabuchi (1697–1769). She rejected Confucianism as a foreign tradition despite her samurai heritage, but she nevertheless conceived of ideal gender relations as hierarchical. She acknowledged in her essay *Hitori kangae* (1817) that she was influenced by Norinaga's *Kojikiden* in formulating her ideas about gender roles. Norinaga's text introduced her to Izanagi and Izanami's roles as the archetypal male and female, one being formed in excess while the other shows a deficiency.[32] She writes,

> Women exist for the sake of men; men do not exist for the sake of women. It would be a mistake to think of them as equal. Even if she is the more intelligent, how can a woman who thinks she is lacking something triumph over a man who always thinks of himself as having a surplus? Because it is with the help of men that women survive in this world, they can live comfortably if men do not find them disagreeable. Realizing that the male body differs from her own, a woman should humble herself in her dealings with men, not only with the man on whom she depends, but also those who have some business with the household, and even the servants he employs. If a woman correctly examines why men find her disagreeable, she will inevitably discover that it is because she is disrespectful. For a woman who ought to obey men to look down on them is contrary to the norms of proper behavior. It is for that reason that she is disliked.[33]

Nevertheless, she also argued that women could have ambitions and cited Amaterasu Ōmikami and the legendary Empress Jingō as ancient successful role models for women.[34] Taseko's and Makuzu's examples illustrate that ancient mythology, despite its strong feminine characters and positive valuation of female fecundity, could serve to reify the Edo period's patriarchal Confucian morality.

Popular Religion and New Religious Movements

During the Edo period, travel and pilgrimage became much easier than in previous periods despite social controls imposed by the authorities. In order to maintain social order and forestall a potential rebellion by hostile forces, the shogunate instituted a hostage system meant to keep daimyo wives in Edo during their husbands' absence. Therefore, the shogunate restricted travel for women, who needed special passports to cross through checkpoints along the major thoroughfares traversing the islands of Japan. Women who had taken the tonsure had an easier time passing checkpoints. Another way women could secure travel documents from their local authorities was to go on pilgrimages. There is ample evidence that female pilgrims traveled the circuits of the Eighty-Eight Sacred Places of Shikoku or the Thirty-Three Sacred Places of Avalokiteśvara in the Saikoku region and that women visited the Ise Shrines and Zenkōji, a temple in Shinano Province. For young commoner women, such pilgrimages might serve as a finishing school of sorts before marriage, while older women might choose to go on pilgrimage for recreation (see figure 6.1).[35] In the case of women in the shogun's Inner Quarters, female employees serving as attendants to the wife or concubines of the shogun could be dispatched on pilgrimages in the place of women who could not go themselves because their status prevented them.[36]

Mount Fuji was one popular site that began to attract female pilgrims toward the end of the Edo period. The cult of Mount Fuji flourished in the Kantō region thanks to the ascetic Jikigyō Miroku (1671–1733), whose teachings emphasized righteousness, benevolence, compassion, and frugality as well as *yin-yang* related fertility practices. In a radically positive evaluation of the female body, Jikigyō understood menstruation, conception, and birth as blessings of divinity of Mount Fuji rather than as impurities. In the early nineteenth century, Jikigyō's descendents founded a subgroup out of Fuji pilgrimage confraternities that became known as Fujidō (The Way of Fuji). Successive Fujidō leaders developed

FIGURE 6.1. *Horinouchi Myōhōji eho mairi no zu.* Utagawa Toyohiro (1763–1828). A group of women visiting Myōhōji in Edo. Japan, ca. 1804. Two sheets of a pentaptych of polychrome woodblock prints; ink and color on paper. Aiban, H. 13 ⅜ in. (34 cm); W. 19 ½ in. (49.5 cm). Gift of Estate of Samuel Isham, 1914 (JP1005). The Metropolitan Museum of Art, New York, NY, U.S.A. Image copyright © The Metropolitan Museum of Art. Image source: Art Resource, NY.

the idea of male-female principles in even more radical ways. Sangyō Rokuō (1745–1809), Jikigyō's second-generation successor, urged his followers to strive for a balance between *yin* and *yang* in order to avoid calamities. In Sangyō's correlative cosmological theory, *yang* corresponded to fire, masculinity, and rising, whereas *yin* corresponded to water, binding, and falling. If *yin* and *yang* were out of balance, calamities such as fires and floods would ensue. Humanity had induced such an imbalance by having placed *yang* above *yin*, thereby allowing *yang*'s rising energy and *yin*'s falling energy to escape without moderating each other. Sexual union between men and women in such a situation could only lead to imbalanced offspring and an inherently pathological society marred by social and gender inequalities. This situation could be ameliorated only through world renewal. Sangyō's successor, Kotani Sanshi (1765–1841), further argued that world renewal could be realized only if people inverted the conventional relationship between *yin* and *yang*, both in social relationships and during sexual intercourse. A couple achieved the latter inversion by positioning the woman on top so that her water property could soothe the fire property of the male and so that she could take on an active sexual role while the male was passive. This action was held to lead to good offspring.[37]

Not only were the teachings of Fujidō inclusive of women, but the pilgrimage cult also attracted female devotees despite their prohibition from ascending the mountain throughout the Edo period. Although Shinto priests controlled the shrines on the summit, the pilgrimage traffic was largely managed by religious professionals called *oshi*, who served as pilgrimage guides and innkeepers in several settlements at the foot of the mountain. In 1800 and 1860, some *oshi* gained permission to extend the limit on the mountain up to which women were allowed to ascend. The *oshi* hoped to encourage more foot traffic through their settlement than their competitors'. Indeed, the 1860 pilgrimage season attracted large numbers of women, many of them Fujidō members.[38]

New religious movements that emerged during the Edo period were also accommodating of women, as their religious leaders questioned traditional notions of female impurity and inferiority, promoted fertility and healing, and allowed women to take leadership roles as divine oracles. One of the first new religious movements was Tenrikyō, founded in 1838 by Nakayama Miki (1798–1887), the daughter of a wealthy peasant. Miki displayed a relatively positive view of women and their sexuality, but ultimately she also operated within a nineteenth-century universe that took hierarchical gender relations for granted. At age forty, she claimed to be possessed by the divinity Tenri Ō no Mikoto while serving as a spirit medium for a mountain ascetic who was trying to cure her son of a pain in his foot. Miki's state of possession continued for three days, until her family acquiesced to the divinity's demand that

Miki become his permanent shrine. As a divine oracle, Miki rejected the common shamanic practice of guided possession during which a male exorcist controlled a female medium. Instead, divine revelations came to her directly without male intercession. Tenri Ō no Mikoto made continuous revelations to Miki, later recorded by Miki in the *Mikagurauta* (1866–1875) and the *Ofudesaki* (1869–1882). Miki attracted followers through her healing abilities, ensuring safe childbirth, and through her teachings promising a happy life through sacred labor that helped shed dust accumulated through one's past lives. Miki also propagated idiosyncratic teachings about the origins of humanity and promoted faith healing, both of which would later cause friction with the authorities. Her activities provoked arrest more than a dozen times in the 1870s and 1880s.[39]

Like the Fujidō movement, Miki took a more positive stance toward women, their bodies, and their role in marriage than did her Neo-Confucian and Buddhist contemporaries. She rejected the idea that menstruation was polluted and argued instead that it served the same essential function as did flowers in the reproductive process of plants.[40] She regarded the human body, male or female, as a divine gift and attributed conception and birth to the work of the divinity rather than considering it a polluted process. She asserted that the divinity had the power to ensure safe childbirth and control the time of delivery.[41] Miki also rejected common dietary taboos and the use of a special belt or special bedding—all means to control the female body—commonly prescribed during pregnancy and for a couple of months after delivery.[42] In her insistence on divinely inspired fertility, she resembled her nativist contemporaries, who also upheld female divinities as models of behavior for ordinary women; however, her telling of how Izanagi and Izanami created the world was highly original, contradicting the creation myths in the national chronicles that nativists would have considered foundational. Some scholars contend that Miki rebelled against the patrilineal household,[43] but others more cautiously argue that Miki was at most dissatisfied with her husband's and son's performance as household heads. While Miki resisted the constrictions the patrilineal household placed on her, she did not envision an alternative to it.[44]

Conclusion

The Edo period has been portrayed as the low point in women's history in Japan because of the hegemony of the patrilineal household and its Confucian ideology. However, a careful examination of the period yields a more nuanced picture. Early modern Japanese society showed considerable variations based on region and class. While status-group membership was not nearly as rigid as it might first seem (especially for women), women beyond the social elites enjoyed much greater freedoms in regard to gender relations than did their privileged counterparts. Despite its restrictions, the patrilineal household also had advantages for women. Women operating outside the patriarchal family and outside religious institutions, such as convents, were often left with few means to survive, and were therefore vulnerable to sexual exploitation. As we shall see in the following chapter, the patrilineal household, which had become pervasive across Edo status groups, remained the fundamental basis of society during Japan's transition into the modern era, while the definition of marriage changed radically during the Meiji period (1868–1912).

Imperial Japan

Good Wives and Wise Mothers

In the latter half of the nineteenth century, Japan transformed into a modern nation-state. As Japan expanded its contact with the West and became a colonial power, religious traditions were redefined and demarcated not only against one another but also against so-called superstitions and suprareligious civic rites. Shortly after the imperial restoration, which marked the beginning of the Meiji period (1868–1912), the worship of Buddhas and *kami* was dissociated into two distinct major traditions, Buddhism and Shinto, which had previously been fused. Religious practices and institutions that did not easily fit these new molds were forced to either identify with one or the other or face suppression. Christianity, which had been prohibited for much of the Tokugawa period, was legalized in 1873. While the Meiji Constitution (1889) nominally guaranteed religious freedom to all Japanese, the extent of freedom was circumscribed in the name of public order. Furthermore, Shrine Shinto was designated as a civic state cult in contradistinction to Sectarian Shinto, which served as an umbrella category for religious organizations identifying as Shinto.

Women's roles in the religious traditions of Japan also changed in this process. Many established religious organizations promoted visions of femininity that reinforced the "good wife, wise mother" ideal, which became prevalent in the late nineteenth century. This ideal proved to be double-edged: it could be empowering by granting women access to education and a means to be publicly active in an era when women were officially barred from the public sphere, but it also limited women to the domestic sphere, reducing them to supportive roles for the men in their lives. Religious women who transgressed against gender norms—such as the founders of new religions and independent shamans—faced conflict with the authorities. Yet eventually, even new, seemingly heterodox religious organizations began to reiterate the ideal of the good wife and wise mother.

Good Wife, Wise Mother

During the transition from an early modern feudal society to a modern nation-state, gender relations in Japan changed significantly. This process was guided, on the one hand, by existing Confucian principles and, on the other, by newly introduced Western concepts. The Meiji state promoted an ideal of building a strong nation populated by physically robust subjects. Emblematic of the times, the Imperial Rescript on Education (1890) reformulated the ideal relationship between husband and wife. In addition to advocating loyalty to the emperor, the Rescript stated, "Ye Our subjects, be filial to your parents, affectionate to your brothers and sisters; as husband and wife be harmonious, as friends true."[1] While the Rescript borrowed, on the surface, the Confucian concept of the five fundamental human relationships (ruler-subject, husband-wife, parent-child, siblings, and friends), it subtly changed the nature of these relationships. For instance, in regard to the relationship between husband and wife, the Rescript advocated marital harmony as ideal rather than reiterating the traditional Confucian principle that "between husband and wife there is distinction." The latter implied mutually chaste behavior and distinct roles within the family, whereas mutual harmony (*aiwa*) acknowledged the new idea of conjugal partnership. However, contemporaneous commentators understood marital harmony to be fundamentally based on the wife's subservience and obedience to the husband.[2]

The Meiji state based its legal and administrative systems on the patrilineal household system. The individual was largely subordinated to the interests of the household and the authority of the head of the household, while the state (*kokka*) itself was conceptualized as a household under the parental authority of the emperor. The importance of the household as the new nation's underlying social unit was already affirmed through the universal household registration system (*koseki seido*), implemented in 1871. According to the system, all imperial subjects, regardless of their social class, had to register the members of their household. However, in the absence of more specific family law, many early modern practices regarding the patrilineal household continued to be enforced until the promulgation of the Civil Code in 1898. According to the new Civil Code, the head of the household had exclusive control of the family property, including assets that women brought into the family through marriage. He also had sole custody of the couple's children and the right to determine marriage partners for sons under thirty and daughters under twenty-five. The headship of the household was passed exclusively along a male line, usually to the eldest son, in effect excluding women from inheritance rights. The household with its ties to an ancestral lineage that received ritual veneration was seen as essential to the preservation of national loyalty and reverence of the emperor. This concept remained central to the state's ideology until the end of World War II.[3] Another important change in the late Meiji period was the exclusion of women from the political sphere. The Law on Political Assembly and Association (1890) and the Public Peace Police Law (1900) prohibited women from attending political meetings and forming political parties. These policies officially relegated women to the private sphere.[4]

Significantly, the Meiji Civil Code redefined the institution of marriage as a mutually monogamous relationship, ending the long-standing practice of concubinage among the social elites. Previous laws promulgated in the early Meiji era had removed the distinctions between wives and concubines, giving both equal rights. In practice, this raised the status of concubines; conversely, however, it also lowered the status of wives. Polygyny remained a tolerated practice until the promulgation of the Civil Code in 1898. Despite the new focus on the conjugal pair at the center of the household, the new system presupposed that the continuity and stability of the household as a collective were more important than the interests of the individual.[5]

During the early Meiji period, reformers debated extensively what the ideal nature of marriage should be. Reformers such as the members of the Meiji Six Society (Meirokusha)—named after the year of its founding, namely, Meiji 6 (1873)—argued for the abandonment of polygyny in favor of monogamy in order to promote civilization and enlightenment. The debates articulated in the *Meiji Six Journal* (published from 1874 to 1875) were influenced by Confucianism, as well as Western utilitarianism and Christianity. While the members of the Meiji Six Society condemned prostitution and concubinage and called for consensual, monogamous marriage, they generally limited equal rights for women only to marriage and the domestic sphere rather than extending such rights to the public, political sphere.[6] In 1875 Nakamura Masanao (1832–1891), a member of the Meiji Six Society, coined a term for the new feminine ideal: "good wife, wise mother" (*ryōsai kenbō*). Nakamura was strongly influenced by contemporaneous Western ideals of the wife as the "better half" of her husband and argued for women's education so that they could better support their husbands and provide religious and moral instruction for their children.[7]

The concept of "good wife, wise mother" became a key objective in women's education in the 1890s, especially after the Sino-Japanese War (1894–1895). The primary objective of women's education was to train women to be better homemakers and mothers rather than training them for skilled work outside the home. The realities of many women's lives, however, did not reflect the ideal of confining women to the home. Women provided essential labor in small businesses, farms, and factories. Furthermore, there were women who resisted their relegation to the domestic sphere. Women in the emerging women's movement advocated for rights such as suffrage, while women influenced by socialism pushed for equal rights to participate politically. Early feminists identifying as "New Women" openly expressed their opposition to prevalent restrictive social conventions regarding female sexuality. Nevertheless, in its various iterations, the ideal of "good wife, wise mother" became an important ideological tool in imperial Japan. As Japan became a colonial power and engaged in a series of wars, women's maternal role was considered important to the state and its pro-natalist policies in order to provide a strong population to staff the army and settle the colonies.[8]

During the Meiji period, the Meiji Six Society reformers were not the only ones calling for an end to prostitution and concubinage, the reformulation of marriage, and improvements in women's education. Christian women's organizations were usually affiliated with charitable Protestant organizations established in nineteenth-century Europe and North America, such as the Woman's Christian Temperance Union in Japan (founded in 1886) and the women's branches of the Red Cross and the Salvation Army in Japan. As the historian Yasutake Rumi notes, the Woman's Christian Temperance Union's "activism was rooted in American Protestant evangelism and the development of the Victorian ideology of womanhood which emphasized 'purity,' 'piety,' 'domesticity,' and 'submissiveness'" and which constructed women as "innately more 'pious' and 'pure' and thus, morally superior to men."[9] Historians have termed this the "cult of true womanhood."[10] As in the United States, this gender ideology, with its emphasis on the moral superiority of women, had the ironic effect of motivating women to move out of the domestic sphere to have an impact in society. In Japan, Christian women's organizations were engaged in social welfare activism and education. Beginning in the early Meiji period, they strongly lobbied against prostitution. Their campaign resumed with new fervor after the Great Kantō Earthquake in 1923 in order to prevent the reconstruction of the pleasure quarters in Tokyo.[11] Furthermore, female Christian missionaries and female Christian converts established educational institutions for women, which helped spread the ideals of companionate, monogamous marriage and Victorian ideals of femininity. Like other social welfare activities, education gave these Christian women a means to be publicly active within socially acceptable boundaries.[12]

FIGURE 7.1. Tsuda Umeko. Image copyright © National
Diet Library, Tokyo. Image source: National Diet Library.

Perhaps the most famous among the Japanese Christian women who
promoted women's education was Tsuda Umeko (1864–1929; see figure
7.1). When Tsuda was six, her father volunteered to have her sent by the
Japanese government to America to receive an education. She returned
to Japan in 1882, having graduated from a girls' school and having
been baptized as a Christian. In 1885 she took a teaching position at
the recently established Peeresses' School (Kazoku Jogakkō), where she
taught until 1899. During a leave of absence, she returned to the United
States for further study in the Northeast from 1889 to 1892, opened her

own women's school, Joshi Eigaku Juku, in Japan in 1900, and became the president of the newly founded Tokyo branch of the Young Women's Christian Association (YWCA) in 1905. Scholars have debated the extent to which Tsuda (who never herself married) supported, accepted, or challenged the prevailing ideal of good wife and wise mother and whether she rejected or implicitly influenced emerging feminist ideals in early twentieth-century Japan. While she acknowledged that traditionally, "a woman's sphere is in her home, and it is she who attends to all the details of every-day life for her husband, performing many acts of services with her own hands,"[13] she confessed in private to her American foster mother, "Do not expect me to ever make such a marriage, or, to marry at all."[14] She understood that in the past women had been disadvantaged because they lacked a formal education and were thus unable to be on equal footing with men. For Tsuda, recent changes in educational opportunities, however, meant that "the girl or woman is called on now to lead a different life and to fill new duties."[15] During her lifetime, Tsuda strongly advocated improving women's education so that women could be more independent and better serve the nation, but she also opposed the suffrage movement and remained staunchly class-conscious, concentrating her educational efforts on the social elites and the upper middle class.[16] Tsuda embodied the difficult balancing act in which socially active women had to engage in order to accomplish their missions.

Monastic Reform Movements and Buddhist Married Women's Associations

In the early Meiji period, the nature of Buddhist monasticism was also redefined. In 1872 the new regime declared that meat eating and marriage were no longer punishable civil offenses for male clerics. In 1873 the same legislation was adopted for nuns.[17] However, clerical marriage was not immediately considered acceptable by the Buddhist denominations, with the noted exception of the Jōdo Shin sect, whose clerics had been allowed to marry freely since the Kamakura period. Clerical marriage came to be debated vigorously; in the late 1910s and early 1920s, most Buddhist denominations permitted the practice for male clerics but did so only reluctantly. By the late 1930s, the majority of male Buddhist clerics were married, even though many denominations continued to view the practice critically from a doctrinal perspective.[18]

In contrast, nuns generally did not practice clerical marriage.[19] Ironically, during an era when the most prominent feminine ideal cast women's natural roles as wives and mothers, nuns completely rejected marriage and motherhood. Nevertheless, when the good-wife-and-wise-mother ideology was used to promote education for women, educational opportunities for nuns also improved even though they were not destined to become wives or mothers. For example, in the 1880s Sōtō Zen nuns took the initiative to establish schools without the support of the sectarian headquarters in order to give other nuns an opportunity to gain access to basic education. In 1902 the Sōtō sect decided to found three schools for nuns, who made up nearly 10 percent of its clergy, in order to provide four years of general education and basic training in sectarian doctrine. While this education was much more modest than that for male Sōtō clerics, who had the option of attending a sectarian university and entering training monasteries to further their education, the three schools for Sōtō nuns founded between 1903 and 1907 at least provided the nuns with the beginnings of an education. Such training was largely made possible by the efforts of nuns who served as teachers at these sectarian schools.[20]

As the emerging feminist and suffrage movements in Japan gained force in the 1920s, Sōtō nuns also began to demand greater equality with their male counterparts. The male sectarian leadership endorsed a division of labor between male clerics and nuns that paralleled the prevailing gender roles in the secular sphere: the study and promulgation of doctrine should be the role of male clerics, while nuns should limit themselves to their role as nurturers of women and children. If nuns were not themselves wives and mothers, then they could teach other women skills (for example, sewing, tea ceremony, and flower arrangement) that would make the latter better wives and mothers. From the mid-1920s to the mid-1940s, the Sōtō nuns submitted numerous petitions to the sectarian leadership calling for the establishment of training nunneries and a voice in sectarian leadership, as well as the rights to maintain female-based monastic lineages, to become missionaries, and to serve as abbots of medium-level temples that had hereditary parishes and thus offered a stable income. While the nuns were not immediately able to receive concessions that granted them full status equality and equal access to financial resources, in the 1920s the Sōtō sect began to issue to nuns monastic titles that had previously been given only to male clerics and that recognized them as teachers. During this time, nuns were also given—as auditors—limited access to the sectarian university.[21]

However, we should not assume that the Meiji period was a time when previously disenfranchised nuns gained new rights and greater access to education. Nuns such as Kumano *bikuni*, who did not fit neatly into new categories, suddenly saw their livelihoods outlawed when, in the late 1860s and early 1870s, the Meiji regime suppressed what it considered heterodox religious practices. For instance, in 1872, male and female itinerant religious professionals were prohibited from collecting donations on alms rounds.[22] This essentially banned what were, for itinerant preachers, important income-generating activities. As we shall see below, other prohibitions affecting common rituals performed by shamans and folk healers were soon to follow.

Furthermore, not all nuns were marginalized and undereducated before the Meiji period. Under the Tokugawa regime, nuns of elite background had enjoyed a privileged status, including state-funded stipends, at over a dozen convents. During the Meiji Restoration, such convents—like their male counterparts—lost their titles, stipends, and lands. During the dissociation of Buddhas and *kami*, male and female clerics from the imperial lineage were forcibly laicized because the imperial family was now supposed to be linked only to Shinto and not to Buddhism.

Such laicization also extended to aristocrats who had been adopted into the imperial lineage to serve as abbots and abbesses of imperial temples. While former imperial male clerics could find a new role in politics, former imperial nuns usually did not have this option. Therefore, they had greater incentives to resist laicization and the closure of their convents than did their male counterparts. Imperial nuns used monastic lineage documents to demonstrate that they were rightful heirs to both Buddhist and imperial traditions. By means of these strategies, some convents avoided closure, but the imperial nuns were still forced to laicize. After laicization, some were able to remain in residence at the convents and some were eventually allowed to become nuns again. In the end, most convents were able to regain their imperial titles in 1885, though members of the imperial lineage no longer functioned as abbesses.[23]

Alongside nuns, laywomen also claimed their institutional place in modern Buddhist organizations. The first Buddhist married women's associations were founded in the late nineteenth and early twentieth centuries. These early associations were partially modeled on early modern Buddhist consororities (*nyoninkō*), but were also inspired by modern Christian women's organizations that were brought to Japan by foreign missionaries in the late nineteenth and early twentieth centuries. For example, Jōdo Shinshū's Ōtani branch established a sect-wide married women's association in 1890 in order to "uplift the way of married women" through sermons and social welfare activities. Similarly, the imperial Nichiren nun Murakumo Nichiei (1855–1920), who also founded a training convent for nuns in 1919 and was involved in the Kyoto branch of the Japanese Red Cross, established a national women's association, Murakumo fujinkai, in the late nineteenth century. Despite the existence of a few sect-wide associations such as these, many of the prewar Buddhist married women's associations were localized and run by individual temples rather than Buddhist sects.[24]

During this era, many religious organizations, including not just Buddhist and Christian but also Shinto groups, began to establish married women's associations and young men's associations. Like their

Christian counterparts such as the YWCA and the YMCA, these associations not only enabled the religious organizations to represent themselves as modern religious institutions but also served to reinforce and shape visions of masculinity and femininity in their era. In the case of *fujinkai*, or married women's associations, the name of the organizations projected an image of cultured femininity and of a wife: *fujin* is commonly translated as "woman," but it also carries the notion of "lady" or "married woman." *Fujinkai* gave women an opportunity to publicly engage in feminine activities in a socially acceptable way but also confined them to the institutional spaces and activities of the married women's associations.

Masculinizing the Shinto Priesthood and Shinto Weddings

Like the Buddhist clergy, the Shinto priesthood was also redefined. During the Edo period, the Shinto priesthood had been very religiously diverse, localized, and largely hereditary. It often overlapped with Buddhist clerics and mountain ascetics and was only partially controlled by sacerdotal Shinto lineages. During the early Meiji period, the Shinto priesthood came under the control of the Department of Divinity, which was later renamed the Ministry of Divinity. In 1871, the priesthood lost their right to hereditary succession and instead became state-appointed bureaucrats certified through national examinations. Shinto rites conducted by the emperor, which were revived under the auspices of the Department of Divinity, were redefined as public state rites rather than private observances. In this process, the Shinto priesthood was largely masculinized and the ceremonial roles that women held at the imperial court were also tightly controlled.[25]

The process of masculinization is apparent at the Ise Shrines. In the Edo period, the position of the master celebrant (*saishu*) had been hereditarily held by women of the Fujinami clan. The master celebrant's most important role was that of leading the divine procession from the old to the new shrine buildings during periodic reconstructions of the precinct as a representative of the imperial house. After the Meiji Restoration, a male member of the imperial family took over this role. The position remained in male hands until the end of World War II.[26]

Women were also prohibited from serving as priests at village Shinto shrines. In 1874 the question arose whether women could, in the absence of suitable male candidates, hold the position of shrine priest and, like Buddhist nuns, participate in the Promulgation Campaign of the Great Teaching (1870–1884), which was meant to indoctrinate the populace with the new imperial ideology. The authorities decided that women could not hold the office of a shrine priest because women could not hold public offices.[27] In general, women who had functioned as shamanic mediums and dancers at shrines lost their positions and were unable to regain their certifications.[28] In the 1910s, Miyamoto Shigetane (1881–1959), the priest at Nisho Yamada Shrine in Yamaguchi Prefecture and founder of Keishin fujinkai, a national Shinto married women's association, stressed the historical precedent for women's priestly roles. Although he called in the association's journal, *Joshidō* (The Way of Women), for the revival of priestly positions for women, female shrine priests did not reappear until after 1945.[29]

Moreover, in 1873 independent shamans such as catalpa-bow shamans and blind shamans (*ichiko*) were officially prohibited from serving as spirit mediums, conducting exorcisms, or performing divination. These injunctions were soon followed by prohibitions against healing rituals.[30] Until 1945, shamans, spirit mediums, and folk healers—many of whom were women—faced continued harassment and suppression by the authorities. The most common charges against them were licentiousness, extortion, and physically harming their clients with folk remedies. As the Meiji regime promoted the adoption of Western medicine and psychology in order to build a strong nation, folk remedies were seen as detrimental to the health of the nation. This meant that ailments commonly treated by folk healers, such as eye ailments and mental afflictions attributed to fox possession, were redefined according to scientific, Western categories. They were supposed to be treated by doctors trained in Western medicine rather than folk healers. However, the authorities did not completely eradicate shamans and healers. In Aomori Prefecture in northeastern Japan, for example, where blind shamans were deeply entrenched, shamans and healers continued to practice widely despite the official harassment and negative mass media coverage. The authorities tacitly tolerated such activities because these religious professionals were able to adjust flexibly to the official ideology of State Shinto. In contrast, in Okinawa (formerly the Ryūkyū Islands), which was annexed by imperial Japan in 1872, female shamans faced systematic eradication campaigns in the 1930s because their practices were considered completely heterodox.[31]

New Shinto practices also affected women who did not have sacerdotal roles at Shinto shrines. In 1901 the Hibiya Daijingū, the Tokyo branch of the Ise Shrines, introduced a ritual novelty: the Shinto wedding. In Tokugawa Japan, wedding rituals were not held at religious institutions or conducted by religious professionals, but rather were celebrated as domestic rituals. If any kind of religious specialist was employed, it was elderly women performers (*katsurame*), who were to protect the bride from demonic harm on her passage into the bridegroom's household, rather than to officiate at the wedding rite per se. By the mid- to late Edo period, several scholars with nativist leanings began to assign divine meanings to the wedding rite, which they saw as paralleling Izanami and Izanagi's nuptial encounter.[32] The idea that religious professionals should take charge of the central nuptial rite, however, is distinctly modern. The first Shinto ritual manual with instructions about weddings presided over by a Shinto priest was published in 1872, and the first recorded Shinto weddings took place in the 1880s, particularly in the families of Shinto priests and within Sectarian Shinto groups. Around this time other forms of religious wedding ceremonies, such as Buddhist weddings and Christian weddings, also were emerging in Japan for the first time. Shinto weddings gained popularity only after the imperial wedding in 1900 of Crown Prince Yoshihito, later known as the Taishō Emperor (1879–1926), and his fifteen-year-old bride, Kujō

Sadako, later known as Empress Teimei (1884–1951). The crown prince's wedding rite took place at the Kashikodokoro in the imperial palace. About a year later, the Hibiya Daijingū in Tokyo (whose head priest had himself had a Shinto wedding in 1882) offered the first Shinto wedding for the urban elites, including the families of politicians, military men, university professors, and financiers.[33]

The motivation for devising such rituals may have been partially economic. During the period between 1880 and 1905, state support for Shinto shrines had been declining, which led to greater need among the Shinto priesthood to provide rituals for the general populace to raise money. Since funerals were prohibited for shrine priests in the 1880s, they looked to other rites of passage, such as shrine visits on the occasion of a child's birth (*hatsumiya mairi*) or on a child's third, fifth, and seventh birthday (*shichigosan*).[34] For the Hibiya Daijingū, the performance of wedding rituals for Tokyo's urban elites must have been a welcome source of income.

There also were ideological in addition to economic factors leading to the popularization of the Shinto wedding rite. Religious wedding rituals emerged precisely when the definition of marriage underwent considerable change. As mentioned above, members of the Meiji Six Society and Christian missionaries had portrayed the practice of concubinage and the country's high divorce rate as inappropriate for a modern nation. Christian missionaries proposed that religious marriage rituals, particularly Christian rites, might counter the problem of systemically high divorce rates. The newly enacted Civil Code of 1898 had redefined marriage as mutually monogamous. Reflecting the new definition of marriage, the Taishō Emperor, whose marriage set the precedent for Shinto weddings, had only one consort. By contrast, his father, the Meiji Emperor (1852–1912), had one principal wife, Empress Shōken (Ichijō Haruko, 1849–1914), but his children were born to five concubines, including Yanagihara Naruko (1859–1943), the Taishō Emperor's mother.[35] Soon after the implementation of the Civil Code and the crown prince's wedding, the Hibiya Daijingū began to offer wedding ceremonies for urban elites. By 1913, the Ueno Shimotani Shrine and the Tokyo branch of the Izumo Grand Shrine (established in 1912) also offered wedding rites. Between 1908 and 1915, the number of Shinto weddings at the Hibiya Daijingū more than tripled, to 1,550 per year. By the 1930s, Shinto weddings had spread to other urban areas, such as Osaka and Kyoto. Although the vast majority of weddings were still conducted at home, home weddings and bridal dowries also became more elaborate and expensive. Such expenses provided an incentive to make marriages last longer and forestall divorce. Indeed, after the promulgation of the Civil Code, the divorce rate dropped sharply.[36]

New Religious Movements: Integration or Suppression

In imperial Japan, new religious movements—several founded by women—played important roles in Japan's modern religious landscape. Like shamans, folk healers, and, from the 1920s, spiritualists, hypnotists, and psychics, they usually faced harassment by the authorities and the news media, both of which accused them of licentiousness, extortion, and quackery. The groups were usually forced to integrate into established religious structures, such as Buddhist sects or Sectarian Shinto, to avoid conflict. Even then they often faced suppression. Tenrikyō, founded in the late Edo period by Nakayama Miki (1798–1887), encountered repeated harassment by the authorities and arrests of its leaders. The communal lifestyle advocated by Miki, combined with dance services that involved the mingling of the sexes, Miki's faith healing, and her idiosyncratic account of human creation made Tenrikyō appear suspicious to the authorities. During the 1880s and 1890s, when Tenrikyō underwent rapid growth, the media strongly attacked the organization for promoting licentiousness and extorting money from its followers.[37] Eventually, Tenrikyō adjusted its doctrines to comply with State Shinto teachings and changed its dance service to allow only men to perform so that the movement could gain recognition as a Shinto sect, which it accomplished in 1908.[38]

As Tenrikyō women were being pushed to more marginal positions in the organization, they founded a married women's association in 1910. In the context of this organization, women began to assert in the mid-1920s and the early 1930s that they were the foundation of the faith (*michi no dai*). This motto meant, first, that they played an essential role within the larger organization and, second, that they played subordinate roles, supporting men's activities.[39] Embodying the motto of "foundation of the faith," the married women's association was involved in establishing a girls' high school, daycare facilities, and an orphanage in the 1910s and 1920s.[40] The focus on children and young women's education allowed Tenrikyō women to be publicly active while nominally fulfilling their roles as good wives and wise mothers. Even today's married women's association remains focused on children's education in its social activities. In the prewar era, married women's associations, which usually subscribed to the good wife and wise mother ideal, became a typical way of mobilizing and confining female participation in new religious movements, a trend that continued into the postwar period.

Other new religious organizations were not as successful as Tenrikyō in gaining official acceptance. For instance, Ōmotokyō, another new religious movement, eventually met with forceful repression in the 1920s and 1930s after the foundress's death. Deguchi Nao (1837–1918) founded the group in 1892 after she experienced spirit possession by a divinity she called Ushitora Konjin. Like Tenrikyō's Nakayama Miki, Nao came from a humble background. Her life as an adolescent and later as a young woman fluctuated between moderate wealth in youth and as a newlywed bride, and complete destitution as first her father and then her husband lost the family fortune and died. Unlike Miki, she had undergone little spiritual training before becoming a spiritual leader in her own right. While her family was affiliated with the Jōdo sect and she had aspired, when young, to become a Buddhist nun, she had not trained as a spirit medium. When one of her adult daughters succumbed to mental illness in 1890, Nao came in contact with Konkōkyō, another new religious movement of the time, through a ritual of exorcism that invoked a divinity called Ushitora Konjin. Shortly after another of her adult daughters also experienced an episode of mental illness in 1891, Nao had her first divine possession.[41]

After a particularly powerful divine possession in 1892, Nao began to write down the revelations she received from Ushitora Konjin. These writings are collectively known as the *Ofudesaki* (Tip of the Writing Brush), like the revelations recorded by Tenrikyō's founder, with whom she shared the technique of spirit writing. Around this time, Nao engaged in a stringent regimen of austerities such as cold-water ablutions. In 1893 she was incarcerated by the authorities—not because the authorities considered her a fraud or a heterodox leader at this point, but because they deemed her insane and suspected her of arson. Upon her release, Nao attempted to form affiliations with Tenrikyō and Konkōkyō in order to legitimize the propagation of her revelations, but neither attempt proved to be successful because both groups were ultimately interested in promoting their own teachings rather than Nao's. Nao was finally able to build a more stable organization with the help of Ueda Kisaburō (1873–1948), who married one of her daughters and took the name Deguchi Onisaburō in 1900. Through Onisaburō's status as a Shinto priest connected to the cult of Inari, Nao was able to become independent of Konkōkyō, but she also had to share power with Onisaburō, who was a charismatic leader in his own right.[42]

Nao's divine revelations, received through unmediated spirit possession, were a source of power and contention in Nao's relationships with her male religious collaborators. Nao's divine possessions allowed her to gain alternative knowledge enabling her to critique society and politics even though she lacked formal education and was of lower-class background. However, despite her charisma and ability to attract followers, her early male collaborators sent by Konkōkyō failed to acknowledge her teachings recorded in the *Ofudesaki*. Whereas Deguchi Onisaburō eventually edited and published parts of Nao's *Ofudesaki*, he also challenged her authority through his emphasis on mediated spirit possession. Onisaburō had been trained as a spirit mediator (*saniwa*), who could guide spirit mediums through divine possession, and he provided this service to members at large. Nao, however, was disturbed that his preoccupation with mediated possession marginalized her teachings and her direct connection with the divine. Nao expected Onisaburō to bow to her authority, not the other way around.[43]

Nao challenged traditional ideas of gender. She considered herself the Transformed Male (*henjō nanshi*), who had a "male nature in a female body" and who could effect the salvation of humanity during this time of world renewal. She believed that only such a Transformed Male could serve in this role, which regular males would not be able to bear because they lacked the necessary endurance and capacity to subordinate themselves completely to the divine will. She also asserted that Onisaburō conversely was the Transformed Female (*henjō nyoshi*), who would collaborate with the Transformed Male in these millennial times. As Helen Hardacre argues, Nao distinguished between the physical sex and gender—a distinction that would later become vital for second-wave feminists in their pursuit of their own political agendas. Nao used this gender construction to wield control over Onisaburō, who often challenged her authority in his joint leadership of Ōmotokyō.[44] However, in contrast to late twentieth-century feminists, who resisted ideas of biological determinism, Nao seems to have maintained that the female sex innately made women perseverant nurturers and that the male sex was marked by egotism. These innate male and female characteristics remained even in the Transformed Male and the Transformed Female although their genders had been changed.

Conclusion

As Japan became a modern imperial state between 1868 and 1945, the religious landscape and women's roles and opportunities within it were also transformed. Paradoxically, while marriage was redefined as monogamous and was ideally supposed to consist of a partnership, the patrilineal household became more hegemonic than ever across all social classes. Women were encouraged to emulate the ideal of the good wife and wise mother, in whose name they were officially excluded from politics and from the public sphere. By strategically invoking this ideal, women gained great access to educational opportunities and representation in their religious organizations and found ways to be active in public through married women's associations. By contrast, women who violated the new imperial order through their religious activities—shamans, faith healers, and founders and adherents of new religious movements—were subjected to varying degrees of suppression and vilification by the modern news media. Nevertheless, certain women demonstrated great persistence, ingenuity, and vigor despite these social constraints. In the postwar era, new religious movements and alternative religious practitioners would win greater legal freedoms, but negative news media coverage would continue to expose them to public criticism.

8

The Postwar Period

Nostalgia, Religion, and the Reinvention of Femininity

The end of World War II brought sweeping social changes to Japan. The Allied Occupation (1945–1952) abolished the restrictive laws of the prewar era, such as the Peace Preservation Law of 1925 and the Religious Organizations Law of 1940. The new constitution of 1947 and other civil and labor laws promised gender equality and gave religious organizations greater freedom from state control. However, despite legal reforms, during the postwar period the figure of the housewife became a hegemonic ideal of femininity that placed women in the domestic sphere. As Vera Mackie notes, "It is one of the paradoxes of that period that the forces of political economy and familial ideology increasingly pushed women into an identification with the domestic sphere as housewives, while the legal changes of that time removed official obstacles to their activities as citizens in the public, political sphere."[1]

Similarly, while Japanese religious institutions affirmed to varying degrees these new ideals of egalitarianism and democracy, they also resisted the resultant changes in the family system and in women's roles. Many Buddhist, Shinto, or new religious organizations chose to promote so-called traditional values that cast women as good wives and wise mothers and placed them in the home. Women reacted in various ways. Some lobbied for changes within existing religious structures, while others took advantage of the new legal system to found their own independent religious organizations. Many women, however, chose to embrace their identities as wives and mothers (at least nominally) by joining the married women's associations of their respective religious organizations, through which they found ways to become publicly active outside the home. On the whole, women in the postwar religious organizations tended to be more socially and politically conservative than were secular feminists, who often belonged to the political left.

The Postwar Constitution and the Permutations of Good Wife and Wise Mother

During the latter half of the Meiji period (1868–1912), women's rights had been severely curtailed. This changed in the postwar era. In 1945 the Allied Occupation granted women political rights Japanese feminists had demanded for decades: the rights to vote, join political parties, stand for office, and unionize. The passing of the new constitution in 1947 made these changes permanent. Drafted by a team of foreign experts, including one woman, the new constitution guaranteed the legal equality of men and women. The document was eventually approved by the Japanese Diet, which by 1946 included thirty-nine women elected to office. Any discrimination based on gender was outlawed (Article 14). Husband and wife became equal partners in marriage (Article 24). Furthermore, the constitution guaranteed women equal rights to an education (Article 26) and the right to vote (Article 44).[2] Of these laws, Article 24 became particularly controversial with its affirmation of gender equality by privileging the rights of the individual and undermining the household as the basic unit of society:

> Marriage shall be based only on the *mutual consent of both sexes* and it shall be maintained through mutual cooperation with the *equal rights of husband and wife* as a basis. With regard to choice of spouse, property rights, inheritance, choice of domicile, divorce and other matters pertaining to marriage and the family, laws shall be enacted from the standpoint of *individual dignity* and the *essential equality of the sexes.*[3] (Emphasis added)

During the 1950s and 1960s, conservative critics of the constitution suggested various revisions of Article 24. For instance, some took issue with the idea of mutual consent, presumably because it problematized arranged marriages, which were still very common during this era but were declining sharply and by 1970 were overtaken in number by love marriages. Others sought to remove the concepts of individualism and gender equality in favor of familial collectivism, and to reinstitute the patrilineal household system of the prewar era.[4]

For many conservatives, the principle of good wife and wise mother remained the normative feminine identity throughout the postwar era. While the term "good wife and wise mother" itself was no longer used officially after the war, government policies and business company rules continued to reaffirm the concept indirectly, thereby reasserting that the ideal femininity consisted of wifehood and motherhood. Trends such as greater urbanization, a higher percentage of wage labor (rather than employment in family businesses), and increases in the number of nuclear families (rather than multigenerational households) made the role of motherhood more important than of wifehood. Technological innovation made household chores less time consuming, giving women the opportunity to focus almost exclusively on their children's education. Women were primarily cast as mothers rather than as daughters-in-law, a role emphasized in earlier periods more strongly influenced by Neo-Confucianism. Conversely, many women began to use their roles as wives and mothers to engage in political activism, often by organizing into married women's associations (*fujinkai*) to advocate social issues that were closely related to their lives as homemakers and mothers.[5] The principle of good wife and wise mother also remained important in many conservative religious organizations. Religious organizations ranging from the Association of Shinto Shrines and Buddhist denominations to new religious and Buddhist lay movements used the concept of good wife and wise mother to formulate policies regarding the roles and rights of women within their institutions.

Modern Buddhist Nuns and Temple Wives:
New Rights, Traditional Ideals

After 1945, the Buddhist denominations pursued reforms such as granting male and female clerics equal legal rights pursuant to the new constitution. This process took several decades to accomplish. In the Sōtō sect, for instance, nuns built on the institutional structures they had established before and during the war to agitate for equality within their denomination. Their demands included equal educational opportunities (including the right to matriculate at Komazawa University, a Sōtō university in Tokyo, and to operate training convents) and advancement opportunities equal to those in the male order. When the Sōtō sect promulgated its own sectarian constitution in 1946, nuns gained greater autonomy and institutional recognition as teachers. Additionally, certified female teachers earned the right to vote within the sectarian assembly. Yet the nuns' order was still under male supervision for dharma transmissions and the oversight of disciples. Nuns were not allowed to manage temples of high rank or seek office in sectarian elections, policies that excluded them from direct representation in the sectarian assembly. Following the passage of the new Japanese constitution, however, Sōtō nuns won the right to stand as candidates in 1948 and sent their first representative, Kojima Kendō (1898–1995), to the sectarian assembly in 1951. Thanks to Kojima's presence, the denomination soon granted nuns further rights and greater autonomy from the male order. But it was not until 1970 that nuns achieved full equality. In the postwar years, nuns also gained educational opportunities on a par with those of male clerics.[6]

Despite the nuns' struggle for equality, their training and practice have remained somewhat distinct from those of their male counterparts. Unlike male clerics, the vast majority of nuns remain unmarried—a fact that allows nuns to claim legitimacy, even greater legitimacy than male clerics, as orthodox guardians of the precepts. This sense has perhaps been heightened by the fact that since the 1960s, in reflection of changing demographics, nuns have increasingly come from families with fewer siblings and no strong previous temple affiliations. In contrast to their predecessors and male contemporaries, who were mostly ordained as teenagers and at the behest of their families, the majority of nuns who ordained after 1960 have done so of their own volition and at an older age. Furthermore, even though nuns, through education, can earn the same ranks as their male colleagues, the content of their education is gendered, containing elements not included in male clerics' education. Sōtō nuns' training, for example, includes the study of traditional Japanese arts such as tea ceremony and flower arrangement as well as the singing of devotional Buddhist hymns (*baika*) (see figure 8.1). While such training is vital preparation for life at their temples, where they often act as teachers of these skills, the study of these arts, which have become associated with genteel feminine refinement, also allows the nuns to perform a conservative, traditional form of femininity in spite of having renounced their lives as wives and mothers.[7] Tea-ceremony culture became increasingly feminized in the early twentieth century, a trend that continued into the postwar period and inhered with the role of the housewife becoming normative. Tea ceremony served as a means to teach women physically disciplined etiquette.[8] The Sōtō nuns' Zen training has similarly emphasized the ritualization of daily activities and bodily discipline, making the practice of tea ceremony particularly appropriate for the nuns. Furthermore, their celibate lifestyle gives them the advantage of teaching traditional arts without having to contend with family demands. While students of tea ceremony rarely question their roles as wives and mothers and tend to subordinate their study of tea ceremony to their family obligations, most female lay teachers of tea ceremony tend to become professionals only later in life, after they have fulfilled their roles as wives and mothers.[9]

In addition to changing the status of nuns, the Buddhist denominations have also had to come to terms with the existence of the Buddhist clerics' wives. While clerical marriage became legal in the Meiji period

FIGURE 8.1. A Sōtō Zen nun teaching Buddhist hymns to temple wives and lay-women. Photograph by the author.

and had been sanctioned by all Japanese Buddhist denominations since the 1920s, temple wives remained largely unacknowledged by sectarian leadership. In most Buddhist denominations, male clerics were still regarded as renunciants, making the presence of temple wives a contradiction in terms. Ironically, Buddhist nuns were at the forefront of claiming that clerical marriage is in principle incompatible with renunciation. Still, Buddhist sectarian leaders justified temple wives' presence in terms of their roles supporting the male cleric and rearing the male heir to the temple. Thus the role of the temple wife was understood similarly to the concept of the good wife and wise mother. Apart from her status as the abbot's wife and mother of the abbot's heir, the temple wife's status as a temple resident remained precarious. This became apparent in cases in which the abbot passed away without leaving a male heir who could succeed him. In such situations, the temple wife lost her standing at the temple and often had to leave the premises, sometimes with little financial assistance. Only in the 1990s, when pressured by temple wives' increased activism, did sectarian leadership begin to address the under-lying institutional structures affecting temple wives.[10]

Shinto Weddings: Symbols of Japaneseness and Ideal Femininity

In the postwar era, Shrine Shinto lost its special status as a suprareligious state cult. Shinto was now legally treated as a religion and no longer received any special monetary support from the state because of the new constitutional separation of religion and the state. It was in this con-text that Shinto weddings, which stressed traditional ideas about gender roles, the family, and Japanese identity, became widely popular. As we have seen, Shinto wedding ceremonies were developed in the early twentieth century, but before World War II they were largely limited to the urban elites. After the war, however, as more people moved to the cities and homes became smaller, it became difficult to host wed-dings at home, as was customary before the war. Mutual aid associations developed, providing members with affordable wedding venues. These cooperatives were modeled on a system similar to the modern funeral industry. Eventually, the associations developed into an elaborate com-mercial wedding industry as they began to serve nonmembers and offer additional services, such as catering and reception hall rentals. The height of specialized wedding parlors was in the 1970s and 1980s. By the 1990s, the most common venues were hotels with facilities similar to wedding parlors. During this period, weddings generally included a Shinto ceremony performed by Shinto priests, even when they were performed at wedding parlors or hotels rather than at Shinto shrines.[11]

At the same time, Shinto wedding ceremonies became highly stan-dardized. Contemporary Shinto weddings include the traditional three-fold sake exchange between the spouses-to-be, food offerings at the altar, purification, ceremonial prayer, offerings of *sakaki* branches, and some-times a ceremonial dance. The groom reads the marriage vow while the bride only offers silent acquiescence—enacting the feminine ideal of the demure and obedient wife. The bride's dress—a formal kimono and large wig—also hampers her movement and accentuates her passivity. The wedding ceremony is followed by a wedding reception, which in contrast to the actual wedding ceremony, is typically attended by a large number of guests beyond the immediate family. Despite their recent origins, such Shinto weddings are perceived as traditional and as enactments of Japaneseness. As such, they inscribe conservative gender values onto the bride. Japanese-style wedding garments not only are physically constrictive but also suppress the individuality of the bride.[12]

In addition to the rite's material aspects, the liturgy of the wedding ritual stresses the "natural" roles for male and female and the preeminence of the household for the married couple. A typical wedding prayer usually implies that this is an arranged marriage by stating that the union of the bridegroom and bride occurred through the mediation of the matchmaker, a central player in an arranged marriage. Even if the marriage was not arranged, someone in the wedding party will perform the matchmaker's role in order to give the union the guise of an arranged marriage. The prayer encourages the couple to emulate the creator divinities, Izanagi and Izanami, who are said to have been the first to institute the marriage ritual, in mutually supporting and complementing each other like the sun and moon in the heavens and mountains and rivers on earth. This phrase implies that male and female have distinct but complementary roles to play as a married couple. The prayer further emphasizes the couple's role in maintaining the household: they must uphold the forefathers' teachings in private, respect the laws of the nation (literally, "the national household"—kokka) in public, dedicate themselves to maintaining the household, strive for the family business, and raise offspring. The bride and groom pledge to uphold the divinities' will and, in return, hope to receive divine protection for their household.[13] In the prayer, the marriage is clearly conceived as serving the maintenance of the patrilineal household and the nation-state, rather than being for the personal fulfillment of the individual bride and groom.

New Religious Movements and Buddhist Lay Movements

After World War II, women secured not only greater legal rights but also greater religious freedom that exceeded the provisions of the Meiji Constitution. Whereas the latter had limited religious freedom to beliefs and had curtailed practice and organizations by stipulating that they must not disturb public order, the new constitution contained no such restrictions. It also demanded a clear separation of religion and the state. Under the postwar legal system, new religious movements were able to incorporate freely with the same rights and privileges as those of more established religious organizations. Registration of new religious movements and Buddhist lay movements spiked after 1945, including those that had their roots in the early twentieth century. The media as well as established religions viewed these developments with concern because they considered new religions superstitious, predatory pseudoreligions that fooled the uneducated masses.[14] Nevertheless, these movements often promoted conservative ideals of femininity. Three prominent movements that emerged in the prewar period and gained a strong following in the postwar period were Tenshō Kōtai Jingūkyō, Reiyūkai, and Sōka Gakkai. Tenshō Kōtai Jingūkyō is a good example of how a female founder transgressively performed gender roles while still affirming the good wife and wise mother ideal. Reiyūkai and Sōka Gakkai are examples of Buddhist lay movements founded before World War II that envisioned women's roles within their organizations along conservative lines that also mirrored the ideal of good wife and wise mother.

Tenshō Kōtai Jingūkyō, also known as the dancing religion, was founded by Kitamura Sayo (1900–1967) in the 1940s. Kitamura was fiercely confrontational in public, criticized the emperor, and claimed privileged access to the imperial ancestress Amaterasu in competition with the Ise imperial cult. Kitamura was a farmer's daughter from rural Yamaguchi Prefecture. At age twenty, she married Kitamura Seinoshin, seventeen years her senior. Although Kitamura Sayo was known since childhood for her masculine behavior and for being argumentative, sectarian sources depict her as an obedient daughter-in-law who served her husband's family faithfully until she became the family matriarch. During the first ten to fifteen years of her marriage, Kitamura endured the harassment of her controlling mother-in-law, who had already made her son divorce six former daughters-in-law. Kitamura, known for her physical strength and perseverance, persisted and bore her husband a son. As her mother-in-law gradually declined physically and mentally in her old age, Kitamura remained dedicated to the old woman. By the time of her mother-in-law's death in 1940, Kitamura Sayo, rather than her husband, inherited the management of the farm.[15]

In her new position as the senior woman in the family, Kitamura transformed from a hardworking, exemplary daughter-in-law into an outspoken prophet whose inner divine voice caused her to become "the most impolite and sharp-tongued person under Heaven."[16] After part of the family property was destroyed by arson, Kitamura engaged in intense prayer and asceticism upon the advice of a healer, who eventually prophesized that she would transform into a living divinity. In 1944 Kitamura experienced her first divine possession by a being that she subsequently identified as the dual-gendered divinity Tenshō Kōtai Jingū, a composite of the female Amaterasu Ōmikami and the male Kōtai Jin. In the state of divine possession, Kitamura upbraided people, calling them maggots and beggars. She even criticized the emperor, and she predicted the disastrous end of the war. When her prophecy proved to be correct in 1945, she began to attract devotees, who soon started calling her Ōgamisama (literally, "great divinity"). After the war, she was quick to register her group under the new legislation and railed against the prewar Japanese establishment, which constituted, in her view, "the maggot world." Her demeanor, language, and dress during her street sermons were decidedly masculine—as she later stated, feminine clothing was inappropriate when preaching in such gruff language. She fiercely rejected other forms of religions, particularly Buddhism, but her teachings incorporated concepts from Shinto, Buddhism, and Christianity, all of which she radically redefined to suit her own purposes. When

Kitamura passed away in 1967, her granddaughter, Kiyokazu (1950–2006), took over as Tenshō Kōtai Jingūkyō's leader.[17]

As eccentric and abrasive as Kitamura was as a religious leader, she still had a conservative vision of gender roles. She justified her own gruff speech and mannerisms, saying that they were the work of the divinity inside her. Kitamura also seems to have embraced the ideal of the good wife and wise mother. She considered her relationship with her mother-in-law as especially formative in her spiritual career. Her uncomplaining attitude and devotion as a daughter-in-law were upheld as a role model for her followers, as was her wisdom in raising her own son. She was said to have taught him to do his chores, chided him when he was at fault, and avoided being an overbearing parent. Rather, she guided him with love and affection, allowing him to become a young man of outstanding character. Despite Kitamura's depiction as a good wife and wise mother, she also appeared highly masculine, whereas her close agnatic kin were implicitly feminized in sectarian sources. She, rather than her husband, was shown as the one working hard on the family farm and inheriting its management. In contrast to her own prototypically masculine conduct, she was said to have made her son do chores that were usually associated with women's work, such as cooking rice and sewing.[18]

The ideal of the good wife and wise mother has also been important in other new religious movements. For instance, in the Nichiren-inspired, lay Buddhist movement Reiyūkai, which combined faith in the *Lotus Sutra* with ancestor veneration, women embraced an exaggerated performance of feminine subservience. Reiyūkai (literally, "spirit friends association") was founded in the early 1920s by Kubo Kakutarō (1892–1944), whose sister-in-law, Kotani Kimi (1901–1971), soon joined him as coleader. The latter appears to have been the driving force behind Reiyūkai's success in attracting members. After Kubo's death in 1944, Kotani took over as the group's sole leader, thus remaining until her death in 1971. Kotani maintained her leadership position through the strong support of the married women's division and through her role as guardian for Kubo's son, who eventually succeeded her.[19]

During the postwar era, Reiyūkai promoted a highly conservative vision of the family and gender roles. Reiyūkai leaders strongly resisted the changes to the family system after the war and attempted to promote the prewar household system, which they perceived as deteriorating with the legal changes under the new constitution, greater urbanization, and an increase in the number of nuclear families. Reiyūkai leadership attempted to reinstitute its conservative vision of the family by emphasizing marriage as religious training, encouraging women to conform to traditional ideals of femininity (for example, subservience and obedience), and advocating Reiyūkai-specific ancestor veneration. Women in particular were encouraged to embrace their roles as housewives and stay-at-home mothers.[20]

During the 1970s, female converts were counseled to treat their husbands with exaggerated respect, even in cases in which the husband was unfaithful, and to accept that they were responsible for marital trouble since they, as women, had more karmic hindrances. Paradoxically, women were empowered through their exaggerated performance of gender ideals, which the scholar of religion Helen Hardacre terms "strategies of weakness."[21] By excelling at ideal feminine behavior such as obedience, subservience, and selflessness, a woman could maneuver her unfaithful husband into fulfilling his expected role as the male breadwinner and responsible husband. Despite a strong emphasis on women's domestic roles, women were also encouraged to become highly active within the religious group. This essentially took the women outside the home and away from their families unless—or until—the other family members ended up joining them in this endeavor. However, in their public role as Reiyūkai leaders, women were primarily expected to serve as role models and counselors for other women and to guide the youth within the movement; thus, they were ultimately portrayed in socially acceptable roles as nurturers. And ironically, because they were thought to be more karmically hindered and exposed to greater hardship, women were also believed to have greater spiritual powers, which allowed them to communicate with the ancestral spirits and made them more capable healers than men.[22]

Many new religious movements have depended heavily on women's voluntary labor while circumscribing their official participation within married women's associations and excluding them from holding leadership positions within the larger organizational hierarchy. For example, Sōka Gakkai—another Nichiren-inspired, *Lotus Sutra*–based group— was founded in 1930 and, with over eight million follower households, has become Japan's largest new religious movement in the postwar period. Sōka Gakkai (literally, "value creation society") promotes a conservative ideal of the family similar to that of Reiyūkai. Echoing the pre–World War II concept of the household as the basic unit of Japanese society, the group counts members not as individuals but as households. In the early postwar era, Sōka Gakkai's second president, Toda Jōsei (1900–1958), simultaneously upheld women as the backbone of the movement and stressed their inferior karmic position. In this stance, he drew heavily on the teachings of the *Lotus Sutra* and of Nichiren (1222–1282), the medieval founder of Nichiren Buddhism. During the early postwar decades in particular, Sōka Gakkai narrowly defined women's roles as wives and mothers within the domestic sphere. Under the leadership of Ikeda Daisaku (b. 1928) from the early 1960s, women's roles within the Married Women's Division have expanded, and the organization also toned down its rhetoric regarding women's karmic hindrances. Women in the Married Women's Division constitute the organization's members who are most actively dedicated to proselytizing, promoting subscriptions to Sōka Gakkai publications, and campaigning for Kōmeitō (a political party closely aligned with Sōka Gakkai). While women's public image, per Sōka Gakkai's ideals, still centers on their roles as mothers and wives, their participation in Sōka Gakkai activities often removes them from their homes and families for substantial amounts of time.[23]

"New" New Religions

In the 1970s and 1980s, several new religious movements emerged that, in distinction from new religious movements that gained popularity during the 1950s and 1960s, exhibited a greater reliance on spirit possession and a stronger millennial streak. To distinguish them from the earlier new religious movements, scholars have often called these groups "new" new religions, despite obvious misgivings about the analytical usefulness of the category. What is evident, however, is that these "new" new religions appeared to ride the crest of the Japanese occult wave of the 1970s and 1980s. Yet despite their seemingly unorthodox teachings, many of these groups reified conventional gender roles in ways quite similar to those perpetuated by established and older new religions.

Since the "new" new religions tend to emphasize spirit possession and spirit communication, practices that have historically been strongly connected with women, we might assume that women should constitute a large constituency in these movements. In the case of Mahikari, this is demonstrably true. In the early 1980s, women constituted about two-thirds of the group's membership.[24] Mahikari (literally, "true light") was founded in 1959 by Okada Kōtama (1901–1974) and is one of several new religious movements whose spiritual heritage can be traced back to Ōmotokyō. The central divinity of Mahikari is the Mioya Motosu Mahikari no Ōkami, or the Revered-Parent Origin-Lord True-Light Great Divinity, whose name is shortened to Su-God. Okada conceptualized Su-God as a highly *yang*, or masculine, divinity. Su-God is associated with fire, light, austerity, righteousness, and strictness, and he is said to have taken the reins from *yin*, or feminine, divinities that are associated with water, sensuality, passivity, and gentleness, who are unable to control malevolent spirits. By purifying the body of spiritual and physical defilement, Su-God aims to heal illness and extend life. The purification is supposed to take the form of a Baptism by Fire, which will heal devotees but scorch unbelievers. Okada also predicted that unless the balance between good and evil were rectified, Su-God would destroy this world by fire in the year 2000.[25]

Mahikari adherents have been drawn not just by this millennial vision, but also by the promise of healing through amulets, purifications, and exorcisms. Once converts have been exposed to Mahikari exorcisms, many manifest dramatic possessions by vengeful spirits, mostly spirits of the ancestors and animal spirits.[26] A survey conducted in the late 1970s showed that a majority of Mahikari members believed that women were more likely to experience spirit possession than were men. The same survey also indicated that women did indeed experience more spirit possessions than did men and that women were more likely than men to be possessed by, in addition to their natal ancestors, their spouses' ancestors, a reflection of the fact that most women, rather than men, are integrated into the affinal household after marriage.[27]

Mahikari embraces belief in karmic retribution, expressing this notion, too, in conventionally gendered fashion. Women are believed to be especially susceptible to sexual karma (*shikijō innen*).[28] Women's sexual karma is thought to manifest itself through spirit possessions. Local leaders tend to attribute various physical and mental ailments to sexual karma even when the female convert herself may not have thus conceptualized her problems previously; eventually the convert, too, will come to understand her afflictions to be caused by sexual karma. The sociologist of religion Winston Davis argues that during the postwar era, the pressure to conform to the conventional life cycle model wherein women married and bore children by their early twenties was so strong that women who did not fulfill the expected norm faced anxiety, leading to mental and physical ailments. In his opinion, "women become Mahikari followers of a serious 'role deprivation': the failure to attract a husband."[29] Mahikari offered women who struggled or failed to find a mate a chance to act out their frustrations and insecurities through spirit possession. Such women displayed the most intense possessions and were more closely identified with the ill effects of sexual karma. The most dramatic case Davis presents is that of a young single woman in her late teens, who under the influence of a fox spirit turned into a willful, sensual drunkard, defying gender norms that prohibit such behavior.[30]

However, married and divorced women also sought help from Mahikari for a variety of troubles, including conflict with their natal families, childlessness, divorce, and spousal infidelity. For instance, during an exorcism a middle-aged mother of two blamed her husband's infidelity on the spirit of a female family dog. According to her account, she had restrained the dog while the latter was in heat, thus preventing the dog from fulfilling her sexual drive. The dog then sought retribution, now driving the husband away from his wife into the arms of another woman.[31] Similar to the role of spirit possession in the Heian period, which offered women a means to voice their anger and jealousy when open expression of such feelings was socially unacceptable, spirit possession in Mahikari offered women a means to voice their discontent. At the same time, the gender roles posited as ideal in Mahikari were not particularly divergent from the prevailing gender ideals in postwar society at large.

Memorial Rites for *Mizuko*

Buddhist temples have also offered rituals that address sexual relations between men and women while upholding conventional gender roles. Many temples specializing in the performance of prayer rituals have long offered rites for family safety and safe childbirth; additionally, since the 1970s and 1980s, some temples have started offering rituals memorializing *mizuko* (literally, "water child")—that is, aborted, miscarried, or stillborn fetuses, and victims of sudden infant death. The postwar emphasis on women as natural mothers who are innate nurturers, paired with the passing of the Eugenic Protection Law (1948), created moral dilemmas with regard to abortion and contraception. In the 1940s, abortion was legal only in cases in which the pregnancy endangered the mother's health or when congenital defects were discovered in the fetus; the postwar legislation expanded to permit abortion in the cases of rape, severe illness, and—from 1949—economic hardship. During the 1950s, abortion served as the predominant method of birth control; subsequently, in the 1960s, contraceptives such as condoms became more popular. Conservative religious leaders—from institutions ranging from the Catholic Church to the new religious movement Seichō no Ie—reacted critically to the 1948 legislation and its corresponding spike in abortions.[32]

The news media gradually became more critical as well. During the first decade after the war, they treated abortion due to economic hardship relatively neutrally, accepting the idea that married women were choosing for the sake of their existing children not to have more children. However, from the late 1950s onward, during years of high economic growth, abortions came to be associated with extramarital affairs and premarital sex: the prototypical image involved a callous male partner convincing the foolish woman to abort the fetus. Additionally, from the mid-1970s, teenage sexuality was linked with abortion and provided another point of contention. In other words, the media coverage of abortion suggested that women ought to feel guilty for having engaged in illicit sex leading to an abortion.[33]

Memorial rites for *mizuko* need to be understood in the context of the motherly ideal that was commonly upheld in the postwar era (see figure 8.2). As the scholar of religion Komatsu Kayoko explains, the sharp rise in the number of Buddhist memorial rites for *mizuko* is linked to the "myth of innate motherly affection," which casts "women who have chosen not to have children . . . as problematic or antisocial."[34] During the 1970s and 1980s, Japan experienced a growing interest in the occult, which also gave rise to the idea that aborted fetuses could act as vengeful spirits, who were said to cause delinquency in existing offspring, sexual abnormalities in women, and marital problems. Women could commission memorial rites conducted primarily at Buddhist temples in order to appease these vengeful spirits and to assuage their own feelings of grief and guilt. Such rituals were not typically standardized by the

FIGURE 8.2. Mizuko Jizō at Hasedera in Kamakura. Photograph by the author.

sectarian headquarters but, rather, relied largely on the individual initiatives of entrepreneurial Buddhist clerics and other religionists such as spirit mediums.[35] Buddhist clerics and local entrepreneurs were not just motivated by financial prospects, but also regarded such rituals as a means to critique the practice of abortion and effect social change.[36] And while many Buddhist clerics, even those who performed memorial rites for *mizuko*, publicly rejected the belief in vengeful spirits, the rituals unilaterally single out women as the ones who have committed a moral offense and must repent their lack of compassion toward the aborted fetus.[37]

The practice of memorial rites for *mizuko* has generated passionate debates in the mass media and among religious professionals. The media reaction to these rituals was ambivalent: while magazines and tabloids directed at a female readership promoted the idea of vengeful spirits, publications targeting a male audience were largely critical of the phenomenon, depicting such rituals as predatory. The reaction of Buddhist institutions has been equally mixed: while the memorial rites for *mizuko* were offered at entrepreneurial Buddhist temples, the Buddhist denominations did not develop any guidelines regarding the ritual, and many Buddhist clerics remained critical of the rites and denied the idea of vengeful spirits.[38] Yet despite such negative perceptions of this ritual practice, it is undeniable that many women turned to memorial rites for *mizuko* as a means to come to terms with the grief caused by pregnancy loss.[39]

Conclusion

New legislation after World War II led to important changes in women's status in Japan and spurred developments toward greater equality between the sexes; at the same time, however, such legislation caused tensions because many religious organizations resisted these developments. Many Shinto, Buddhist, and new religious organizations chose to adhere to prewar definitions of the family, rejecting individualism in favor of an identity based on the household and limiting women's roles to the domestic sphere as wives and mothers. Some women chose to embrace these domestic roles and performed them in exaggerated ways, perhaps in order to subvert gender differences.[40] Kitamura Sayo's exaggerated performance of femininity *and* masculinity effectively divorced the assumed unity of sex and gender, revealing them as constructed categories. However, many women were not seeking to parody or deconstruct gender norms when they enacted them in excess; rather, they sought to fulfill those norms in earnest, which conversely gave them strength vis-à-vis their husbands and other family members. They espoused ultraconservative gender roles in order to serve their own agendas.[41] Yet not everyone has accepted this normative vision of femininity. Some women within the religious organizations have used the new legislation to call for reform and for religious organizations to face postwar demographic realities, rather than cling to nostalgic longing for an idealized past. As we shall see in the following chapter, such voices grew stronger during the 1990s.

9

The Lost Decades

Gender and Religion in Flux

The death of the Shōwa Emperor in 1989 signaled the end of the postwar era. In contrast to the confidence that filled the 1980s, the Heisei era (1989–present) has been marked by a sense of millennial crisis, social malaise, and economic stagnation, which together have earned the last twenty-some years the name "the Lost Decades." The financial bubble burst in the early 1990s, leading to a prolonged recession and a sluggish labor market. Society's rapid aging and low birthrate became the focus of intense public scrutiny. The year 1995 was particularly traumatic. On January 17, a large earthquake struck the Kobe area, causing massive destruction and 6,200 fatalities, and on March 20, followers of the apocalyptic Aum Shinrikyō movement released sarin gas on several subway lines in Tokyo, killing twelve people and injuring over five thousand.[1]

Aum's sarin attack intensified an already critical attitude toward religion. Critical of institutionalized religion, which was perceived as calcified, predatory, and, in the case of new religious movements, dangerous, many people have turned away from communally oriented, established religions and older new religious movements. Instead, they have sought out new spiritual practices promising more individual choices and customization, seemingly more appropriate in the uncertain, complex environment of contemporary Japan.[2] Simultaneously, the rise of new communication media, particularly the mobile phone and the Internet, has created new opportunities for religious institutions and independent spiritual entrepreneurs to establish translocal, personalized networks. Older religious organizations in return have criticized the upsurge of individualism and social fragmentation, but the dismantling of traditional social structures has also opened up new opportunities. While social conservatives deemed the disintegration of traditional values to be a crisis, many who had felt constricted by the rigid hierarchies and social conformity of the bubble years have experienced this new era as liberating. These two decades have brought greater legal protections for women at work and at home and better benefits for the socially disadvantaged.[3] In this malleable climate, debates about the family and gender have emerged with new intensity as religious organizations try to come to terms with the economic and demographic realities of contemporary Japan.

Demographic Changes and Gender Debates

The low birthrate and dramatically aging population have sparked heated debates about the family and gender. Both masculine and feminine ideals and attitudes toward marriage appear to be in flux: gendered labor divisions according to which men work outside the home and women are professional homemakers are disappearing. While the postwar labor market was clearly gendered, with men occupying full-time positions and women working as part-timers and temporary workers, this division has become blurred during the Lost Decades as larger numbers of young men began to take positions as "freeters," a term referring to flexible temporary and part-time workers. Social conservatives have criticized both male and female freeters as parasitic, presuming that they have not accepted the self-sacrificial ideology of the postwar era and are deliberately avoiding full-time employment and all that it entails.[4] Meanwhile, women have joined the wage labor market in greater numbers, and new legislation in the 1990s theoretically guaranteed women equal educational and advancement opportunities. In turn, women's increased participation in the labor force and high educational achievement are regarded as causes for the low birthrate.[5]

The institution of marriage has also been in transition. Many young people postpone, or simply opt out of, marriage and parenthood. This trend has been perceived as a major cause for the low birthrate and has caused much consternation. By the late 1990s, unmarried young people living with their parents were perceived as freeloaders. Women in particular were faulted for staying single and enjoying luxurious lifestyles rather than getting married and having children.[6] Meanwhile, the divorce rate climbed to new heights compared to the postwar era—a reflection of legal changes and the prevalence of love marriages, which are associated with higher expectations than arranged marriage with regard to compatibility and personal fulfillment. While divorce rates are still much lower in Japan than in the United States, Japan now has divorce rates on a par with much of Europe. The divorce rate among the middle-aged and elderly particularly has risen since 2004, when divorcing women were granted the right to a share of their husbands' pension. In contrast to the Edo and early Meiji periods, when divorce rates were even higher, it is not the young, spurned wife who is regarded as the representative victim, but rather the elderly male retiree who is suddenly abandoned by his longtime spouse.[7]

The prevalence of love marriages and an emphasis on personal fulfillment have affected not only divorce rates but also wedding rituals. At the end of the twentieth century, Shinto weddings, which incorporated the matchmaker as an important participant, fell out of favor, whereas chapel weddings based on a Christian format have rapidly risen in popularity. The popularity of chapel weddings cannot be correlated with a similar rise in Christian adherents, but is likely linked to celebrity fashion trends publicized by the mass media. Many of the officiants at chapel weddings are not even Christian ministers or priests but rather temporary workers, preferably Westerners, hired to give the ceremony an exotic atmosphere. Just as Shinto weddings are performances of Japaneseness, chapel weddings, which are sometimes performed in English rather than in Japanese, serve as performances of non-Japaneseness by appearing to break with formal traditions and embodying a more individualized, cheerful celebration even though the chapel wedding tends to be just as formally orchestrated as a Shinto wedding. In addition, chapel weddings allow the participants to perform the love marriage's romantic ideal, which contrasts sharply with the arranged-marriage narrative underlying a Shinto wedding.[8]

Burial customs have also been affected by demographic shifts and changing gender roles. As we have seen, there are historical precedents for women being buried separately from their husbands, but since the Edo period, most women have tended to join their husbands' temple affiliation and be interred in the husbands' family grave after death. In the postwar era, the family was no longer defined as exclusively patrilineal, but burial customs have upheld patrilineality as a central principle. While the majority of Japanese still favor being buried with one's spouse, a sizable number of women—single women, divorcees, and widows—prefer to have their own graves. To realize their wish for a grave of their own but also ensure continual memorialization, some women have formed burial associations. The existence of such associations suggests that women prefer their friendship ties over their conjugal or natal ties.[9] Recently, burial with household pets, particularly dogs and cats, has also become a popular option. During fieldwork on this issue, several of my informants would jokingly point out that women nowadays preferred to be buried *petto to issho ni* (with their pets) rather than *otto to issho ni* (with their husbands), playing on the phonetic resemblance of *petto* (pet) and *otto* (husband).[10] Whatever these women's circumstances, making their own choices about their graves gives them considerable agency.

Reactions by Religious Organizations: Conservatism and Feminism

The conservative elements of religious organizations have been perturbed by the seeming eradication of gender differences. Since the implementation of the Fundamental Law on Gender Equality (1999), which reaffirmed and strengthened gender equality in education, debates about Article 24 of the Japanese constitution have reemerged.

Conservative politicians belonging to the Liberal Democratic Party (LDP) and supported by the Association of Shinto Shrines have criticized the principle of gender equality and its inherent individualism and have called for a revision of the law. Many proposals for revisions call for the reinstitution of traditional Japanese family values; this includes support for such measures as the removal of the stipulation of mutual consent and the addition of language recognizing the family as the basic unit of society (with the understanding that "family" does not mean "single-parent households" or "same-sex households"). The Association of Shinto Shrines has backed up its calls for a revision with claims about the detrimental effects for childhood development of denying so-called natural gender differences; moreover, it has blamed Article 24 for the breakdown of the family and society at large. Conservative politicians have also advocated a reaffirmation of the household system dismantled by the 1947 constitution. In 2003, the Association of Shinto Shrines published an article in its association newspaper encouraging female shrine priests to strive to be good wives and wise mothers, while other articles in the newspaper blamed the disintegration of traditional gender roles in Japan for the moral and physical destruction of Japanese society. Such rhetoric has been strongly criticized by Japanese feminists.[11]

The conservative wing of Tenrikyō maintains a similar stance. *Araki tōryō*, the Tenrikyō Young Men's Association journal, regularly publishes articles by right-wing intellectuals who depict women's status elevation as the cause for Japan's social disintegration and who seek a reinstitution of a normative, "traditional" family.[12] For instance, in 1990 Iida Teruaki (b. 1929), a professor at Tenri University, published an article in *Araki tōryō* entitled "Women, Motherhood, Marriage, and the Home," in which he laments the decline of family values in contemporary Japan. Iida places the blame on the changes in women's status during the postwar era: more women have chosen to work rather than have children, and their financial independence has allowed them to seek divorce more frequently. Thus, he claims, women have become masculinized and Westernized, ignoring the inherent physical, mental, and psychological differences between the genders and rejecting their innate, feminine inclinations toward motherhood. They no longer strive toward the sacred ideal of selfless motherhood and self-effacing love. Advancing an argument of biological determinism, he stresses that just as there is male and female in all species, men and women must play their distinct roles. Iida sees this as an essential teaching of Tenrikyō.[13] An article in the 25 August 2002 edition of *Tenri jihō*, the sectarian weekly, similarly proposes what healthy gender equality means. It asserts that equality between the sexes "does not discriminate between men and women, but rather differentiates between the two based on the sexual distinction of the two." In contrast, "genderless" is defined in the newsletter as "a special concept that denies sexual distinction and even dismisses differentiation," and as such is socially harmful.[14]

Not all voices in Tenrikyō have acquiesced to Iida's conservative vision. For instance, scholars such as Horiuchi Midori (b. 1959) and Kaneko Juri (b. 1962), both female professors at Tenri University, have historicized the role of women in Tenrikyō and problematized the view that women are merely to serve as passive foundations for male (religious) activity. They have presented evidence from within the foundress Nakayama Miki's teachings that point to an egalitarian conceptualization of gender and identified historical role models that show acceptance of alternative family structures within the early movement.[15] While neither Kaneko nor Horiuchi present a radical reconceptualization of Tenrikyō doctrine, they subtly seek to question and moderate from within the tradition the highly conservative stance of the Tenrikyō establishment in regard to women and the family.

Women in Buddhist organizations have also pushed back against the conservative rhetoric of the male establishment. During the mid-1990s, Japanese Buddhist women formed transsectarian networks inspired by transdenominational alliances among Christian women in Europe and America and the domestic feminist movement, whose political influence grew during the 1970s and 1980s. A network of Buddhist women in the Tōkai region was founded in 1996 in Nagoya. Personal connections of Buddhist women in Tokyo with this network led to the founding of a similar network for the Kantō region the following year. The two networks have collaborated by hosting transsectarian conferences and producing publications on women and Buddhism. Instead of rejecting their traditions outright, these women have sought to reform the traditions from within by drawing on potentially empowering doctrines (for example, the teaching of nondualism) and by becoming socially engaged. The women have reached out to other socially marginalized domestic and international populations (outcasts, comfort women, and the disabled), supported charitable aid programs, and given political support to women running for office. [16]

According to Kawahashi Noriko (b. 1960), a Buddhist feminist who has been personally involved in the establishment of these networks, these transsectarian efforts are better able than those operating within sectarian boundaries to transcend rigid, traditional institutional structures and accommodate pluralistic perspectives. Temple wives, for example, were previously organized only into sectarian married women's associations. These associations may have granted temple wives some recognition within their respective denominations, but, like other married women's associations, also limited their involvement to such associations and sectarian frameworks. In contrast, members of the transsectarian network have ties that transcend denominational boundaries. These members have lobbied their respective denominations to change discriminatory policies, including the subordination of temple wives, and exhorted women from different denominations to recognize that being a temple wife and being a nun are equally viable paths, even when some denominations value one or the other more highly.[17]

In fact, the Buddhist denominations are responding, though not always successfully, to the demands of temple wives for greater institutional recognition. In order to address the tenuous position of the temple wife after the death of the abbot, most denominations have encouraged abbots to register their marriages with the denomination and to pay into an insurance fund for their wives in order to assure the latters'

financial security. In 1996 the Tendai sect also tried to introduce ordination certifications for temple wives, an initiative that did not prove
to be successful and was terminated in 2000. Gradually, daughters are
also becoming more accepted as heirs to the temple if they are willing
to become ordained. As far as Buddhist sectarian leadership generally
is concerned, however, temple wives have remained important as paragons of good wives and wise mothers.[18]

In their choice to transcend sectarian boundaries and different constituencies, women's network members have clearly learned lessons
from the women's liberation movement of the 1970s and international
feminist cooperation of the 1980s, which pressured Japanese legislators
to pass laws during the 1980s and 1990s in order to ensure equal education, job opportunities, and parental protections within the workplace.
Particularly after the Fourth United Nations World Conference on
Women, held in Beijing in 1995, Japanese feminists became engaged not
just with domestic women's issues but also with pan-Asian issues such
as sex tourism, migration, and imperialism, and with issues concerning domestic minority groups such as Koreans, Okinawans, and outcasts.[19] Buddhist women's networks are similarly engaged socially on a
broader scale.

New Religious Movements: Adapting to New Realities

New religions have also responded to the realities of changing demographics and altered gender roles. Many of the new religious movements
that saw explosive growth during the postwar era have recently experienced slower growth, or even decline, and have begun to focus on
retaining the new generation of members born into the movement.
While much of the scholarship through the 1980s on women and the
new religions focused on why women chose to join new religious movements, more recent scholarship on these older new religions has focused
on the roles of women who might be second- or third-generation members. This also means that scholarship on older new religions has moved

away from the standard narrative that women become members of new religious movements in times of crisis, when they are particularly vulnerable. The "crisis explanation" has several major shortcomings: it limits women's agency and does not address adequately women's sustained membership, or women who are second-, third-, or even fourth-generation members.

A clear example is Sōka Gakkai. The group split from its monastic parent organization, Nichiren Shōshū, in 1991 after a protracted conflict between Nichiren leadership and that of Sōka Gakkai. Around this time, Sōka Gakkai was additionally embattled because of its political involvement through the party Kōmeitō, which was officially separate from the Sōka Gakkai institution but relied heavily on Sōka Gakkai's married women's association to mobilize election voters. In political circles, criticism of Sōka Gakkai deepened as Kōmeitō gained more political influence, becoming a coalition partner of the ruling party in the 1990s. In the aftermath of the 1995 Aum incident, Sōka Gakkai's opponents took advantage of the widespread anxiety concerning new religious movements in order to criticize Sōka Gakkai and Kōmeitō.[20]

In response to the political strife and the group's expulsion from Nichiren Shōshū, Sōka Gakkai turned inward, focusing on the retention of the younger generation. This was a profound shift from its aggressive proselytization during the postwar era and significantly affected the lives of women in the movement. Contemporary Sōka Gakkai women, whom the scholar of religion Levi McLaughlin has studied, were often active in local home meetings and in the Married Women's Division; however, they have admitted having difficulty converting new members since they themselves were born into the tradition, rather than having joined the movement through conversion. These women have also noted negative reactions from potential converts and from nonmembers approached on behalf of Kōmeitō candidates due to the negative attitude toward religion in the post-Aum climate.[21]

Women's overall involvement in Gakkai activities is likely to encourage their children to remain dedicated to Sōka Gakkai. The new generation's commitment to Sōka Gakkai—especially in the case of young women—is strongly determined by the mothers' level of commitment to Sōka Gakkai, particularly if the young women have had good relationships with their families. In general, Gakkai women, old or young, have a higher religious engagement than do Gakkai men; women are particularly active either in the Married Women's Division or the Young Women's Division, for unmarried women under the age of forty.[22] Given the movement's high level of reliance on women's volunteer labor, it remains to be seen whether Sōka Gakkai will eventually have to change in order to allow women greater participation in its bureaucratic system. Indeed, while the organization as a whole still casts the ideal woman as a homemaker, Ikeda Daisaku, the movement's honorary president, has since the 1990s begun to express a more moderate stance, emphasizing gender equality, especially in regard to education.[23]

What emerges most poignantly from the examples of these Gakkai women is that even though new converts are often recruited in moments of personal crisis, longtime members are not motivated by a continued sense of crisis in their day-to-day involvement in the religious organization; in fact, they have life trajectories very similar to those of women outside the movement. Like other contemporary Japanese women, Gakkai women might successfully balance their commitments to work and family. Or they might delay or forgo marriage and childbearing or seek divorce in the case of unsuccessful marriages, despite the movement's idealized characterization of women as wives or mothers. Indeed, in extreme cases of familial conflict, Sōka Gakkai does not seem any more prepared than other religious organizations to deal effectively with household friction. Where Gakkai women differ from non-Gakkai women is that their intense commitment to the Married Women's Division leads them to spend much time on Gakkai activities outside the home, creating pressures within their familial relationships.[24]

Some of the "new" new religious movements, which experienced significant growth from the late postwar period, have displayed less rigid gender boundaries and have been more accommodating to integrating women into their institutional structures than have older new religions. This has been the case even when such integration met resistance within the groups' own senior ranks. As the scholar of religion Usui Atsuko and the anthropologist Christal Whelan have suggested in their studies of the Buddhist groups Shinnyoen and GLA, respectively, a significant factor may have been these groups' incorporation of practices such as spirit communication in the case of Shinnyoen and glossolalia (speaking in tongues) in the case of GLA (God Light Association). As Usui notes, such spiritual faculties have been traditionally associated with women but are not gender-exclusive.[25] According to Whelan, "Past-life glossolalia . . . bestowed on men and women a kind of androgyny."[26]

At least initially, both Shinnyoen and GLA endorsed traditional gender roles to a certain extent. For instance, Shinnyoen (literally, "garden of thusness") is a Shingon-affiliated Buddhist movement that combines the teachings of the *Nirvana Sutra* and communication with its deceased founders in order to give practitioners spiritual guidance. The movement promotes, even now, dualistic gender associations linked to the founders, Itō Shinjō (1906–1989)—male, heaven, dharma, intelligence—and his wife, Itō Tomoji (1912–1967)—female, earth, practice, training. Tomoji was cast as a model wife and mother and dispensed advice on domestic matters to female adherents, whom she expected to be housewives, as most Japanese women were expected to be in the 1950s and 1960s. However, Shinnyoen's leadership has not applied feminine virtues exclusively to women; it has also encouraged male adherents to cultivate Tomoji's ideals as summarized in her *Josei ni ataeru jū nana kun* (literally, "seventeen lessons for women," but now officially translated gender-neutrally as *Seventeen Teachings*). Additionally, Shinnyoen does not have a married women's association, and positions of leadership are open to both genders. In the 1990s, Shinnyoen's spiritual guides were 54 percent female, an increase from 46 percent in 1970. By 2001, the teachers of the faith, who earn their qualification by completing a training course, included nearly thirty thousand women and eight thousand men. As of 2011, there were about fifty-nine thousand

FIGURE 9.1. Shinnyoen's present leader, Itō Shinsō, dressed in Buddhist robes, performing an esoteric fire ritual (*goma*) in Taibei, Taiwan. Image copyright © Shinnyoen. Image source: Shinnyoen.

female and fourteen thousand male teachers, indicating that women are strongly represented in the organization. After Itō Shinjō's death, the group's leadership passed to his third daughter, Shinsō (b. 1942) (see figure 9.1).[27]

Similarly, after the death of GLA's founder, Takahashi Shinji (1926–1976), leadership passed to his daughter Keiko (b. 1957). However, disputes over the succession centering on Keiko's youth at the time led to several splits within the movement. Keiko's supporters responded by promoting her as an incarnation of the Archangel Michael, giving her by implication a masculine identity. Under Keiko's father, Shinji, GLA combined Buddhist and Judeo-Christian concepts with spirit communication and glossolalia. GLA continued to emphasize glossolalia through the 1970s as Keiko established her leadership, but since the 1990s the group has reshaped itself as an educational movement de-emphasizing shamanistic practices in favor of teachings that embrace psychology and the celebrity of Keiko, who has remained unmarried. GLA's leadership structure is thus organized like a traditional patrilineal household, other than the fact of leadership succession to an unmarried daughter. Keiko's mother, Takahashi Shinji's widow, Kazue, serves as GLA's honorary director. Keiko's only sibling, her sister Mayumi, inherited her father's secular company instead of taking a position in GLA. Takahashi Kōwa, Shinji's brother, is the only closely related male to hold an official position within GLA.[28]

GLA does not have an official married women's association. Instead, the group offers five types of educational courses that are targeted at specific age groups and constituencies: children, adolescents, working adults, caregiving adults, and seniors. Four of these are open to both men and women. One of these courses, Frontier College, was established in 1994. While it initially recruited men aged thirty to fifty-nine, recently, in recognition of women's increased presence in the wage-labor market, Frontier College has started to admit working women. Only the course for caregivers, Kokoro no Kango Gakkō, is still addressed to a specific gender, namely, women aged thirty to fifty-nine. This course is attended mostly by homemakers and occasionally by working women who might additionally attend Frontier College.[29]

Women and New Age Spirituality

As the scholar of religion Shimazono Susumu has pointed out, there has been a growing interest in spirituality in Japan's highly urbanized late twentieth-century society. In contrast to "religion," the concept of "spirituality" is particularly compatible with the postmodern world because it plays on the notion of complexity and uncertainty, which it appears to make somewhat controllable through the manipulation of spirits and fortune. It is also appealing because it works well in the context of disintegrating traditional family structures and weakening ties with established religious institutions. Shimazono notes the emphasis on individuality and personal gratification in this new spirituality culture in contrast to the communally oriented ancestral practices in established Buddhism and older new religions.[30] Engagement in spirituality often takes place in commercialized channels. Practitioners who call themselves spiritual counselors use seemingly scientific language borrowed from psychology to market their trade as spiritual therapy. Clients seek a variety of services, from fortune-telling and communication with the spirits to self-help programs and healing.[31]

Similar developments have occurred elsewhere in the industrialized world during late modernity, and in Japan the development away from religion toward spirituality began in the 1970s. In 1978, for instance, bookstores in Japan established "spiritual world" (*seishin sekai*) sections.[32] The popularity of spirituality has been spurred on by the fact that from the 1990s, particularly after the Aum incident in 1995, organized religion has faced a considerable public backlash. Established religious organizations struggled against the image that they were moribund and socially irrelevant, whereas new religious movements were largely considered suspect. Some alternative religious professionals rejected the category of "religion" and instead adopted a different kind of vocabulary to refer to their profession in order to escape stigmatization as heterodox religious practitioners. For instance, the socially conservative celebrity fortune-teller Hosoki Kazuko (b. 1938), who has been dispensing various spiritual advice to her audience in numerous print publications and during regular television appearances since the mid-1980s, firmly claimed that her activities were not religious, even when she talked about divinities or ancestor veneration. Hosoki's refusal to accept the concept of "religion" began in the 1980s, when claims that Japan was a modern, rational, and secular society were commonly voiced in scholarly surveys and mass media reports.[33] Activities such as visiting shrines and temples, purchasing amulets, and memorializing the ancestors were characterized as "Japanese customs" rather than "religious practice," because such activities involved little consideration of engagement of faith, a presumed component of Western Protestant Christian models of religion. Such claims of secularism fit neatly into the climate of cultural uniqueness and superiority that was pervasive during the years of the bubble economy. The rejection of "religion" also proved useful during a time when established and alternative religious groups were exposed to criticism and suspicion, which only intensified after the Aum incident in 1995.

The interest in spirituality and healing has clearly influenced women's engagement with institutionalized religions. Rituals for *mizuko*, which received much negative public attention through the mid-1990s, have been accommodated to fit New Age concepts. The development of New Age spirituality since the 1990s—with its individualized practices, loose networks, stress on quasi-therapeutic healing practices, and new conceptualizations of the afterlife—has changed the way people think about *mizuko* rituals, lessening the feelings of guilt associated with the ritual and heightening women's agency. For instance, rather than stressing cyclical reincarnation driven by karma—the presumed motivating factor behind Buddhist rites of posthumous memorialization—New Age views of the afterlife, promoted predominantly by female spiritualists, tend to emphasize an evolutionary model, according to which spirits progress through several lifetimes to achieve spiritual perfection. In the process of spiritual progression, spirits, including those of fetuses, are assumed to have agency over their chosen rebirth, which will then teach them valuable lessons for future lives. From this perspective, abortion is seen no longer as a moral transgression but rather as a potential learning experience for both the mother and the fetus. Therefore, the fetus is not just a passive victim of abortion who needs rites of pacification to ameliorate its vengeful potential but an active agent who chooses the birth mother with the full knowledge and acceptance of the pending abortion. Similarly, the mother can make reproductive choices without feeling guilty. Memorialization of the aborted fetus therefore serves to help women to come to terms with the abortion, rather than to avert the vengeful power of the fetus.[34]

The Internet and contemporary theories of bereavement developed in the United States have reshaped how contemporary Japanese women deal with the memorialization of *mizuko*. In the new millennium, online memorial sites have allowed women to post their personal memorial without the intercession of a Buddhist priest. Through Internet-based networks, self-help groups for women who have lost children to miscarriage and sudden infant death syndrome have positively reevaluated rites for *mizuko* through contemporary bereavement theories and New Age spirituality, which stress self-discovery and self-improvement through reflection. The spirits of such fetuses and infants are no longer considered menacing entities but little angels who can serve as guardian spirits for the parents they chose to leave behind. Rather than sending off the harmful spirit, such groups stress the continuing bonds between parent and child as a means to accept and live with the grief of losing a child.[35]

Significantly, the vast majority of participants in this New Age and spirituality culture are female. In a 1995 survey of divination-hall clients in an entertainment district popular with young people, women constituted 95 percent of the respondents. More than half of the clients were full-time employees, and about one-third were high school or university students. Part-time employees and homemakers each constituted only a small percentage. Most of the women were singles in their late teens or twenties. Most clients regularly read divination columns in magazines and had close friends, mothers, or sisters who also relied on divination. Such networks, however, were loosely organized rather than consisting of tight-knit communities. Similar to horoscopes, divination serves as a form of counseling that addresses the clients' uncertainties regarding their professional and love lives and allows them to engage in self-discovery and self-actualization.[36] Likewise, in a more recent study, the vast majority of spiritual therapists were female, and they arguably constituted a representative sample of contemporary practitioners.[37]

Scholars have argued that this gender imbalance is caused by precarious economic conditions that disproportionately affected women. According to critics of alternative spirituality, clients who were socially and emotionally adrift sought advice from diviners and clairvoyants, in hopes of finding a direction in life. This position implies that spiritual counselors are ultimately preying on vulnerable populations, particularly women.[38] This argument raises the question of whether contemporary women who frequent spiritual conventions (*supikon*)—more recently also known as spiritual markets (*supima*)—think of themselves as disadvantaged and emotionally unstable. In contrast, another scholar proposes that from the mid-1990s, many, especially women, who struggled in Japan's depressed economy and sluggish labor market joined training programs to become spiritual therapists. This training allowed them to construct themselves as nonreligious, professional healers in a climate that was hostile toward organized religion.[39] In other words, rather than being passive victims, the women took an active role in promoting spiritual practices.

Moreover, women, particularly young women, are powerful consumers whose aesthetic tastes have shaped contemporary spirituality. In her analysis of tarot and cartomancy in contemporary Japan, the anthropologist Laura Miller shows how tarot decks have been adapted to appeal to Japanese women's tastes, such as the immensely popular culture of cuteness. Japanese decks modify standard Western tarot decks to incorporate cute cartoon figures. In some decks, the High Priestess and other figures are depicted as cute, cartoonish animals such as Hello Kitty. Other decks show the figure of the High Priestess as a sexy young woman, embodying contemporary *manga*-style ideals of femininity. In yet other decks, the High Priestess is transformed into a shrine priestess or Himiko, the prehistoric shamanic female ruler of Wa, to suit traditional Japanese cultural concepts. Tarot cards are promoted in magazines targeted at young women, and tarot readings are available in dedicated urban cafés.[40] Importantly, Laura Miller notes, "in the past, the focus of *uranai* [divination] was primarily on the family, especially on the fate of the kinship group through marriages and births. But these days it is firmly fixed on the individual and her life trajectories, job prospects, love interests, and self-development." She further argues, "It is women and girls who dominate the world of divination cards, and their production and circulation activities often by-pass mainstream and male-controlled routes of distribution."[41] In other words, tarot cards provide women with a tactile, interactive, self-reflective, and individualized spiritual experience that suits their needs.[42]

Conclusion

During the Lost Decades, the intersection between gender and religion has been in great flux as new economic and demographic realities spurred deep social changes. As a result, many religious organizations may have become defensive and ultraconservative. However, some religious organizations, particularly new religious movements, have been eager to accommodate changing gender roles. Even conservative religious institutions are not monolithic in their attitudes toward gender: the younger generation may strongly disagree with the conservative positions of the senior establishment.[43] Female members of religious organizations have also taken active and varied roles in this debate: from Japanese feminists challenging traditional norms to conservatives nostalgically promoting traditional values. It remains to be seen how Japanese religious organizations will reshape themselves to respond to the gendered challenges of the coming decades and what places Japanese women will claim in this new order. If trends continue, religious groups and specialists who stress an individualized spirituality will remain particularly appealing to women.

Conclusion

By focusing on women, this book has provided an important corrective to androcentric narratives of Japanese religions. Rather than serving as marginal actors, Japanese women have taken leading roles. They are, to use the feminist Hiratsuka Raichō's metaphor, radiant suns rather than moons reflecting the brilliance of others. Women's roles in Japanese religious history—as shamans, nuns, patrons of religious institutions, lay devotees, and religious founders—were diverse and complex, and so were religious discourses about them: some idealized them as goddesses, Daoist immortals, Buddhist saints, or Confucian paragons of virtue, and others vilified them as demonic, polluted, and karmically hindered beings.

This text has contextualized women's religious lives within social, economic, political, and legal history and demonstrated that women's religious opportunities and choices were circumscribed by marriage patterns and concomitant inheritance rights. The case of women in Japanese religions is particularly instructive because the *longue durée* of Japanese history offers a culturally bounded case with an exceptionally rich variety of marital arrangements. From the ancient through the medieval and early modern periods, marriage patterns shifted from duolocal to uxorilocal, then to neolocal, and finally to virilocal polygynous marriage arrangements—particularly among the socioeconomic elites, about whom the most detailed information is available. In ancient Japan, women were tightly integrated into their natal families. While men generally wielded greater political and economic power, women were not completely excluded from inheriting land and wealth transmitted among their natal kin. However, as the virilocal, patrilineal household (*ie*) became prevalent in medieval Japan, women lost the right to inherit land in perpetuity and became more economically dependent on their husbands' families. Such changes affected women's ability to act as patrons for religious institutions, their qualifications for serving as members of village shrine associations, their motivations for seeking renunciation as Buddhist nuns, and their place of burial after death. Women's changing status within the family also led to their increasing association with ritual pollution and the demonization of female jealousy and sexuality.

Changes in marriage patterns continued to influence women's religious practices in the modern era. The Civil Code of 1898 redefined marriage as monogamous and ended the practice of concubinage, but the patrilineal household became even more hegemonic since married women lost the right to hold property independently. At the same time, women were increasingly excluded from the public sphere, and women's education promoted the ideal of the good wife and wise mother. This ideal was soon adopted by various religious organizations as they formed married women's associations and rationalized the roles of women married to shrine priests and Buddhist clerics. Despite these limitations, resourceful women found ways to remain publicly active in married women's associations by embracing their roles as nurturers. And although Buddhist nuns opted out of becoming wives and mothers, they managed to employ late nineteenth- and early twentieth-century discourses about women's education to demand greater educational and professional opportunities.

In the postwar era, marriage was redefined again. By constitutional law, marriage became an arrangement into which the couple entered by mutual consent rather than by an agreement between their families. With increasing urbanization and the rise in nuclear families, many couples began living in neolocal rather than virilocal arrangements, at least while the husband's parents were still healthy. This gave wives greater independence from their husbands' families, although they remained financially dependent on their husbands. The ideal of the full-time homemaker and stay-at-home mother became normative and was encouraged by many religious organizations.

Since the 1990s, however, profound demographic changes have shifted traditional gender boundaries. These developments again have affected women in religious organizations, many of which have given women greater participatory and administrative roles. Despite a backlash against feminism from the conservative religious establishment, women within religious organizations have lobbied successfully for structural changes. Women have successfully employed networking strategies in various contexts, from transdenominational groups of nuns and temple wives to women's burial associations. Especially in the wake of the 1995 Fourth World Conference on Women in Beijing, women activists within religious organizations began to collaborate across denominational boundaries to demand change from the male-dominated religious establishment and to question a wide range of social inequities.

Confronting Orientalist stereotypes, this book has demonstrated that Japanese women have not simply been passive victims of subjugation: they have actively resisted, subverted, or employed patriarchal ideologies to promote their own interests. Arguably the most perplexing case has been that of the *Blood Pool Sutra*. Some premodern women rejected the idea that women's uterine blood was so polluting that it universally condemned women to hell. Tenrikyō's founder, Nakayama Miki, for example, denied that menstruation was polluting and instead regarded it as a natural process as necessary for reproduction as the flowers of fruit-bearing plants. Nevertheless, Kumano *bikuni* made a living preaching the misogynistic teachings of the *Blood Pool Sutra*, and female devotees gathered in consororities to honor this scripture. On the one hand, the Kumano *bikuni*'s preaching contributed to an increasing association of the female body with defilement; on the other hand, the menstrual taboos gave the itinerant preachers a powerful tool to reach their female audience. Ironically, Kumano *bikuni* may also have given women agency by promoting the idea that women could take control of their own posthumous salvation. Female members of con-sororities likewise must have seen advantages in venerating the *Blood Pool Sutra*. They may have been motivated by the companionship that they found in their gatherings. Moreover, belief in this scripture may also have provided them with a means to demand posthumous care at a time when the patriline was becoming the central focus of the ances-tral cult. Above all, this example—like many others covered in this text—demonstrates that Japanese women have held a wide range of positions in their encounters with even the most patriarchal religious traditions. In voicing her postcolonial feminist critique, the theologian Kwok Pui-lan has stressed that it is important for feminist readings of Asian women to pay attention to historical contexts and to avoid con-structing Asian cultures as uniform.[1] It is precisely for this reason that this historical survey has emphasized change and diversity in a specific, culturally bounded context.

QUESTIONS FOR DISCUSSION

1. What kind of political powers, if any, did Himiko have? How did these relate to her spiritual powers? How should we understand Himiko's relationship with her brother? What do we make of the fact that she remained unmarried? What role did Himiko's relationship with Wei China play in securing her political power?

2. What, if anything, do the Chinese records about Himiko teach us about women in prehistoric Japan? What do they not teach us?

3. What images of femininity and masculinity do we gain from the early Japanese myths about Izanami and Izanagi, and about Amaterasu and Susanoo? What do these myths suggest about the relationship between the sexes and about kinship structures?

4. What roles did women play in the introduction of Buddhism to Japan? How did the establishment of the female monastic order in Japan affect the lives of women? What new options did this path offer them? Do you see anything distinctly Japanese about the roles women took in the tradition?

5. Does it matter that orthodox ordinations for women were not transmitted to Japan? Did it matter to women in ancient Japan? Why or why not?

6. Do you think that Heian accounts of spirit possession depict women as weak, passive victims or do they show women as active and empowered? Provide evidence for both interpretations. Which do you find more convincing? In what respects did spirit possession allow women to cope with the problems generated by polygyny?

7. Why did the institution of state-sponsored convents decline in the Heian period? How did this decline affect the opportunities women

had in the monastic orders? Why did women choose renunciation during this period? In what respects did becoming a nun allow women to cope with the problems generated by polygyny?

8. How did the concept of marriage change from the ancient to the medieval period in premodern Japan? How did these changes affect the status of women within the family? How did premodern marriage customs influence religious practices?

9. How did views of women change during the medieval period? How do you reconcile the fact that new theories of salvation for women and a revival of the nuns' order emerged just as women became increasingly associated with impurity and spiritual hindrances?

10. How do you explain the fact that women found meaning in the Japanese Buddhist tradition despite its androcentrism?

11. Give your own interpretation of the *Blood Pool Sutra*. How does the idea of the Blood Pool Hell correlate to the increasing demonization of women and the shift toward patriarchal family structures during the medieval period? How do you explain the fact that women themselves had a hand in the propagation of the *Blood Pool Sutra*?

12. What roles did women play in the introduction of Christianity to Japan? What new options did Christianity offer them?

13. What kind of ideal feminine virtues did the *Great Learning for Women* and other early modern Confucian texts promote? How do the ideals of the *Great Learning for Women* compare to medieval Buddhist conceptualizations of women?

14. Scholars have often dismissed Confucianism as a quintessentially patriarchal tradition that exemplifies the oppression of East Asian women in the premodern era. How do you explain the fact that women found meaning in Confucianism despite its androcentrism?

15. Some scholars contend that the new religions offered radically different ways of participation and access to salvation for women than more established religions. Do you agree?

16. Explain the concept of "good wife and wise mother." How did this concept arise? How did it shift from the late nineteenth through the mid-twentieth centuries? How did it construct ideal femininity in prewar Japan? To what extent was this concept indebted to Confucian constructions of gender? To what extent was it indebted to bourgeois nineteenth-century Euro-American constructions of gender? How did this concept simultaneously constrain and provide opportunities for women? How has the concept of "good wife and wise mother" influenced religious practices and religious institutions?

17. How did the concept of marriage change in modern Japan? How did these changes affect the status of women within the family? How did changing marriage customs influence religious practices?

18. How did the status of nuns change during the modern period? Did it improve for all types of nuns? What drove these changes? How did clerical marriage affect nuns? Why has the relationship between nuns and temple wives been at times contentious? Who benefits from this situation?

19. How has clerical marriage challenged the ideal of the world renouncer? How have Buddhist sects handled this tension? What have the consequences been for temple families, particularly for temple wives?

20. How has the prewar concept of "good wife, wise mother" been reified, adapted, and contested in postwar and contemporary Japan? How have religious organizations responded to this debate? How did postwar women appropriate the concept of "good wife, wise mother" to further their own agendas and to become active in the public sphere?

21. How have demographic changes during the Lost Decades affected women's religious practices and modes of organization within religious institutions?

NOTES

INTRODUCTION

1. Cited in Sharon Sievers, *Flowers in Salt: The Beginnings of Feminist Consciousness in Modern Japan* (Stanford: Stanford University Press, 1983), 163.
2. Hiratsuka Raichō, *In the Beginning Was the Sun: The Autobiography of a Japanese Feminist*, trans. Teruko Craig (New York: Columbia University Press, 2010), 160.
3. Cited in Vera Mackie, *Feminism in Modern Japan* (Cambridge: Cambridge University Press, 2003), 120.
4. Bernard Faure, *The Power of Denial: Buddhism, Purity, and Gender* (Princeton: Princeton University Press, 2003).
5. Saba Mahmood, *Politics of Piety: The Islamic Revival and the Feminist Subject* (Princeton: Princeton University Press, 2005), 5–6.
6. Mahmood, *Politics of Piety*, 6.
7. Faure, *Power of Denial*, 53.
8. Dorothy Ko, *Teachers of the Inner Chambers: Women and Culture in Seventeenth-Century China* (Stanford: Stanford University Press, 1994).
9. Ueno Chizuko, "In the Feminine Guise: A Trap of Reverse Orientalism," *U.S.-Japan Women's Journal*, English supplement, 13 (1997): 15.

CHAPTER 1. THE PREHISTORICAL JAPANESE ARCHIPELAGO

1. Richard Bowring, *The Religious Traditions of Japan, 500–1600* (Cambridge: Cambridge University Press, 2005), 1.
2. Idojiri kōkokan, eds., *Yasugatake Jōmon sekai saigen* (Tokyo: Shinchōsha, 1988), 110–11.
3. Esaka Teruya, *Nihon dogū* (Tokyo: Rokkō Shuppan, 1990), 172.
4. Edward Kidder, *Himiko and Japan's Elusive Chiefdom of Yamatai: Archaeology, History, and Mythology* (Honolulu: University of Hawai'i Press, 2007), 141, 146.
5. Imamura Keiji, *Prehistoric Japan: New Perspectives on Insular East Asia* (Honolulu: University of Hawai'i Press, 1996), 95–97.
6. Imamura, *Prehistoric Japan*, 97.
7. Yoshida Atsuhiko, "The Beginning of the Cult of Mother Earth in Europe and in Japan," in *Women and Religion* (Tenri City: Tenri Jihosha, 2003), 341–46.
8. Donald Philippi, trans., *Kojiki* (Tokyo: University of Tokyo Press, 1989), 87; Yoshida, "Beginning of the Cult of Mother Earth," 348–49.

9. William George Aston, trans., *Nihongi: Chronicles of Japan from the Earliest Times to A.D. 697* (Rutland, VT: Charles Tuttle, 1972), 1:32–33; Yoshida, "Beginning of the Cult of Mother Earth," 348–49.

10. Imamura, *Prehistoric Japan*, 99–109.

11. Shitara Hiromi, "Jōmonjin no dōbutsukan," in *Hito to dōbutsu no nihon shi*, vol. 1, *Dōbutsu no kōkogaku*, ed. Nishimoto Toyohiro (Tokyo: Yoshikawa Kōbunkan, 2008); Nishimoto Toyohiro, "Buta to Nihonjin," in Nishimoto, *Hito to dōbutsu no nihon shi*, vol. 1, *Dōbutsu no kōkogaku*, 216–17.

12. Yoshida, "Beginning of the Cult of Mother Earth," 353–54.

13. Aston, *Nihongi*, 2:5.

14. Kidder, *Himiko and Japan's Elusive Chiefdom of Yamatai*, 143.

15. Yoshida, "Beginning of the Cult of Mother Earth," 346–47.

16. Cited in Kidder, *Himiko and Japan's Elusive Chiefdom of Yamatai*, 16–17.

17. Kidder, *Himiko and Japan's Elusive Chiefdom of Yamatai*, 16–18.

18. For detailed overviews of the Yamatai controversy, see Kidder, *Himiko and Japan's Elusive Chiefdom of Yamatai*, 21–35; William Wayne Farris, *Sacred Texts and Buried Treasures: Issues in the Historical Archaeology of Ancient Japan* (Honolulu: University of Hawai'i Press, 1998), 15–23.

19. Kidder, *Himiko and Japan's Elusive Chiefdom of Yamatai*, 8–9.

20. One scholar prefers to view Himiko not as a shaman but as a healer by means of dispensing medicine. Kidder, *Himiko and Japan's Elusive Chiefdom of Yamatai*, 132.

21. Joan Piggott, *The Emergence of Japanese Kingship* (Stanford: Stanford University Press, 1997), 26–27; Kidder, *Himiko and Japan's Elusive Chiefdom of Yamatai*, 132.

22. Kidder, *Himiko and Japan's Elusive Chiefdom of Yamatai*, 128–29, 132, 145–46.

23. Adapted from Aston, *Nihongi*, 1:225.

24. Kidder, *Himiko and Japan's Elusive Chiefdom of Yamatai*, 138–39.

25. Piggott, *Emergence of Japanese Kingship*, 37–39; Kidder, *Himiko and Japan's Elusive Chiefdom of Yamatai*, 132; Matsumura Kazuo, "Ancient Japan and Religion," in *Nanzan Guide to Japanese Religions*, ed. Paul Swanson and Clark Chilson (Honolulu: University of Hawai'i Press, 2006), 136–38.

26. Yoshie Akiko, "When Antiquity Meets the Modern: Representing Female Rulers in the Making of Japanese History," paper presented at the Conference of the International Federation for Research in Women's History: Women's History Revisited—Historiographical Reflections on Women and Gender in a Global Context, Sydney, Australia, 9 July 2005, http://www.historians.ie/women/Akiko.pdf.

27. Aston, *Nihongi*, 1:221–32; Philippi, *Kojiki*, 257–65.

28. Kidder, *Himiko and Japan's Elusive Chiefdom of Yamatai*, 21–24.

29. Kidder, *Himiko and Japan's Elusive Chiefdom of Yamatai*, 27.

30. Aston, *Nihongi*, 1:176–77, 1:205, 1:211; Philippi, *Kojiki*, 210–11, 233, 238–40.

31. Piggott, *Emergence of Japanese Kingship*, 17–37.

32. Cited in Kidder, *Himiko and Japan's Elusive Chiefdom of Yamatai*, 15–16.

33. Kidder, *Himiko and Japan's Elusive Chiefdom of Yamatai*, 291.

34. Kidder, *Himiko and Japan's Elusive Chiefdom of Yamatai*, 18, 298.

35. Farris, *Sacred Texts and Buried Treasures*, 27–29; Kidder, *Himiko and Japan's Elusive Chiefdom of Yamatai*, 297.

36. Farris, *Sacred Texts and Buried Treasures*, 26–27.

37. Kidder, *Himiko and Japan's Elusive Chiefdom of Yamatai*, 293–94.

38. Yoshie Akiko, "Tamayori saikō: *Imo no chikara* hihan," in *Miko to joshin*, ed. Ōsumi Kazuo and Nishiguchi Junko (Tokyo: Heibonsha, 1989), 51–90; Yoshie, "When Antiquity Meets the Modern."

CHAPTER 2. ANCIENT JAPANESE MYTHOLOGY

1. Sekiguchi Hiroko, "The Patriarchal Family Paradigm in Eighth-Century Japan," in *Women and Confucian Cultures in Premodern China, Korea, and Japan*, ed. Dorothy Ko, JaHyun Kim Haboush, and Joan Piggott (Berkeley: University of California Press, 2003), 27–46; Serinity Young, ed., *An Anthology of Sacred Texts by and about Women* (New York: Crossroad, 1993), 359.

2. Sekiguchi, "The Patriarchal Family Paradigm in Eighth-Century"; Hongō Masatsugu, "State Buddhism and Court Buddhism: The Role of Court Women in the Development of Buddhism from the Seventh to Ninth Centuries," in *Engendering Faith: Women and Buddhism in Premodern Japan*, ed. Barbara Ruch (Ann Arbor: University of Michigan Center for Japanese Studies, 2002), 50; Nomura Ikuyo, *Bukkyō to onna no seishinshi* (Tokyo: Yoshikawa Kōbunkan, 2004), 106–7; Lori Meeks, "Buddhist Renunciation and the Female Life Cycle: Understanding Nunhood in Heian and Kamakura Japan," *Harvard Journal of Asiatic Studies* 70, no. 1 (2010): 17. Japanologists tend to use the terms "virilocal" and "uxorilocal" rather than "patrilocal" and "matrilocal" even though the latter are more common in many other disciplines. This may be a reflection of the Japanese terminology, which similarly foregrounds marital rather than parental relationships. Japanese scholars speak of "taking a daughter-in-law" (*yometori*) and "taking a son-in-law" (*mukotori*). The corresponding Japanese term for a duolocal marriage is "visiting a wife" (*tsumadoi*). The English terms, however, do not completely replicate Japanese usage: while the English concepts emphasize the location of the marital residence, the Japanese terms stress personal relationships and bodily movements, that is, who is incorporated into the household through marriage or who moves between households. See Tonomura Hitomi, "Re-envisioning Women in the Post-Kamakura Age," in *The Origins of Japan's Medieval World: Courtiers, Clerics, Warriors, and Peasants in the Fourteenth Century*, ed. Jeffrey Mass (Stanford: Stanford University Press, 1997), 146–47.

3. Ronald Toby, "Why Leave Nara? Kammu and the Transfer of the Capital," *Monumenta Nipponica* 40, no. 3 (1985): 331–47.

4. Donald Philippi, trans., *Kojiki* (Tokyo: University of Tokyo Press, 1989), 50.

5. Allan Grapard, "Visions of Excess and Excesses of Vision: Women and Transgression in Japanese Myth," *Japanese Journal of Religious Studies* 18, no. 1 (1991): 8.

6. William George Aston, trans., *Nihongi: Chronicles of Japan from the Earliest Times to A.D. 697* (Rutland, VT: Charles Tuttle, 1972), 1:13.

7. See, for instance, Young, *Anthology of Sacred Texts by and about Women*, 341–47.

8. On such spirit-shaking rites, see Michael Como, *Weaving and Binding: Immigrant Gods and Female Immortals in Ancient Japan* (Honolulu: University of Hawai'i Press, 2009), 161.

9. Philippi, *Kojiki*, 61–67.

10. Philippi, *Kojiki*, 68–70.

11. Edward Kidder, *Himiko and Japan's Elusive Chiefdom of Yamatai: Archaeology, History, and Mythology* (Honolulu: University of Hawai'i Press, 2007), 15, 293.

12. Como, *Weaving and Binding*, 184–85.

13. Grapard, "Visions of Excess and Excesses of Vision."

14. Aston, *Nihongi*, 1:18–19.

15. Arne Kalland and Pamela Asquith, *Japanese Images of Nature: Cultural Perspectives* (Richmond, Surrey: Curzon, 1997), 10–15.

16. Philippi, *Kojiki*, 79.

17. Gary Ebersole, *Ritual Poetry and the Politics of Death in Early Japan* (Princeton: Princeton University Press, 1989), 79.

18. Joan Piggott, *The Emergence of Japanese Kingship* (Stanford: Stanford University Press, 1997), 66–69, 79–83, 99, 113–17, 161–64.

19. Aston, *Nihongi*, 1:44.

20. The *sakaki* (*Cleyera japonica*) is a flowering, leafy evergreen tree. To this day, *sakaki* branches are used as an offering at Shintō shrines.

21. Aston, *Nihongi*, 1:77–79.

22. John Breen and Mark Teeuwen, *A New History of Shinto* (Chichester: Wiley-Blackwell, 2010), 132.

23. Como, *Weaving and Binding*, 176–92.

24. Mark Teeuwen, "The Creation of a *honji suijaku* Deity: Amaterasu as the Judge of the Dead," in *Buddhas and kami in Japan: Honji suijaku as a Combinatory Paradigm*, ed. Mark Teeuwen and Fabio Rambelli (New York: RoutledgeCurzon, 2003), 115.

25. Como, *Weaving and Binding*, 167, 180–82; Breen and Teeuwen, *A New History of Shinto*, 134–35.

26. Piggott, *Emergence of Japanese Kingship*, 127; Richard Bowring, *The Religious Traditions of Japan, 500–1600* (Cambridge: Cambridge University Press, 2005), 36–38, 45.

27. Felicia Bock, *Engishiki: Procedures of the Engi Era, Books I–V* (Tokyo: Sophia University, 1970), 51–52.

28. Michiko Yusa, "Women in Shinto: Images Remembered," in *Women and Religion*, ed. Arvind Sharma (Albany: State University of New York Press, 1994), 107–8.

29. Yusa, "Women in Shinto," 108–11; Bock, *Engishiki I–V*, 55.

30. Bock, *Engishiki I–V*, 152–53.

31. Teeuwen, "The Creation of a *honji suijaku* Deity," 115–44; Breen and Teeuwen, *A New History of Shinto*, 145–48.
32. Como, *Weaving and Binding*, 144–92.

CHAPTER 3. THE INTRODUCTION OF BUDDHISM

1. William George Aston, trans., *Nihongi: Chronicles of Japan from the Earliest Times to A.D. 697* (Rutland, VT: Charles Tuttle, 1972), 2:101–2.
2. Brian Ruppert, *Jewel in the Ashes: Buddha Relics and Power in Early Medieval Japan* (Cambridge: Harvard University Asia Center, 2000), 1–9; Dan Martin, "Pearls from Bones: Relics, Chortens, Tertons and the Signs of Saintly Death in Tibet," *Numen* 41, no. 3 (1994): 273–324.
3. Paula Arai, *Women Living Zen: Japanese Sōtō Buddhist Nuns* (New York: Oxford University Press, 1999), 31–32.
4. Bernard Faure, *The Power of Denial: Buddhism, Purity, and Gender* (Princeton: Princeton University Press, 2003), 29.
5. Aston, *Nihongi*, 2:103–4; George Sansom, "Early Japanese Law and Administration," pt. 2, *Transactions of the Asiatic Society of Japan*, 2nd ser., 11 (1934): 132.
6. Chikusa Masaaki, "The Formation and Growth of Buddhist Nun Communities in China," in *Engendering Faith: Women and Buddhism in Premodern Japan*, ed. Barbara Ruch (Ann Arbor: University of Michigan Center for Japanese Studies, 2002), 4–11.
7. Paul Groner, "The Vicissitudes in the Ordination of Japanese 'Nuns' during the Eighth through the Tenth Centuries," in Ruch, *Engendering Faith*, 65–108.
8. Lori Meeks, *Hokkeji and the Reemergence of Female Monastic Orders in Premodern Japan* (Honolulu: University of Hawai'i Press, 2010).
9. Aston, *Nihongi*, 2:113, 2:117–18.
10. Miwa Stevenson, "The Founding of the Monastery Gangōji and a List of Its Treasures," in *Religions of Japan in Practice*, ed. George Tanabe (Princeton: Princeton University Press, 1999), 307.
11. Stevenson, "Founding of the Monastery Gangōji," 305–14.
12. Sonoda Kōyū, "Early Buddha Worship," in *The Cambridge History of Japan*, vol. 1, *Ancient Japan*, ed. Delmer Brown (Cambridge: Cambridge University Press, 1993), 386, 390.
13. Joan Piggott, *The Emergence of Japanese Kingship* (Stanford: Stanford University Press, 1997), 93–95.
14. Piggott, *Emergence of Japanese Kingship*, 95–96; Sonoda, "Early Buddha Worship," 383.
15. Yoshida Kazuhiko, "The Enlightenment of the Dragon King's Daughter in the *Lotus Sutra*," in Ruch, *Engendering Faith*, 304.
16. Serinity Young, ed., *An Anthology of Sacred Texts by and about Women* (New York: Crossroad, 1993), 317–20.
17. Piggott, *Emergence of Japanese Kingship*, 96.

18. Yoshida, "Enlightenment of the Dragon King's Daughter," 304.

19. Burton Watson, trans., *The Lotus Sutra* (New York: Columbia University Press, 1993), 190–92; Jan Nattier, "Gender and Hierarchy in the *Lotus Sūtra*," in *Readings of the Lotus Sūtra*, ed. Stephen Teiser and Jacqueline Stone (New York: Columbia University Press, 2009), 93.

20. Mikoshiba Daisuke, "Empress Kōmyō's Buddhist Faith: Her Role in the Founding of the State Temple and Convent System," in Ruch, *Engendering Faith*, 26–30.

21. Mikoshiba, "Empress Kōmyō's Buddhist Faith," 30–33, 36–38; Piggott, *Emergence of Japanese Kingship*, 246–47; Hongō Masatsugu, "State Buddhism and Court Buddhism: The Role of Court Women in the Development of Buddhism from the Seventh to Ninth Centuries," in Ruch, *Engendering Faith*, 49–50.

22. Richard Bowring, *The Religious Traditions of Japan, 500–1600* (Cambridge: Cambridge University Press, 2005), 94–97; Mikoshiba, "Empress Kōmyō's Buddhist Faith," 33; Piggott, *Emergence of Japanese Kingship*, 280–81.

23. Kyōko Motomuchi Nakamura, *Miraculous Stories from the Japanese Buddhist Tradition: The Nihon Ryōiki of the Monk Kyōkai* (Cambridge: Harvard University Press, 1973), 24. Hereafter cited as *Nihon Ryōiki*.

24. Sansom, "Early Japanese Law and Administration," pt. 2, 127–33.

25. Hubert Seiwert, *Popular Religious Movements and Heterodox Sects in Chinese History* (Leiden: Brill, 2003), 105.

26. Cited in Mikoshiba, "Empress Kōmyō's Buddhist Faith," 33.

27. Sansom, "Early Japanese Law and Administration," pt. 2, 128–30.

28. Mikoshiba, "Empress Kōmyō's Buddhist Faith," 34.

29. Nakamura, *Nihon Ryōiki*, 69, 71–72.

30. Hongō, "State Buddhism and Court Buddhism," 50.

31. Nakamura, *Nihon Ryōiki*, 75.

32. Yoshida, "Enlightenment of the Dragon King's Daughter," 304.

33. Nakamura, *Nihon Ryōiki*, 124–25.

34. Faure, *Power of Denial*, 114.

CHAPTER 4. THE HEIAN PERIOD

1. William McCullough, "Japanese Marriage Institutions in the Heian Period," *Harvard Journal of Asiatic Studies* 27 (1967): 127–35.

2. Doris Bargen, *A Woman's Weapon: Spirit Possession in "The Tale of Genji"* (Honolulu: University of Hawai'i Press, 1997), 1–3.

3. Michelle Osterfeld Li, *Ambiguous Bodies: Reading the Grotesque in Japanese Setsuwa Tales* (Stanford: Stanford University Press, 2009), 116–53.

4. Tonomura Hitomi, "Coercive Sex in the Medieval Japanese Court: Lady Nijō's Memoir," *Monumenta Nipponica* 61, no. 3 (2006): 286–89; Margaret Childs, "The Value of Vulnerability: Sexual Coercion and the Nature of Love in Japanese Court Literature," *Journal of Asian Studies* 58, no. 4 (1999): 1059–79.

5. McCullough, "Japanese Marriage Institutions in the Heian Period," 105–18; Wakita Haruko, "The Medieval Household and Gender Roles within the Imperial Family, Nobility, Merchants, and Commoners," in *Women and Class in Japanese History*, ed. Tonomura Hitomi, Anne Walthall, and Wakita Haruko (Ann Arbor: Center for Japanese Studies, University of Michigan, 1999), 82–84.
6. Yoshikawa Shinji, "Ladies-in-Waiting in the Heian Period," in *Gender and Japanese History*, vol. 2, ed. Wakita Haruko, Anne Bouchy, and Ueno Chizuko (Osaka: Osaka University Press, 1999), 283–311.
7. Jeffrey Mass, *Lordship and Inheritance: A Study of the Kamakura Sōryō System* (Stanford: Stanford University Press, 1989), 9–17.
8. Mass, *Lordship and Inheritance*, 17.
9. Mass, *Lordship and Inheritance*, 17–18.
10. Li, *Ambiguous Bodies*, 154–91.
11. Michael Bathgate, *The Fox's Craft in Japanese Religion and Folklore: Shapeshifters, Transformations, and Duplicities* (New York: Routledge, 2004), 35–60.
12. Li, *Ambiguous Bodies*, 179–89.
13. Terry Kawashima, *Writing Margins: The Textual Construction of Gender in Heian and Kamakura Japan* (Cambridge: Harvard University Asia Center, 2001), 255–87.
14. Bargen, *A Woman's Weapon*, 1–27.
15. Lori Meeks, "The Disappearing Medium: Reassessing the Place of *Miko* in the Religious Landscape of Premodern Japan," *History of Religions* 50, no. 3 (2011): 213–14; Nishiguchi Junko, *Onna no chikara: kodai no josei to Bukkyō* (Tokyo: Heibonsha, 1987), 220–54.
16. Felicia Bock, *Engishiki: Procedures of the Engi Era, Books VI–X* (Tokyo: Sophia University, 1972), 2–3.
17. Bock, *Engishiki VI–X*, 3–7; Felicia Bock, *Engishiki: Procedures of the Engi Era, Books I–V* (Tokyo: Sophia University, 1970), 52.
18. Ivan Morris, trans., *The Pillow Book of Sei Shōnagon* (New York: Columbia University Press, 1967), 192.
19. Bock, *Engishiki VI–X*, 7–8, 10.
20. Edward Kamens, *The Buddhist Poetry of the Great Kamo Priestess: Daisaiin Senshi and the "Hosshin Wakashū"* (Ann Arbor: University of Michigan Center for Japanese Studies, 1990).
21. Kamens, *Buddhist Poetry of the Great Kamo Priestess*, 16.
22. Kamens, *Buddhist Poetry of the Great Kamo Priestess*, 16–18, 76–138.
23. Paul Groner, "The Vicissitudes in the Ordination of Japanese 'Nuns' during the Eighth through the Tenth Centuries," in *Engendering Faith: Women and Buddhism in Premodern Japan*, ed. Barbara Ruch (Ann Arbor: University of Michigan Center for Japanese Studies, 2002), 65–78; Yoshida Kazuhiko, "The Enlightenment of the Dragon King's Daughter in the *Lotus Sutra*," in Ruch, *Engendering Faith*, 308–11; Bernard Faure, *The Power of Denial: Buddhism, Purity, and Gender* (Princeton: Princeton University Press, 2003), 114–15.

24. Groner, "Vicissitudes in the Ordination of Japanese 'Nuns,'" 65–78; Yoshida, "Enlightenment of the Dragon King's Daughter," 308–11.

25. Yoshida, "Enlightenment of the Dragon King's Daughter," 306–8, 311–17; Ōsumi Kazuo, "Historical Notes on Women and the Japanization of Buddhism," in Ruch, *Engendering Faith*, xxvii–xxix.

26. Faure, *Power of Denial*, 114–15.

27. Yoshiko Dykstra, *Miraculous Tales of the Lotus Sutra from Ancient Japan* (Honolulu: University of Hawai'i Press, 1983), 121.

28. Faure, *Power of Denial*, 114–15.

29. Faure, *Power of Denial*, 115.

30. Brian Ruppert, *Jewel in the Ashes: Buddha Relics and Power in Early Medieval Japan* (Cambridge: Harvard University Asia Center, 2000), 221–23.

31. Faure, *Power of Denial*, 115.

32. William Deal, "Women and Japanese Buddhism: Tales of Birth in the Pure Land," in *Religions of Japan in Practice*, ed. George Tanabe (Princeton: Princeton University Press, 1999), 179–84.

33. James Dobbins, "Women's Birth in the Pure Land as Women: Intimations from the Letters of Eshinni," *Eastern Buddhist* 28, no. 1 (1995): 119–20.

34. Dykstra, *Miraculous Tales of the Lotus Sutra*, 136.

35. Dykstra, *Miraculous Tales of the Lotus Sutra*, 137.

36. Dykstra, *Miraculous Tales of the Lotus Sutra*, 140.

37. Obara Hitoshi, "The Rebirth of Women into Paradise: Women in Fujiwara no Munetada's Diary Chūyūki (1087–1138)," in Ruch, *Engendering Faith*, 443–52.

38. Lori Meeks, "Reconfiguring Ritual Authority: The Ordination of Aristocratic Women in Premodern Japan," *Japanese Journal of Religious Studies* 33, no. 1 (2006): 51–74; Lori Meeks, "Buddhist Renunciation and the Female Life Cycle: Understanding Nunhood in Heian and Kamakura Japan," *Harvard Journal of Asiatic Studies* 70, no. 1 (2010): 1–5, 11–18.

39. Meeks, "Buddhist Renunciation and the Female Life Cycle," 5–10, 36–42.

40. Meeks, "Buddhist Renunciation and the Female Life Cycle," 18–34; Katsuura Noriko, "Tonsure Forms for Nuns: Classification of Nuns according to Hairstyle," in Ruch, *Engendering Faith*, 114–26.

41. Groner, "Vicissitudes in the Ordination of Japanese 'Nuns,'" 81–84.

42. Edward Kamens, *The Three Jewels: A Study and Translation of Minamoto Tamenori's "Sanbōe"* (Ann Arbor: University of Michigan, 1988), 272–73.

43. Ruppert, *Jewel in the Ashes*, 192–229.

44. Barbara Ambros, "Liminal Journeys: Noblewomen's Pilgrimages in the Heian Period," *Japanese Journal of Religious Studies* 24, nos. 3–4 (1997): 302–45.

45. Chung Young-Ah, "Heian Noblewomen's Pilgrimage: The Language of Gendered Discontent and (Re)construction of the Self," *West Virginia University Philological Papers* 48 (2001): 1–8.

46. Edwin Cranston, *The Izumi Shikibu Diary: A Romance of the Heian Court* (Cambridge: Harvard University Press, 1969), 153–54.

CHAPTER 5. THE MEDIEVAL PERIOD

1. Tonomura Hitomi, "Re-envisioning Women in the Post-Kamakura Age," in *The Origins of Japan's Medieval World: Courtiers, Clerics, Warriors, and Peasants in the Fourteenth Century*, ed. Jeffrey Mass (Stanford: Stanford University Press, 1997), 146–53.

2. Wakita Haruko, "The Medieval Household and Gender Roles within the Imperial Family, Nobility, Merchants, and Commoners," in *Women and Class in Japanese History*, ed. Tonomura Hitomi, Anne Walthall, and Wakita Haruko (Ann Arbor: Center for Japanese Studies, University of Michigan, 1999), 81–84.

3. Tabata Yasuko, "Female Attendants and Wives of the Medieval Warrior Class," in *Gender and Japanese History*, vol. 2, ed. Wakita Haruko, Anne Bouchy, and Ueno Chizuko (Osaka: Osaka University Press, 1999), 314–31; Hata Hisako, "Servants of the Inner Quarters," in *Servants of the Dynasty: Palace Women in World History*, ed. Anne Walthall (Berkeley: University of California Press, 2008), 172–90.

4. Wakita, "Medieval Household and Gender Roles," 87.

5. Hank Glassman, "Chinese Buddhist Death Ritual and the Transformation of Japanese Kinship," in *The Buddhist Dead: Practices, Discourses, Representations*, ed. Brian Cuevas and Jacqueline Stone (Honolulu: University of Hawai'i Press, 2007), 381.

6. Jeffrey Mass, *Lordship and Inheritance: A Study of the Kamakura Sōryō System* (Stanford: Stanford University Press, 1989), 48–49, 101–3.

7. Mass, *Lordship and Inheritance*, 104.

8. Jurgis Elisonas, "The Evangelic Furnace: Japan's First Encounter with the West," in *Sources of Japanese Tradition*, vol. 2, *1600–2000*, pt. 1, *1600–1868*, comp. William de Bary, Carol Gluck, and Arthur Tiedemann (New York: Columbia University Press, 2006), 143.

9. Amino Yoshihiko, *Rethinking Japanese History* (Ann Arbor: Center for Japanese Studies, University of Michigan, 2012), 230–33.

10. William Lindsey, *Fertility and Pleasure: Ritual and Sexual Values in Tokugawa Japan* (Honolulu: University of Hawai'i Press, 2007), 79–80.

11. Katō Mieko, "Women's Associations and Religious Expression in the Medieval Japanese Village," in Tonomura, Walthall, and Wakita, *Women and Class in Japanese History*, 120–27.

12. Ushiyama Yoshiyuki, "Buddhist Convents in Medieval Japan," in *Engendering Faith: Women and Buddhism in Premodern Japan*, ed. Barbara Ruch (Ann Arbor: University of Michigan Center for Japanese Studies, 2002), 132–36.

13. Lori Meeks, "Buddhist Renunciation and the Female Life Cycle: Understanding

Nunhood in Heian and Kamakura Japan," *Harvard Journal of Asiatic Studies* 70, no. 1 (2010): 45.

14. Ushiyama, "Buddhist Convents in Medieval Japan," 137–40.

15. Lori Meeks, *Hokkeji and the Reemergence of Female Monastic Orders in Premodern Japan* (Honolulu: University of Hawai'i Press, 2010), 93–95, 104–16.

16. Meeks, *Hokkeji and the Reemergence of Female Monastic Orders*, 133–40.

17. Meeks, *Hokkeji and the Reemergence of Female Monastic Orders*, 7.

18. Meeks, *Hokkeji and the Reemergence of Female Monastic Orders*, 140–55.

19. Hosokawa Ryōichi, "Ōken to amadera: chūsei josei to shari shinkō," *Rettō no bunkashi* 5 (1988): 95–142; Bernard Faure, *The Power of Denial: Buddhism, Purity, and Gender* (Princeton: Princeton University Press, 2003), 32; see also Brian Ruppert, *Jewel in the Ashes: Buddha Relics and Power in Early Medieval Japan* (Cambridge: Harvard University Asia Center, 2000).

20. This pairing is also found in the Devadatta chapter of the *Lotus Sutra*, which promises Buddhahood to both Devadatta (the Buddha's evil cousin) and the Dragon Girl, seemingly implying that both evil men and women bear similar moral hindrances on their way to salvation.

21. Faure, *Power of Denial*, 71–72, 110–12; Simone Heidegger, *Die Frau im japanischen Buddhismus der Kamakurazeit* (Copenhagen: Seminar for Buddhist Studies, 1995), 53–62, 94–105.

22. Heidegger, *Die Frau im japanischen Buddhismus der Kamakurazeit*, 72–77, William Deal, "Women and Japanese Buddhism: Tales of Birth in the Pure Land," in *Religions of Japan in Practice*, ed. George Tanabe (Princeton: Princeton University Press, 1999); James Dobbins, *Letters of the Nun Eshinni: Images of Pure Land Buddhism in Medieval Japan* (Honolulu: University of Hawai'i Press, 2004).

23. Nomura Ikuyo, *Bukkyō to onna no seishinshi* (Tokyo: Yoshikawa Kōbunkan, 2004), 106–7; Meeks, *Hokkeji and the Reemergence of Female Monastic Orders*, 17.

24. Virginia Skord, *Tales of Tears and Laughter: Short Fiction of Medieval Japan* (Honolulu: University of Hawai'i Press, 1991), 97.

25. Skord, *Tales of Tears and Laughter*, 197.

26. Yoshida Kazuhiko, "The Enlightenment of the Dragon King's Daughter in the *Lotus Sutra*," in Ruch, *Engendering Faith*, 309–11.

27. Hank Glassman, "At the Crossroads of Birth and Death: The Blood Pool Hell and Postmortem Fetal Extraction," in *Death and the Afterlife in Japanese Buddhism*, ed. Jacqueline I. Stone and Mariko Namba Walter (Honolulu: University of Hawai'i Press, 2008), 176–78, 180–81; Barbara Ruch, "Woman to Woman: *Kumano bikuni* Proselytizers in Medieval and Early Modern Japan," in Ruch, *Engendering Faith*, 567, 572–73.

28. Duncan Ryūken Williams, "Funerary Zen: Sōtō Zen Death Management in Tokugawa Japan," in Stone and Walter, *Death and the Afterlife in Japanese Buddhism*, 220–28.

29. Faure, *Power of Denial*, 76.

30. Jessey Choo, "Historicized Ritual and Ritualized History: Women's Lifecycle in Late Medieval China (600–1000 AD)" (Ph.D. diss., Princeton University, 2009), 138–39, 144–45.
31. Cited in Williams, "Funerary Zen," 226.
32. Faure, *Power of Denial*, 225–35; Keller Kimbrough, *Buddhist Sermon-Ballads and Miracle Plays of Seventeenth-Century Japan* (New York: Columbia University Press, 2012).
33. Donald Keene, trans., *Essays in Idleness: The Tsurezuregusa of Kenkō* (New York: Columbia University Press, 1967), 90.
34. Robert Morrell, "Mirror for Women: Mujō Ichien's *Tsuma kagami*," *Monumenta Nipponica* 35, no. 1 (1980): 67–68.
35. Keller Kimbrough, "Translation: The Tale of Fuji Cave" (online only), *Japanese Journal of Religious Studies* 33, no. 2 (2006): 12. http://nirc.nanzan-u.ac.jp/nfile/290712.
36. Kimbrough, "The Tale of Fuji Cave."
37. Terry Kawashima, *Writing Margins: The Textual Construction of Gender in Heian and Kamakura Japan* (Cambridge: Harvard University Asia Center, 2001), 219–87.
38. Marian Ury, trans., *Tales of Times Now Past: Sixty-Two Stories from a Medieval Japanese Collection* (Ann Arbor: Center for Japanese Studies, 1979), 93–96.
39. Susan Klein, "Woman as Serpent: The Demonic Feminine in the Noh Play *Dōjōji*," in *Religious Reflections on the Human Body*, ed. Jane Marie Law (Bloomington: Indiana University Press, 1995), 109.
40. Klein, "Woman as Serpent," 112–13.
41. Klein, "Woman as Serpent," 105–7, 119; Donald Keene, trans., *Twenty Plays of the Nō Theatre* (New York: Columbia University Press, 1970), 237–52. For a translation of an early Edo-period *otogizōshi* version that incorporates elements of the Noh play, see Skord, *Tales of Tears and Laughter*, 129–55.
42. Kawashima, *Writing Margins*, 27–30; Faure, *Power of Denial*, 250–61; Amino, *Rethinking Japanese History*, 233–35; Janet Goodwin, *Selling Songs and Smiles: The Sex Trade in Heian and Kamakura Japan* (Honolulu: University of Hawai'i Press, 2007).
43. Lori Meeks, "The Disappearing Medium: Reassessing the Place of *Miko* in the Religious Landscape of Premodern Japan," *History of Religions* 50, no. 3 (2011).
44. Haruko Ward, *Women Religious Leaders in Japan's Christian Century, 1549–1650* (Burlington, VT: Ashgate, 2009).
45. Ward, *Women Religious Leaders in Japan's Christian Century*; Pierre Humberclaude, "*Myōtei Mondō*: Une apologétique chrétienne japonais de 1605," *Monumenta Nipponica* 1 (1938): 223–56; Pierre Humberclaude, "*Myōtei Mondō*: Une apologétique chrétienne japonais de 1605," *Monumenta Nipponica* 2 (1939): 237–67; Haruko Ward, "Jesuits, Too: Jesuits, Women Catechists and Jezebels in Christian-Century Japan," in *The Jesuits II: Cultures, Sciences, and the Arts, 1540–1773*, ed. John W.

O'Malley, Gauvin Alexander Bailey, Steven J. Harris, and T. Frank Kennedy (Toronto: University of Toronto Press, 2006), 656.

CHAPTER 6. THE EDO PERIOD

1. Okuda Akiko, Introduction to *Women and Religion in Japan*, ed. Okuda Akiko and Okano Haruko (Wiesbaden: Harrassowitz, 1998), 10.
2. Okuda, Introduction to *Women and Religion in Japan*, 10–11.
3. Igeta Midori, "Women's Role: A Channel for Power," in Okuda and Okano, *Women and Religion in Japan*, 127.
4. Anne Walthall, "Preparation for Marriage through Service in Households of the Great: The Late Tokugawa Period," *Annual Report of the Institute for International Studies (Meijigakuin University)* 11 (2008): 105.
5. Hur Namlin, *Death and Social Order in Tokugawa Japan: Buddhism, Anti-Christianity, and the Danka System* (Cambridge: Harvard University Asia Center, 2007), 126–27; Fukuta Ajio, *Tera, haka, senzo no minzokugaku* (Tokyo: Taiga Shobō, 2004), 158–61; Morimoto Kazuhiko, *Senzo saishi to ie no kakuritsu: handanka kara ikka ichiji e* (Kyoto: Mineruva Shobō, 2006), 68–69, 71–74, 91–94, 215–17.
6. Harald Fuess, *Divorce in Japan: Family, Gender, and the State* (Stanford: Stanford University Press, 2004), 18–46.
7. Ann Dutton, "Temple Divorce in Tokugawa Japan: A Survey of Documentation on Tōkeiji and Mantokuji," in *Engendering Faith: Women and Buddhism in Premodern Japan*, ed. Barbara Ruch (Ann Arbor: University of Michigan Center for Japanese Studies, 2002), 211–14.
8. Dutton, "Temple Divorce in Tokugawa Japan."
9. Bernard Faure, *The Power of Denial: Buddhism, Purity, and Gender* (Princeton: Princeton University Press, 2003), 45.
10. Diana Wright, "The Power of Religion/the Religion of Power: Religious Activities as *Upaya* for Women of the Edo Period—The Case of Mantokuji" (Ph.D. diss., University of Toronto, 1996); Gina Cogan, "Time Capsules for Tradition: Repositioning Imperial Convents for the Meiji Period," *U.S.-Japan Women's Journal* 30–31 (2006): 80–104; Sharon Yamamoto, "Visual and Material Culture at Hōkyōji Imperial Convent: The Significance of 'Women's Art' in Early Modern Japan" (Ph.D. diss., University of California at Berkeley, 2010); Gina Cogan, *The Princess Nun: Bunchi, Buddhist Reform, and Gender in Early Edo Japan* (Cambridge: Harvard University Asia Center, 2014).
11. Walthall, "Preparation for Marriage," 109.
12. Amy Stanley, *Selling Women: Prostitution and the Household in Early Modern Japan* (Berkeley: University of California Press, 2012), 6–7.
13. William Lindsey, *Fertility and Pleasure: Ritual and Sexual Values in Tokugawa Japan* (Honolulu: University of Hawai'i Press, 2007), 1–3.

14. Ikegami Eiko, *Bonds of Civility: Aesthetic Networks and the Political Origins of Japanese Culture* (Cambridge: Cambridge University Press, 2005), 167–69.

15. Gerald Groemer, "Female Shamans in Eastern Japan during the Edo Period," *Asian Folklore Studies* 66 (2007): 27–53.

16. Nishida Kahoru, "Miko," in *Minkan ni ikiru shūkyōsha*, ed. Takano Toshihiko (Tokyo: Yoshikawa Kōbunkan, 2000), 79–80.

17. Theresa Kelleher, "Women's Education," in *Sources of East Asian Tradition*, vol. 1, *Premodern East Asia*, comp. William Theodore de Bary (New York: Columbia University Press, 2008), 410–27.

18. Lily Xiao Hong Lee, *The Virtue of Yin: Studies on Chinese Women* (Sydney: Wild Peony, 1994), 11–16.

19. Dorothy Perkins, *Encyclopedia of China: The Essential Reference to China, Its History and Culture* (New York: Roundtable Press, 2000), 25.

20. Theresa Kelleher, "Confucianism," in *Women in World Religions*, ed. Arvind Sharma (Albany: State University of New York Press, 1987), 145–50.

21. Dorothy Ko, *Teachers of the Inner Chambers: Women and Culture in Seventeenth-Century China* (Stanford: Stanford University Press, 1994), 18–19.

22. Mary Evelyn Tucker, "Kaibara Ekken," in *Sources of Japanese Tradition*, vol. 2, *1600 to 1868*, comp. William Theodore de Bary, Carol Gluck, and Arthur E. Tiedemann (New York: Columbia University Press, 2006), 229–35.

23. Sekiguchi Sumiko, "Gender in the Meiji Renovation: Confucian 'Lessons for Women' and the Making of Modern Japan," *Social Science Japan Journal* 11, no. 2 (2008): 201–21.

24. Walthall, "Preparation for Marriage," 110–15.

25. Sugano Noriko, "State Indoctrination of Filial Piety in Tokugawa Japan: Sons and Daughters in the *Official Records of Filial Piety*," in *Women and Confucian Cultures in Premodern China, Korea, and Japan*, ed. Dorothy Ko, JaHyun Kim Haboush, and Joan Piggott (Berkeley: University of California Press, 2003), 170–88.

26. Martha Tocco, "Norms and Texts for Women's Education in Tokugawa Japan," in Ko, Haboush, and Piggott, *Women and Confucian Cultures in Premodern China, Korea, and Japan*, 194–201, 211–13.

27. Robert Bellah, *Tokugawa Religion: The Cultural Roots of Modern Japan* (New York: Free Press, 1985), 133–77; Janine Sawada, *Confucian Values and Popular Zen: Sekimon Shingaku in Eighteenth Century Japan* (Honolulu: University of Hawai'i Press, 1993), 28–61.

28. Jennifer Robertson, "The Shingaku Woman: Straight from the Heart," in *Recreating Japanese Women, 1600–1945*, ed. Gail Lee Bernstein (Berkeley: University of California Press, 1992), 93–99.

29. Robertson, "Shingaku Woman," 99–103.

30. Anne Walthall, *The Weak Body of a Useless Woman: Matsuo Taseko and the Meiji Restoration* (Chicago: University of Chicago Press, 1998), 122.

31. Walthall, *Weak Body of a Useless Woman*, 125–31.
32. Janet R. Goodwin, Bettina Gramlich-Oka, Elizabeth A. Leicester, Yuki Terazawa, and Anne Walthall, "Solitary Thoughts: A Translation of Tadano Makuzu's *Hitori Kangae* (1)," *Monumenta Nipponica* 56, no. 1 (2001): 24–25.
33. Goodwin et al., "Solitary Thoughts," 25.
34. Goodwin et al., "Solitary Thoughts," 25–26, 30; Bettina Gramlich-Oka, "Tadano Makuzu and Her *Hitori Kangae*," *Monumenta Nipponica* 56, no. 1 (2001): 13–15.
35. Constantine Vaporis, *Breaking Barriers: Travel and the State in Early Modern Japan* (Cambridge: Council on East Asian Studies, Harvard University, 1994); Anne Walthall, "The Life Cycle of Farm Women in Tokugawa Japan," in Bernstein, *Recreating Japanese Women, 1600–1945*, 48–49, 66–67.
36. Hata Hisako, "Servants of the Inner Quarters," in *Servants of the Dynasty: Palace Women in World History*, ed. Anne Walthall (Berkeley: University of California Press, 2008), 186; Mitamura Engyo, *Goten jochū* (Tokyo: Seiabō, 1982), 34, 52–54.
37. Janine Sawada, "Sexual Relations as Religious Practice in the Late Tokugawa Period: Fujidō," *Journal of Japanese Studies* 32, no. 2 (2006): 346–49, 351–62; Miyazaki Fumiko, "Female Pilgrims and Mt. Fuji: Changing Perspectives on the Exclusion of Women," *Monumenta Nipponica* 60, no. 3 (2005): 348–51.
38. Miyazaki, "Female Pilgrims and Mt. Fuji," 353–76.
39. Robert Ellwood, *Tenrikyo: A Pilgrimage Faith* (Tenri City: Tenri University, 1982), 37–51; Helen Hardacre, "The Shaman and Her Transformations: The Construction of Gender in Motifs of Religious Action," in *Gender and Japanese History*, vol. 1, ed. Wakita Haruko, Anne Bouchy, and Ueno Chizuko (Osaka: Osaka University Press, 1999), 100–112.
40. Ulrike Wöhr, *Frauen und die neuen Religionen: Die Religionsbegründerinnen Nakayama Miki und Deguchi Nao* (Vienna: Universität Wien Institut für Japanologie, 1989), 63; Yamashita Akiko, "Tenrin-o and Henjo-nanshi: Two Women Founders of New Religions," *Japanese Religions* 25, no. 1 (2002): 94; Hardacre, "The Shaman and Her Transformations," 110.
41. Barbara Ambros, "Nakayama Miki's Views of Women and Their Bodies in the Context of Nineteenth Century Japanese Religions," *Tenri Journal of Religion* 41 (2012): 1–31.
42. Wöhr, *Frauen und die neuen Religionen*, 62–63.
43. Oguri Junko, *Nihon no kindai shakai to Tenrikyō* (Tokyo: Hyōronsha, 1969); Kasahara Kazuo, "Mizukara kami ni natta josei," in *Nihon joseishi 5: teikō ni mezameru onna*, ed. Kasahara Kazuo (Tokyo: Hyōronsha, 1973), 167–216; Yamashita, "Tenrin-o and Henjo-nanshi," 97; Hardacre, "The Shaman and Her Transformations," 106–7.
44. Wöhr, *Frauen und die neuen Religionen*, 38, 54–55; Ambros, "Nakayama Miki's Views of Women and Their Bodies," 99–105.

CHAPTER 7. IMPERIAL JAPAN

1. Cited in Sekiguchi Sumiko, "Confucian Morals and the Making of a 'Good Wife and Wise Mother': From 'Between Husband and Wife There Is Distinction' to 'As Husbands and Wives Be Harmonious,'" *Social Science Japan Journal* 13, no. 1 (2010): 101.

2. Sekiguchi, "Confucian Morals and the Making of a 'Good Wife and Wise Mother,'" 101–2.

3. Igeta Midori, "Women's Role: A Channel for Power," in *Women and Religion in Japan*, ed. Okuda Akiko and Okano Haruko (Wiesbaden: Harrassowitz, 1998), 129–33; Toshitani Nobuyoshi, "The Reform of Japanese Family Law and Changes in the Family System," *U.S.-Japan Women's Journal*, English supplement, 6 (1994): 66–82; Kaneko Sachiko, "The Struggle for Legal Rights and Reforms: A Historical View," in *Transforming Japan: How Feminism and Diversity Are Making a Difference*, ed. Kumiko Fujimura-Fanselow (New York: Feminist Press, 2011), 4–5.

4. Shibahara Takeo, "Through Americanized Japanese Woman's Eyes: Tsuda Umeko and the Women's Movement in Japan in the 1910s," *Journal of Asia Pacific Studies* 1, no. 2 (2010): 227.

5. Harald Fuess, *Divorce in Japan: Family, Gender, and the State* (Stanford: Stanford University Press, 2004), 56–57; Yasutake Rumi, "Transnational Women's Activism: The Woman's Christian Temperance Union in Japan and Beyond, 1858–1920" (Ph.D. diss., University of California, Los Angeles, 1998), 18–19.

6. Sharon Sievers, *Flowers in Salt: The Beginnings of Feminist Consciousness in Modern Japan* (Stanford: Stanford University Press, 1983), 16–22; Sekiguchi, "Confucian Morals and the Making of a 'Good Wife and Wise Mother,'" 96–98; Vera Mackie, *Feminism in Modern Japan* (Cambridge: Cambridge University Press, 2003), 16–19.

7. Sievers, *Flowers in Salt*, 22–24.

8. Kathleen Uno, "Womanhood, War and Empire: Transmutations of 'Good Wife, Wise Mother' before 1931," in *Gendering Modern Japanese History*, ed. Barbara Molony and Kathleen Uno (Cambridge: Harvard University Asia Center, 2005), 493–519; Kathleen Uno, "The Death of 'Good Wife, Wise Mother,'" in *Postwar Japan as History*, ed. Andrew Gordon (Berkeley: University of California Press, 1993), 293–322; Mackie, *Feminism in Modern Japan*, 32–36; Katō Shūichi, "Ai seyo, umeyo, yori takaki shuzoku no tame ni," in *Shirīzu sei o tou 3: kyōdōtai*, ed. Ōba Takeshi et al. (Tokyo: Senshū Daigaku Shuppankyoku, 1997), 203–53.

9. Yasutake, "Transnational Women's Activism," 2.

10. Barbara Welter, "The Cult of True Womanhood: 1820–1860," *American Quarterly* 18, no. 2.1 (1966): 151–74.

11. Mackie, *Feminism in Modern Japan*, 29–30; Yasutake, "Transnational Women's Activism"; Yang Sunyoung, "Kantō daishinsai to baishō undō: Nihon Kirisutokyō

fujin kyōfūkai no katsudō o chūshin ni," *Kokuritsu josei kyōiku kaikan kenkyū kiyō* 9 (2005): 95–105; Amy Stanley, *Selling Women: Prostitution and the Household in Early Modern Japan* (Berkeley: University of California Press, 2012).

12. Mackie, *Feminism in Modern Japan*, 36; Yasutake, "Transnational Women's Activism," 17, 24–66.

13. Tsuda Ume, *Woman's Life in Japan* (Philadelphia: Board of Foreign Missions, Reformed Church in the United States, n.d.), 7.

14. Tsuda Ume, *The Attic Letters: Ume Tsuda's Correspondence to Her American Mother*, ed. Furuki Yoshiko (New York: Weatherhill, 1991), 105.

15. Tsuda, *Woman's Life in Japan*, 8.

16. Sally Hasting, "American Culture and Higher Education for Japanese Women," *Feminist Studies* 19, no. 3 (1993): 617–27; Linda Johnson, "Tsuda Umeko and a Transnational Network Supporting Women's Higher Education in Japan during the Victorian Era," *American Educational History Journal* 37, nos. 1–2 (2010): 475–79; Helen Parker, "Women, Christianity, and Internationalism in Early Twentieth-Century Japan: Tsuda Ume, Caroline Macdonald and the Founding of the Young Women's Christian Association in Japan," in *Japanese Women Emerging from Subservience, 1868–1945*, ed. Hiroko Tomida and Gordon Daniels (Folkestone: Global Oriental, 2005), 178–91; Shibahara, "Through Americanized Japanese Woman's Eyes."

17. Uchino Kumiko, "The Status Elevation Process of Sōtō Sect Nuns in Modern Japan," *Japanese Journal of Religious Studies* 10, nos. 2–3 (1983): 179.

18. Richard Jaffe, *Neither Monk nor Layman: Clerical Marriage in Modern Japanese Buddhism* (Princeton: Princeton University Press, 2001), 8, 234.

19. Uchino, "Status Elevation Process of Sōtō Sect Nuns," 180.

20. Paula Arai, *Women Living Zen: Japanese Sōtō Buddhist Nuns* (New York: Oxford University Press, 1999), 52–53; Uchino, "Status Elevation Process of Sōtō Sect Nuns," 180–81.

21. Uchino, "Status Elevation Process of Sōtō Sect Nuns," 181–85.

22. Miyake Hitoshi, "Kingendai no sangaku shūkyō to shugendo: shinbutsu bunrirei to shintō shirei e no taiō o chūshin ni," *Meiji shōtoku kinen gakkai kiyō* 43 (2006): 48.

23. Gina Cogan, "Time Capsules for Tradition: Repositioning Imperial Convents for the Meiji Period," *U.S.-Japan Women's Journal* 30–31 (2006): 81–83, 87–97.

24. Ishizuki Shizue, "Kindai Nihon Bukkyō fujinkai ni tsuite: Gifuken ni kansuru shiryō shōkai o chūshin ni," *Ōka gakuen daigaku kenkyū kiyō* 2 (2000): 117–29; Nishiguchi Junko, "Murakumo Nichiei," in *Asahi Nihon rekishi jinbutsu jiten*, ed. Asahi Shinbunsha (Tokyo: Asahi Shinbunsha, 1994), 1677; Ichikawa Seigaku, *Kinsei joryū shodō meika shiden* (Tokyo: Nihon Tosho Sentā, 1991), 76.

25. Helen Hardacre, *Shinto and the State, 1868–1988* (Princeton: Princeton University Press, 1989), 60–63; Odaira Mika, *Josei shinshoku no kindai* (Tokyo: Perikansha, 2009), 201–21.

26. Personal communication with Helen Hardacre, 13 May 2011; Jingūshichō, eds., *Jingū: Meiji hyakunenshi*, vol. 1 (Ise-shi: Jingūshchō, 1968), 192–95, 369.

27. Odaira, *Josei shinshoku no kindai*, 221–26.

28. Hardacre, *Shinto and the State*, 63.

29. Odaira, *Josei shinshoku no kindai*, 251–52.

30. Miyake, "Kingendai no sangaku shūkyō to shugendō," 48; Odaira, *Josei shinshoku no kindai*, 247–48.

31. Gerald Figal, *Civilization and Monsters: Spirits of Modernity in Meiji Japan* (Durham: Duke University Press, 1999), 92–104; Ikegami Yoshimasa, "Local Newspaper Coverage of Folk Shamans in Aomori Prefecture," in *Folk Beliefs in Modern Japan*, ed. Inoue Nobutaka (Tokyo: Kokugakuin University, 1994), 9–91; Ōhashi Hidetoshi, "Okinawa shamanizumu no rekishi: yuta kin'atsu no shosō to haikei," *Tōhoku daigaku bungakubu kenkyū nenpō* 32 (1982): 106–41.

32. William Lindsey, *Fertility and Pleasure: Ritual and Sexual Values in Tokugawa Japan* (Honolulu: University of Hawai'i Press, 2007), 71–87.

33. Ishii Kenji, "Shinzen kekkonshiki ni miru 'ie' no henbō to kojin no sōshutsu," *Meiji shōtoku kinen gakkai kiyō* 43 (2006): 95–98.

34. Hardacre, *Shinto and the State*, 22–23, 49, 111.

35. Donald Keene, *Emperor of Japan: Meiji and His World, 1852–1912* (New York: Columbia University Press, 2002), 172–73, 321, 554–55, 717–18.

36. Fuess, *Divorce in Japan*, 119–43; Ishii, "Shinzen kekkonshiki ni miru 'ie' no henbō to kojin no sōshutsu," 94–98.

37. Kaneko Juri, "'Onna wa dai' saikō," in *Josei to shūkyō no kindaishi*, ed. Okuda Akiko (Tokyo: San'ichi Shobō, 1995), 52; Ikegami, "Local Newspaper Coverage of Folk Shamans in Aomori Prefecture," 16–21.

38. Johannes Laube, *Oyagami: Die heutige Gottesvorstellung der Tenrikyō* (Wiesbaden: Harrassowitz, 1978), 64–68; Kaneko, "'Onna wa dai' saikō."

39. Kaneko, "'Onna wa dai' saikō," 48–53; Horiuchi Midori, "'Michi no dai' to josei," *Tenri kyōgaku kenkyū* 32 (1994): 63–78; Horiuchi Midori, "The 'Foundation of the Path' and Women: Women Appearing in 'Senjin no omokage' in the *Michinodai*," *Tenri Journal of Religion* 30 (2002): 65–82.

40. Tenrikyō Church Headquarters, ed., *A Short History of Tenrikyō* (Tenri City: Headquarters of Tenrikyō Church, 1958), 165.

41. Emily Groszos Ooms, *Women and Millenarian Protest in Meiji Japan: Deguchi Nao and Ōmotokyō* (Ithaca: East Asia Program, Cornell University, 1993), 23–32; Helen Hardacre, "Gender and the Millennium in Ōmoto: The Limits of Religious Innovation," in *Innovation in Religious Traditions*, ed. Michael Williams and Collette Cox (The Hague: Mouton, 1992), 217.

42. Ooms, *Women and Millenarian Protest in Meiji Japan*, 5–9, 45–53; Hardacre, "Gender and the Millennium in Ōmoto," 217–18.

43. Ooms, *Women and Millenarian Protest in Meiji Japan*, 17–19, 50–57.

44. Hardacre, "Gender and the Millennium in Ōmoto," 220–23.

CHAPTER 8. THE POSTWAR PERIOD

1. Vera Mackie, *Feminism in Modern Japan* (Cambridge: Cambridge University Press, 2003), 122–23.

2. Mackie, *Feminism in Modern Japan*, 121–26; John Dower, *Embracing Defeat: Japan in the Wake of World War II* (New York: Norton, 1999), 364–70; Inoue Kyōko, *MacArthur's Japanese Constitution: A Linguistic and Cultural Study of Its Making* (Chicago: University of Chicago Press, 1991), 276–79, 282–83.

3. Inoue, *MacArthur's Japanese Constitution*, 279.

4. Christian Winkler, *The Quest for Japan's New Constitution: An Analysis of Visions and Constitutional Reform Proposals, 1980–2009* (London: Routledge, 2011), 163, 186–87; Hashimoto Akiko and John Traphagan, eds., *Imagined Families, Lived Families: Culture and Kinship in Contemporary Japan* (Albany: State University of New York Press, 2008), 6–7.

5. Kathleen Uno, "The Death of 'Good Wife, Wise Mother,' " in *Postwar Japan as History*, ed. Andrew Gordon (Berkeley: University of California Press, 1993).

6. Uchino Kumiko, "The Status Elevation Process of Sōtō Sect Nuns in Modern Japan," *Japanese Journal of Religious Studies* 10, nos. 2–3 (1983): 185–88; Paula Arai, *Women Living Zen: Japanese Sōtō Buddhist Nuns* (New York: Oxford University Press, 1999), 63–74.

7. Arai, *Women Living Zen*, 125–29, 138–45, 162–63; Christlieb Jobst, "Befriedigung aus Tee und Blumen: Traditionelle Formen der Selbstverwirklichung," in *Die Frau in Japan*, ed. Gebhard Hielscher (Berlin: Erich Schmidt Verlag, 1984), 137–50.

8. Katō Etsuko, " 'Art' for Men, 'Manners' for Women: How Women Transformed the Tea Ceremony in Modern Japan," in *Women as Sites of Culture: Women's Roles in Cultural Formation from the Renaissance to the Twentieth Century*, ed. Susan Shifrin (Burlington, VT: Ashgate, 2002), 139–49; Katō Etsuko, *The Tea Ceremony and Women's Empowerment in Modern Japan: Bodies Re-Presenting the Past* (New York: RoutledgeCurzon, 2004), 61–68, 89–99.

9. Barbara Mori, "The Traditional Arts as Leisure Activities for Contemporary Women," in *Re-imagining Japanese Women*, ed. Anne Imamura (Berkeley: University of California Press, 1996), 123.

10. Kawahashi Noriko, "*Jizoku* (Priests' Wives) in Sōtō Zen Buddhism: An Ambiguous Category," *Japanese Journal of Religious Studies* 22, nos. 1–2 (1995): 163–83; Kawahashi Noriko, "Feminist Buddhism as Praxis: Women in Traditional Buddhism," *Japanese Journal of Religious Studies* 30, nos. 3–4 (2003): 291–313; Stephen Covell, *Japanese Temple Buddhism: Worldliness in a Religion of Renunciation* (Honolulu: University of Hawai'i Press, 2005), 109–39; Jessica Starling, "A Family of Clerics: Temple Wives, Tradition and Change in Contemporary Jōdo Shinshū Temples" (Ph.D. diss., University of Virginia, 2012), 204–58.

11. Walter Edwards, *Modern Japan through Its Weddings: Gender, Person, and Society in Ritual Portrayal* (Stanford: Stanford University Press, 1989), 15–19, 42–47, 50–51; Ofra Goldstein-Gidoni, *Packaged Japaneseness: Weddings, Business and Brides*

(Honolulu: University of Hawai'i Press, 1997), 22–24, 33–47, 59; Robert Smith, "Wedding and Funeral Ritual: Analysing a Moving Target," in *Ceremony and Ritual in Japan: Religious Practices in an Industrialized Society*, ed. Jan van Bremen and Dolores Martinez (London: Routledge, 1995), 29.

12. Joy Hendry, *Marriage in Changing Japan: Community and Society* (Rutland, VT: Charles Tuttle, 1981), 178–81; Smith, "Wedding and Funeral Ritual," 28–29; Goldstein-Gidoni, *Packaged Japaneseness*, 110–17, 124–25, 136.

13. Asoya Masahiko, "Shintō no kekkonkan," *Heiwa to shūkyō* 25 (2006): 61–63.

14. Benjamin Dorman, *Celebrity Gods: New Religion, Media, and Authority in Occupied Japan* (Honolulu: University of Hawai'i Press, 2011), 108–11, 115–18.

15. Dorman, *Celebrity Gods*, 79–81; Tensho-Kotai-Jingu-Kyo, *Prophet of Tabuse* (Tabuse: Tensho Kotai Jingu Kyo, 1954), 1–10.

16. Tensho-Kotai-Jingu-Kyo, *Prophet of Tabuse*, 121.

17. Dorman, *Celebrity Gods*, 81–89, 168–203; Carmen Blacker, *The Catalpa Bow: A Study of Shamanistic Practices in Japan* (London: George Allen and Unwin, 1986), 134–35; Tensho-Kotai-Jingu-Kyo, *Prophet of Tabuse*, 13–70.

18. Tensho-Kotai-Jingu-Kyo, *Prophet of Tabuse*, 8–9.

19. Helen Hardacre, *Lay Buddhism in Contemporary Japan: Reiyūkai Kyōdan* (Princeton: Princeton University Press, 1984), 11–53.

20. Hardacre, *Lay Buddhism in Contemporary Japan*, 98–126.

21. Hardacre, *Lay Buddhism in Contemporary Japan*, 208.

22. Hardacre, *Lay Buddhism in Contemporary Japan*, 188–223.

23. Levi McLaughlin, "Sōka Gakkai in Japan" (Ph.D. diss., Princeton University, 2009), 201–315.

24. Miyanaga Kuniko, "Social Reproduction and Transcendence: An Analysis of the Sekai Mahikari Bunmei Kyōdan, a Heterodox Religious Movement in Contemporary Japan" (Ph.D. diss., University of British Columbia, 1983), 74.

25. Richard Young, "Magic and Morality in Modern Japanese Exorcistic Technologies: A Study of Mahikari," *Japanese Journal of Religious Studies* 17, no. 1 (1990): 35–36.

26. Young, "Magic and Morality in Modern Japanese Exorcistic Technologies," 36–39.

27. Winston Davis, *Dōjō: Magic and Exorcism in Modern Japan* (Stanford: Stanford University Press, 1980), 162.

28. Davis, *Dōjō*, 167.

29. Davis, *Dōjō*, 147.

30. Davis, *Dōjō*, 162–85.

31. Davis, *Dōjō*, 187–97; Miyanaga, "Social Reproduction and Transcendence," 216–17.

32. Elizabeth Harrison, "Strands of Complexity: The Emergence of *mizuko kuyō* in Postwar Japan," *Journal of the American Academy of Religion* 67 (1999): 769–96; Helen Hardacre, *Marketing the Menacing Fetus in Japan* (Berkeley: University of California Press, 1997), 56–60.

33. Hardacre, *Marketing the Menacing Fetus in Japan*, 60–73.

34. Komatsu Kayoko, "*Mizuko kuyō* and New Age Concepts of Reincarnation," *Japanese Journal of Religious Studies* 30, nos. 3–4 (2003): 263.

35. Hardacre, *Marketing the Menacing Fetus in Japan*, 77–91, 155–56.

36. Harrison, "Strands of Complexity."

37. Kawahashi Noriko, "Mizuko kuyō," in *Josei to kyōdan: Nihon shūkyō no omote to ura*, ed. Nomura Fumiko and Usui Atsuko (Tokyo: Hābetsutosha, 1996), 139.

38. Hardacre, *Marketing the Menacing Fetus in Japan*, 77–97; Nitta Mitsuko, "Nihon no shūkyō to mizuko kuyō," in *Mizuko kuyō: gendai shakai no fuan to iyashi*, ed. Takahashi Saburō (Kyoto: Kōrosha, 1999), 177–84.

39. Bardwell Smith, *Narratives of Sorrow and Dignity: Japanese Women, Pregnancy Loss, and Modern Rituals of Grieving* (New York: Oxford University Press, 2013).

40. On gender performance, see Judith Butler, *Gender Trouble: Feminism and the Subversion of Identity* (New York: Routledge, 1990), 134–41.

41. They resemble the Islamic women studied by Saba Mahmood who affirmed conservative religious ideas in order to further their own agendas. Saba Mahmood, *Politics of Piety: The Islamic Revival and the Feminist Subject* (Princeton: Princeton University Press, 2005), 5–6.

CHAPTER 9. THE LOST DECADES

1. Jeff Kingston, *Japan's Quiet Transformation: Social Change and Civil Society in the Twenty-First Century* (New York: RoutledgeCurzon, 2004), 1–17.

2. Barbara Ambros, *Bones of Contention: Animals and Religion in Contemporary Japan* (Honolulu: University of Hawai'i Press, 2012), 91–93; Ben Dorman, "Representing Ancestor Worship as 'Non-Religious': Hosoki Kazuko's Divination in the Post-Aum Era," *Nova Religio* 10, no. 3 (2006): 45–46; Shimazono Susumu, *From Salvation to Spirituality: Popular Religious Movements in Modern Japan* (Melbourne: Transpacific Press, 2004), 275–76; Shimazono Susumu, *Supirichuariti no kōryū: shinreisei bunka to sono shūhen* (Tokyo: Iwanami Shoten, 2007), 275–78.

3. Kingston, *Japan's Quiet Transformation*, 32–39.

4. Mark Driscoll, "Debt and Denunciation in Post-Bubble Japan: On the Two Freeters," *Cultural Critique* 65 (2007): 170–71, 175–77.

5. Florian Coulmas, *Population Decline and Ageing in Japan: The Social Consequences* (New York: Routledge, 2007), 11–12, 51–52; Kingston, *Japan's Quiet Transformation*, 279.

6. Coulmas, *Population Decline and Ageing in Japan*, 9–12; Kingston, *Japan's Quiet Transformation*, 279.

7. Harald Fuess, *Divorce in Japan: Family, Gender, and the State* (Stanford: Stanford University Press, 2004), 144–66; Hoshino Yutaka, "Rikonji no nenkin jukyūken bunkatsu seido ni taisuru jakkan no kentō: kaisei kōsei nenkin hokenhō no kōzō to mondaiten," *Tsukuba hōsei* 38 (2005): 173–92.

8. Michael Fisch, "The Rise of the Chapel Wedding in Japan: Simulation and

Performance," *Japanese Journal of Religious Studies* 28, nos. 1–2 (2001): 58, 64–65, 70–75.

9. Mark Rowe, "Grave Changes: Scattering Ashes in Contemporary Japan," *Japanese Journal of Religious Studies* 30, nos. 1–2 (2003): 87, 111; Mark Rowe, *Bonds of the Dead: Temples, Burial, and the Transformation of Contemporary Japanese Buddhism* (Chicago: University of Chicago Press, 2011), 87–99; Inoue Haruyo, *Haka o meguru kazokuron: dare ga hairu ka, dare ga mamoru ka* (Tokyo: Heibonsha, 2000), 28–52.

10. Ambros, *Bones of Contention*, 144–53.

11. Christian Winkler, *The Quest for Japan's New Constitution: An Analysis of Visions and Constitutional Reform Proposals, 1980–2009* (London: Routledge, 2011), 162–66; Helen Hardacre, "Constitutional Revision and Japanese Religions," *Japanese Studies* 25, no. 3 (2005): 240–45.

12. Kaneko Juri, "Can Tenrikyō Transcend the Modern Family? From a Humanistic Understanding of *Hinagata* and Narratives of Foster Care Activities," *Japanese Journal of Religious Studies* 30, nos. 3–4 (2003): 246.

13. Iida Teruaki, "Josei, bosei, kekkon, katei ni tsuite," *Araki tōryō* 161 (1990): 20–31.

14. Cited in Kaneko, "Can Tenrikyō Transcend the Modern Family?," 245–46.

15. Horiuchi Midori, "'Michi no dai' to josei," *Tenri kyōgaku kenkyū* 32 (1994): 63–78; Horiuchi Midori, "The 'Foundation of the Path' and Women: Women Appearing in 'Senjin no omokage' in the *Michinodai*," *Tenri Journal of Religion* 30 (2002): 65–82; Horiuchi Midori, "No Distinction between Male and Female Pines: Environmental Issues and Women," *Tenri Journal of Religion* 31 (2003): 53–76; Kaneko Juri, "'Onna wa dai' saikō," in *Josei to shūkyō no kindaishi*, ed. Okuda Akiko (Tokyo: San'ichi Shobō, 1995); Kaneko, "Can Tenrikyō Transcend the Modern Family?"; Kaneko Juri, "Tenrikyō ni okeru satooya katsudō to jendā," *Shūkyō kenkyū* 77, no. 4 (2004): 1237–38.

16. Kawahashi Noriko, "Feminist Buddhism as Praxis: Women in Traditional Buddhism," *Japanese Journal of Religious Studies* 30, nos. 3–4 (2003): 300–309; Kawahashi Noriko, "Hajime ni," in *Shin Bukkyō to jendā: joseitachi no chōsen*, ed. Josei to Bukkyō Tōkai-Kantō Nettowāku (Tokyo: Nashi no Ki Sha, 2011), 3.

17. Kawahashi, "Feminist Buddhism," 300–309.

18. Kawahashi Noriko, "*Jizoku* (Priests' Wives) in Sōtō Zen Buddhism: An Ambiguous Category," *Japanese Journal of Religious Studies* 22, nos. 1–2 (1995): 163–83; Kawahashi, "Feminist Buddhism"; Stephen Covell, *Japanese Temple Buddhism: Worldliness in a Religion of Renunciation* (Honolulu: University of Hawai'i Press, 2005), 120–39.

19. Vera Mackie, *Feminism in Modern Japan* (Cambridge: Cambridge University Press, 2003), 174–225.

20. Levi McLaughlin, "Did Aum Change Everything?," *Japanese Journal of Religious Studies* 39, no. 1 (2012): 51–75.

21. Levi McLaughlin, "Sōka Gakkai in Japan" (Ph.D. diss., Princeton University, 2009), 201–315; McLaughlin, "Did Aum Change Everything?"

22. Inose Yūri, "Influential Factors in the Intergenerational Transmission of Religion: The Case of Sōka Gakkai in Hokkaido," *Japanese Journal of Religious Studies* 32, no. 2 (2005): 371–82.

23. Inose, "Influential Factors in the Intergenerational Transmission of Religion."

24. McLaughlin, "Sōka Gakkai in Japan," 201–315.

25. Usui Atsuko, "Women's 'Experience' in New Religious Movements: The Case of Shinnyoen," *Japanese Journal of Religious Studies* 30, nos. 3–4 (2003): 235–36.

26. Christal Whelan, "Shifting Paradigms and Mediating Media: Redefining a New Religion as 'Rational' in Contemporary Society," *Nova Religio* 10, no. 3 (2006): 59.

27. Usui, "Women's 'Experience' in New Religious Movements"; Bunkachō, eds., *Shūkyō nenkan: Heisei 23 nenban* (Tokyo: Gyōsei, 2012), 71.

28. Whelan, "Shifting Paradigms and Mediating Media," 61–68; Christal Whelan, "Religious Responses to Globalization in Japan: The Case of the God Light Association" (Ph.D. diss., Boston University, 2007), 92–93.

29. Whelan, "Religious Responses to Globalization in Japan," 78–84.

30. Shimazono, *From Salvation to Spirituality*, 164–77, 275–79, 290–92, 304; Shimazono, *Supirichuariti no kōryū*, 275–306.

31. Ioannis Gaitanidis, "At the Forefront of a 'Spiritual Business': Independent Professional Spiritual Therapists in Japan," *Japan Forum* 23, no. 2 (2011): 185–206.

32. Shimazono, *From Salvation to Spirituality*, 275–76.

33. Dorman, "Representing Ancestor Worship as 'Non-Religious,'" 32–53.

34. Komatsu Kayoko, "*Mizuko kuyō* and New Age Concepts of Reincarnation," *Japanese Journal of Religious Studies* 30, nos. 3–4 (2003): 268–74.

35. Katherine Matsuura, "Transformation and Expressions of Grief in *Mizuko Kuyō*: Mourning the Stillborn and Still-to-Be-Born" (M.A. thesis, Duke University, 2010), 21–27.

36. Suzuki Kentarō, "Divination in Contemporary Japan," *Japanese Journal of Religious Studies* 22, nos. 3–4 (1995): 256–63.

37. Gaitanidis, "At the Forefront of a 'Spiritual Business,'" 189–90.

38. Sakurai Yoshihide, "Gendai Nihon shakai to supirichuariti būmu," in *Karuto to supiritchuariti: gendai Nihon ni okeru "sukui" to "iyashi" no yukue*, ed. Sakurai Yoshihide (Kyoto: Minerva Shobō, 2009), 270; Sakurai Yoshihide, *Rei to kane: supiricharu bijinesu no kōzō* (Tokyo: Shinchōsha, 2009), 10.

39. Ioannis Gaitanidis, "Socio-Economic Aspects of the 'Spiritual Business' in Japan: A Survey of Professional Spiritual Therapists," *Shūkyō to shakai* 16 (2010): 143–60; Gaitanidis, "At the Forefront of a 'Spiritual Business.'"

40. Laura Miller, "Tantalizing Tarot and Cute Cartomancy in Japan," *Japanese Studies* 31, no. 1 (2011): 73–91.

41. Miller, "Tantalizing Tarot and Cute Cartomancy in Japan," 85, 88.

42. Miller, "Tantalizing Tarot and Cute Cartomancy in Japan," 89.

43. Kumata Katsuo, "Shūkyō shinri fukkō undo ni okeru Nihon teki bosei no isō: GLAkei shokyōdan no jirei kenkyū yori," *Shūkyō to shakai* 3 (1997): 38.

CONCLUSION

1. Kwok Pui-lan, "Unbinding Our Feet: Saving Brown Women and Feminist Religious Discourse," in *Postcolonialism, Feminism and Religious Discourse*, ed. Laura Donaldson and Kwok Pui-lan (New York: Routledge, 2002), 70–71.

WORKS CITED

Ambros, Barbara. *Bones of Contention: Animals and Religion in Contemporary Japan.* Honolulu: University of Hawai'i Press, 2012.

———. "Liminal Journeys: Noblewomen's Pilgrimages in the Heian Period." *Japanese Journal of Religious Studies* 24, nos. 3–4 (1997): 302–45.

———. "Nakayama Miki's Views of Women and Their Bodies in the Context of Nineteenth Century Japanese Religions." *Tenri Journal of Religion* 41 (2012): 1–31.

Amino, Yoshihiko. *Rethinking Japanese History.* Ann Arbor: Center for Japanese Studies, University of Michigan, 2012.

Arai, Paula. *Women Living Zen: Japanese Sōtō Buddhist Nuns.* New York: Oxford University Press, 1999.

Asoya, Masahiko. "Shintō no kekkonkan." *Heiwa to shūkyō* 25 (2006): 60–72.

Aston, William George, trans. *Nihongi: Chronicles of Japan from the Earliest Times to A.D. 697.* Rutland, VT: Charles Tuttle, 1972.

Bargen, Doris. *A Woman's Weapon: Spirit Possession in "The Tale of Genji."* Honolulu: University of Hawai'i Press, 1997.

Bathgate, Michael. *The Fox's Craft in Japanese Religion and Folklore: Shapeshifters, Transformations, and Duplicities.* New York: Routledge, 2004.

Bellah, Robert. *Tokugawa Religion: The Cultural Roots of Modern Japan.* New York: Free Press, 1985.

Blacker, Carmen. *The Catalpa Bow: A Study of Shamanistic Practices in Japan.* London: George Allen and Unwin, 1986.

Bock, Felicia. *Engishiki: Procedures of the Engi Era, Books I–V.* Tokyo: Sophia University, 1970.

———. *Engishiki: Procedures of the Engi Era, Books VI–X.* Tokyo: Sophia University, 1972.

Bowring, Richard. *The Religious Traditions of Japan, 500–1600.* Cambridge: Cambridge University Press, 2005.

Breen, John, and Mark Teeuwen. *A New History of Shinto.* Chichester: Wiley-Blackwell, 2010.

Bunkachō, ed. *Shūkyō nenkan: Heisei 23 nenban.* Tokyo: Gyōsei, 2012.

Butler, Judith. *Gender Trouble: Feminism and the Subversion of Identity.* New York: Routledge, 1990.

Chikusa, Masaaki. "The Formation and Growth of Buddhist Nun Communities in China." In *Engendering Faith: Women and Buddhism in Premodern Japan*, edited by Barbara Ruch, 3–20. Ann Arbor: University of Michigan Center for Japanese Studies, 2002.

Childs, Margaret. "The Value of Vulnerability: Sexual Coercion and the Nature of Love in Japanese Court Literature." *Journal of Asian Studies* 58, no. 4 (1999): 1059–79.

Choo, Jessey. "Historicized Ritual and Ritualized History: Women's Lifecycle in Late Medieval China (600–1000 AD)." Ph.D. diss., Princeton University, 2009.

Chung, Young-Ah. "Heian Noblewomen's Pilgrimage: The Language of Gendered Discontent and (Re)construction of the Self." *West Virginia University Philological Papers* 48 (2001): 1–8.

Cogan, Gina. *The Princess Nun: Bunchi, Buddhist Reform, and Gender in Early Edo Japan.* Cambridge: Harvard University Asia Center, 2014.

———. "Time Capsules for Tradition: Repositioning Imperial Convents for the Meiji Period." *U.S.-Japan Women's Journal* 30–31 (2006): 80–104.

Como, Michael. *Weaving and Binding: Immigrant Gods and Female Immortals in Ancient Japan.* Honolulu: University of Hawai'i Press, 2009.

Coulmas, Florian. *Population Decline and Ageing in Japan: The Social Consequences.* New York: Routledge, 2007.

Covell, Stephen. *Japanese Temple Buddhism: Worldliness in a Religion of Renunciation.* Honolulu: University of Hawai'i Press, 2005.

Cranston, Edwin. *The Izumi Shikibu Diary: A Romance of the Heian Court.* Cambridge: Harvard University Press, 1969.

Davis, Winston. *Dōjō: Magic and Exorcism in Modern Japan.* Stanford: Stanford University Press, 1980.

Deal, William. "Women and Japanese Buddhism: Tales of Birth in the Pure Land." In *Religions of Japan in Practice*, edited by George Tanabe, 176–84. Princeton: Princeton University Press, 1999.

Dobbins, James. *Letters of the Nun Eshinni: Images of Pure Land Buddhism in Medieval Japan.* Honolulu: University of Hawai'i Press, 2004.

———. "Women's Birth in the Pure Land as Women: Intimations from the Letters of Eshinni." *Eastern Buddhist* 28, no. 1 (1995): 108–22.

Dorman, Benjamin. *Celebrity Gods: New Religion, Media, and Authority in Occupied Japan.* Honolulu: University of Hawai'i Press, 2011.

———. "Representing Ancestor Worship as 'Non-Religious': Hosoki Kazuko's Divination in the Post-Aum Era." *Nova Religio* 10, no. 3 (2006): 32–53.

Dower, John. *Embracing Defeat: Japan in the Wake of World War II.* New York: Norton, 1999.

Driscoll, Mark. "Debt and Denunciation in Post-Bubble Japan: On the Two Freeters." *Cultural Critique* 65 (2007): 164–87.

Dutton, Ann. "Temple Divorce in Tokugawa Japan: A Survey of Documentation on Tōkeiji and Mantokuji." In *Engendering Faith: Women and Buddhism in Premodern Japan*, edited by Barbara Ruch, 209–45. Ann Arbor: University of Michigan Center for Japanese Studies, 2002.

Dykstra, Yoshiko. *Miraculous Tales of the Lotus Sutra from Ancient Japan*. Honolulu: University of Hawai'i Press, 1983.

Ebersole, Gary. *Ritual Poetry and the Politics of Death in Early Japan*. Princeton: Princeton University Press, 1989.

Edwards, Walter. *Modern Japan through Its Weddings: Gender, Person, and Society in Ritual Portrayal*. Stanford: Stanford University Press, 1989.

Elisonas, Jurgis. "The Evangelic Furnace: Japan's First Encounter with the West." In *Sources of Japanese Tradition*, vol. 2, *1600–2000*, pt. 1, *1600–1868*, compiled by William Theodore de Bary, Carol Gluck, and Arthur E. Tiedemann, 127–57. New York: Columbia University Press, 2006.

Ellwood, Robert. *Tenrikyo: A Pilgrimage Faith*. Tenri City: Tenri University, 1982.

Esaka, Teruya. *Nihon dogū*. Tokyo: Rokkō Shuppan, 1990.

Farris, Wayne. *Sacred Texts and Buried Treasures: Issues in the Historical Archaeology of Ancient Japan*. Honolulu: University of Hawai'i Press, 1998.

Faure, Bernard. *The Power of Denial: Buddhism, Purity, and Gender*. Princeton: Princeton University Press, 2003.

Figal, Gerald. *Civilization and Monsters: Spirits of Modernity in Meiji Japan*. Durham: Duke University Press, 1999.

Fisch, Michael. "The Rise of the Chapel Wedding in Japan: Simulation and Performance." *Japanese Journal of Religious Studies* 28, nos. 1–2 (2001): 57–76.

Fuess, Harald. *Divorce in Japan: Family, Gender, and the State*. Stanford: Stanford University Press, 2004.

Fukuta, Ajio. *Tera, haka, senzo no minzokugaku*. Tokyo: Taiga Shobō, 2004.

Gaitanidis, Ioannis. "At the Forefront of a 'Spiritual Business': Independent Professional Spiritual Therapists in Japan." *Japan Forum* 23, no. 2 (2011): 185–206.

———. "Socio-Economic Aspects of the 'Spiritual Business' in Japan: A Survey of Professional Spiritual Therapists." *Shūkyō to shakai* 16 (2010): 143–60.

Glassman, Hank. "At the Crossroads of Birth and Death: The Blood Pool Hell and Postmortem Fetal Extraction." In *Death and the Afterlife in Japanese Buddhism*, edited by Jacqueline I. Stone and Mariko Namba Walter, 175–206. Honolulu: University of Hawai'i Press, 2008.

———. "Chinese Buddhist Death Ritual and the Transformation of Japanese Kinship." In *The Buddhist Dead: Practices, Discourses, Representations*, edited by Brian Cuevas and Jacqueline Stone, 378–404. Honolulu: University of Hawai'i Press, 2007.

Goldstein-Gidoni, Ofra. *Packaged Japaneseness: Weddings, Business and Brides*. Honolulu: University of Hawai'i Press, 1997.

Goodwin, Janet. *Selling Songs and Smiles: The Sex Trade in Heian and Kamakura Japan*. Honolulu: University of Hawai'i Press, 2007.

Goodwin, Janet R., Bettina Gramlich-Oka, Elizabeth A. Leicester, Yuki Terazawa, and Anne Walthall. "Solitary Thoughts: A Translation of Tadano Makuzu's *Hitori kangae* (1)." *Monumenta Nipponica* 56, no. 1 (2001): 21–38.

Gramlich-Oka, Bettina. "Tadano Makuzu and Her *Hitori kangae*." *Monumenta Nipponica* 56, no. 1 (2001): 1–20.

Grapard, Allan. "Visions of Excess and Excesses of Vision: Women and Transgression in Japanese Myth." *Japanese Journal of Religious Studies* 18, no. 1 (1991): 3–22.

Groemer, Gerald. "Female Shamans in Eastern Japan during the Edo Period." *Asian Folklore Studies* 66 (2007): 27–53.

Groner, Paul. "The Vicissitudes in the Ordination of Japanese 'Nuns' during the Eighth through the Tenth Centuries." In *Engendering Faith: Women and Buddhism in Premodern Japan*, edited by Barbara Ruch, 65–108. Ann Arbor: University of Michigan Center for Japanese Studies, 2002.

Hardacre, Helen. "Constitutional Revision and Japanese Religions." *Japanese Studies* 25, no. 3 (2005): 235–47.

———. "Gender and the Millennium in Ōmoto: The Limits of Religious Innovation." In *Innovation in Religious Traditions*, edited by Michael Williams and Collette Cox, 215–39. The Hague: Mouton, 1992.

———. *Lay Buddhism in Contemporary Japan: Reiyūkai Kyōdan*. Princeton: Princeton University Press, 1984.

———. *Marketing the Menacing Fetus in Japan*. Berkeley: University of California Press, 1997.

———. "The Shaman and Her Transformations: The Construction of Gender in Motifs of Religious Action." In *Gender and Japanese History*, vol. 1, edited by Wakita Haruko, Anne Bouchy, and Ueno Chizuko, 87–119. Osaka: Osaka University Press, 1999.

———. *Shinto and the State, 1868–1988*. Princeton: Princeton University Press, 1989.

Harrison, Elizabeth. "Strands of Complexity: The Emergence of *mizuko kuyō* in Postwar Japan." *Journal of the American Academy of Religion* 67 (1999): 769–96.

Hashimoto, Akiko, and John Traphagan, eds. *Imagined Families, Lived Families: Culture and Kinship in Contemporary Japan*. Albany: State University of New York Press, 2008.

Hasting, Sally. "American Culture and Higher Education for Japanese Women." *Feminist Studies* 19, no. 3 (1993): 617–27.

Hata, Hisako. "Servants of the Inner Quarters." In *Servants of the Dynasty: Palace Women in World History*, edited by Anne Walthall, 172–90. Berkeley: University of California Press, 2008.

Heidegger, Simone. *Die Frau im japanischen Buddhismus der Kamakurazeit*. Copenhagen: Seminar for Buddhist Studies, 1995.

Hendry, Joy. *Marriage in Changing Japan: Community and Society*. Rutland, VT: Charles Tuttle, 1981.

Hiratsuka, Raichō. *In the Beginning Was the Sun: The Autobiography of a Japanese Feminist*. Translated by Teruko Craig. New York: Columbia University Press, 2010.

Hongō, Masatsugu. "State Buddhism and Court Buddhism: The Role of Court Women in the Development of Buddhism from the Seventh to Ninth Centuries."

In *Engendering Faith: Women and Buddhism in Premodern Japan*, edited by Barbara Ruch, 41–61. Ann Arbor: University of Michigan Center for Japanese Studies, 2002.

Horiuchi, Midori. "The 'Foundation of the Path' and Women: Women Appearing in 'Senjin no omokage' in the *Michinodai*." *Tenri Journal of Religion* 30 (2002): 65–82.

———. "'Michi no dai' to josei." *Tenri kyōgaku kenkyū* 32 (1994): 63–78.

———. "No Distinction between Male and Female Pines: Environmental Issues and Women." *Tenri Journal of Religion* 31 (2003): 53–76.

Hoshino, Yutaka. "Rikonji no nenkin jukyūken bunkatsu seido ni taisuru jakkan no kentō: kaisei kōsei nenkin hokenhō no kōzō to mondaiten." *Tsukuba hōsei* 38 (2005): 173–92.

Hosokawa, Ryōichi. "Ōken to amadera: chūsei josei to shari shinkō." *Rettō no bunkashi* 5 (1988): 95–142.

Humberclaude, Pierre. "*Myōtei Mondō*: Une apologétique chrétienne japonais de 1605." *Monumenta Nipponica* 1 (1938): 223–56.

———. "*Myōtei Mondō*: Une apologétique chrétienne japonais de 1605." *Monumenta Nipponica* 2 (1939): 237–67.

Hur, Namlin. *Death and Social Order in Tokugawa Japan: Buddhism, Anti-Christianity, and the Danka System*. Cambridge: Harvard University Asia Center, 2007.

Ichikawa, Seigaku. *Kinsei joryū shodō meika shiden*. Tokyo: Nihon Tosho Sentā, 1991.

Idojiri kōkokan, ed. *Yasugatake Jōmon sekai saigen*. Tokyo: Shinchōsha, 1988.

Igeta, Midori. "Women's Role: A Channel for Power." In *Women and Religion in Japan*, edited by Okuda Akiko and Okano Haruko, 125–50. Wiesbaden: Harrassowitz, 1998.

Iida, Teruaki. "Josei, bosei, kekkon, katei ni tsuite." *Arakitōryō* 161 (1990): 20–31.

Ikegami, Eiko. *Bonds of Civility: Aesthetic Networks and the Political Origins of Japanese Culture*. Cambridge: Cambridge University Press, 2005.

Ikegami, Yoshimasa. "Local Newspaper Coverage of Folk Shamans in Aomori Prefecture." In *Folk Beliefs in Modern Japan*, edited by Inoue Nobutaka, 9–91. Tokyo: Kokugakuin University, 1994.

Imamura, Keiji. *Prehistoric Japan: New Perspectives on Insular East Asia*. Honolulu: University of Hawai'i Press, 1996.

Inose, Yūri. "Influential Factors in the Intergenerational Transmission of Religion: The Case of Sōka Gakkai in Hokkaido." *Japanese Journal of Religious Studies* 32, no. 2 (2005): 371–82.

Inoue, Haruyo. *Haka o meguru kazokuron: dare ga hairu ka, dare ga mamoru ka*. Tokyo: Heibonsha, 2000.

Inoue, Kyōko. *MacArthur's Japanese Constitution: A Linguistic and Cultural Study of Its Making*. Chicago: University of Chicago Press, 1991.

Ishii, Kenji. "Shinzen kekkonshiki ni miru 'ie' no henbō to kojin no sōshutsu." *Meiji shōtoku kinen gakkai kiyō* 43 (2006): 92–109.

Ishizuki, Shizue. "Kindai Nihon Bukkyō fujinkai ni tsuite: Gifuken ni kansuru shiryō shōkai o chūshin ni." *Ōka gakuen daigaku kenkyū kiyō* 2 (2000): 117–29.

Jaffe, Richard. *Neither Monk nor Layman: Clerical Marriage in Modern Japanese Buddhism.* Princeton: Princeton University Press, 2001.

Jingūshichō, ed. *Jingū: Meiji hyakunenshi.* Vol. 1. Ise-shi: Jingūshchō, 1968.

Jobst, Christlieb. "Befriedigung aus Tee und Blumen: Traditionelle Formen der Selbstverwirklichung." In *Die Frau in Japan,* edited by Gebhard Hielscher, 137–50. Berlin: Erich Schmidt Verlag, 1984.

Johnson, Linda. "Tsuda Umeko and a Transnational Network Supporting Women's Higher Education in Japan during the Victorian Era." *American Educational History Journal* 37, nos. 1–2 (2010): 473–91.

Kalland, Arne, and Pamela Asquith. *Japanese Images of Nature: Cultural Perspectives.* Richmond, Surrey: Curzon, 1997.

Kamens, Edward. *The Buddhist Poetry of the Great Kamo Priestess: Daisaiin Senshi and the "Hosshin Wakashū."* Ann Arbor: University of Michigan Center for Japanese Studies, 1990.

———. *The Three Jewels: A Study and Translation of Minamoto Tamenori's "Sanbōe."* Ann Arbor: University of Michigan Center for Japanese Studies, 1988.

Kaneko, Juri. "Can Tenrikyō Transcend the Modern Family? From a Humanistic Understanding of *Hinagata* and Narratives of Foster Care Activities." *Japanese Journal of Religious Studies* 30, nos. 3–4 (2003): 243–58.

———. "'Onna wa dai' saikō." In *Josei to shūkyō no kindaishi,* edited by Okuda Akiko, 45–77. Tokyo: San'ichi Shobō, 1995.

———. "Tenrikyō ni okeru satooya katsudō to jendā." *Shūkyō kenkyū* 77, no. 4 (2004): 1237–38.

Kaneko, Sachiko. "The Struggle for Legal Rights and Reforms: A Historical View." In *Transforming Japan: How Feminism and Diversity Are Making a Difference,* edited by Kumiko Fujimura-Fanselow, 3–14. New York: Feminist Press, 2011.

Kasahara, Kazuo. "Mizukara kami ni natta josei." In *Nihon joseishi 5: teikō ni mezameru onna,* edited by Kasahara Kazuo, 167–216. Tokyo: Hyōronsha, 1973.

Katō, Etsuko. "'Art' for Men, 'Manners' for Women: How Women Transformed the Tea Ceremony in Modern Japan." In *Women as Sites of Culture: Women's Roles in Cultural Formation from the Renaissance to the Twentieth Century,* edited by Susan Shifrin, 139–49. Burlington, VT: Ashgate, 2002.

———. *The Tea Ceremony and Women's Empowerment in Modern Japan: Bodies Re-Presenting the Past.* New York: RoutledgeCurzon, 2004.

Katō, Mieko. "Women's Associations and Religious Expression in the Medieval Japanese Village." In *Women and Class in Japanese History,* edited by Tonomura Hitomi, Anne Walthall, and Haruko Wakita, 119–33. Ann Arbor: University of Michigan, 1999.

Katō, Shūichi. "Ai seyo, umeyo, yori takaki shuzoku no tame ni." In *Shirīzu sei o tou 3: kyōdōtai,* edited by Ōba Takeshi, Kanegae Haruhiko, Hasegawa Mariko, Yamazaki

Kaoru, and Yamazaki Tsutomu, 203–53. Tokyo: Senshū Daigaku Shuppankyoku, 1997.

Katsuura, Noriko. "Tonsure Forms for Nuns: Classification of Nuns according to Hairstyle." In *Engendering Faith: Women and Buddhism in Premodern Japan*, edited by Barbara Ruch, 109–29. Ann Arbor: University of Michigan Center for Japanese Studies, 2002.

Kawahashi, Noriko. "Feminist Buddhism as Praxis: Women in Traditional Buddhism." *Japanese Journal of Religious Studies* 30, nos. 3–4 (2003): 291–313.

———. "Hajime ni." In *Shin Bukkyō to jendā: joseitachi no chōsen*, edited by Josei to Bukkyō Tōkai-Kantō Nettowāku, 3–9. Tokyo: Nashi no Ki Sha, 2011.

———. "*Jizoku* (Priests' Wives) in Sōtō Zen Buddhism: An Ambiguous Category." *Japanese Journal of Religious Studies* 22, nos. 1–2 (1995): 163–83.

———. "Mizuko kuyō." In *Josei to kyōdan: Nihon shūkyō no omote to ura*, edited by Nomura Fumiko and Usui Atsuko, 138–39. Tokyo: Hābetsutosha, 1996.

Kawashima, Terry. *Writing Margins: The Textual Construction of Gender in Heian and Kamakura Japan*. Cambridge: Harvard University Asia Center, 2001.

Keene, Donald. *Emperor of Japan: Meiji and His World, 1852–1912*. New York: Columbia University Press, 2002.

———, trans. *Essays in Idleness: The Tsurezuregusa of Kenkō*. New York: Columbia University Press, 1967.

———, trans. *Twenty Plays of the Nō Theatre*. New York: Columbia University Press, 1970.

Kelleher, Theresa. "Confucianism." In *Women in World Religions*, edited by Arvind Sharma, 135–59. Albany: State University of New York Press, 1987.

———. "Women's Education." In *Sources of East Asian Tradition*, vol. 1, *Premodern East Asia*, compiled by William Theodore de Bary, 410–27. New York: Columbia University Press, 2008.

Kidder, Edward. *Himiko and Japan's Elusive Chiefdom of Yamatai: Archaeology, History, and Mythology*. Honolulu: University of Hawai'i Press, 2007.

Kimbrough, Keller. *Buddhist Sermon-Ballads and Miracle Plays of Seventeenth-Century Japan*. New York: Columbia University Press, 2012.

———. "Translation: The Tale of Fuji Cave." Online only. *Japanese Journal of Religious Studies* 33, no. 2 (2006): 1–22. http://nirc.nanzan-u.ac.jp/nfile/2907.

Kingston, Jeff. *Japan's Quiet Transformation: Social Change and Civil Society in the Twenty-First Century*. New York: RoutledgeCurzon, 2004.

Klein, Susan. "Woman as Serpent: The Demonic Feminine in the Noh Play *Dōjōji*." In *Religious Reflections on the Human Body*, edited by Jane Marie Law, 100–136. Bloomington: Indiana University Press, 1995.

Ko, Dorothy. *Teachers of the Inner Chambers: Women and Culture in Seventeenth-Century China*. Stanford: Stanford University Press, 1994.

Komatsu, Kayoko. "*Mizuko kuyō* and New Age Concepts of Reincarnation." *Japanese Journal of Religious Studies* 30, nos. 3–4 (2003): 259–78.

Kumata, Katsuo. "Shūkyō shinri fukkō undo ni okeru Nihon teki bosei no isō: GLAkei shokyōdan no jirei kenkyū yori." *Shūkyō to shakai* 3 (1997): 37–61.

Kwok, Pui-lan. "Unbinding Our Feet: Saving Brown Women and Feminist Religious Discourse." In *Postcolonialism, Feminism and Religious Discourse*, edited by Laura Donaldson and Kwok Pui-lan, 62–81. New York: Routledge, 2002.

Laube, Johannes. *Oyagami: Die heutige Gottesvorstellung der Tenrikyō*. Wiesbaden: Harrassowitz, 1978.

Lee, Lily Xiao Hong. *The Virtue of Yin: Studies on Chinese Women*. Sydney: Wild Peony, 1994.

Li, Michelle Osterfeld. *Ambiguous Bodies: Reading the Grotesque in Japanese Setsuwa Tales*. Stanford: Stanford University Press, 2009.

Lindsey, William. *Fertility and Pleasure: Ritual and Sexual Values in Tokugawa Japan*. Honolulu: University of Hawai'i Press, 2007.

Mackie, Vera. *Feminism in Modern Japan*. Cambridge: Cambridge University Press, 2003.

Mahmood, Saba. *Politics of Piety: The Islamic Revival and the Feminist Subject*. Princeton: Princeton University Press, 2005.

Martin, Dan. "Pearls from Bones: Relics, Chortens, Tertons and the Signs of Saintly Death in Tibet." *Numen* 41, no. 3 (1994): 273–324.

Mass, Jeffrey. *Lordship and Inheritance: A Study of the Kamakura Sōryō System*. Stanford: Stanford University Press, 1989.

Matsumura, Kazuo. "Ancient Japan and Religion." In *Nanzan Guide to Japanese Religions*, edited by Paul Swanson and Clark Chilson, 131–43. Honolulu: University of Hawai'i Press, 2006.

Matsuura, Katherine. "Transformation and Expressions of Grief in Mizuko Kuyō: Mourning the Stillborn and Still-to-Be-Born." M.A. thesis, Duke University, 2010.

McCullough, William. "Japanese Marriage Institutions in the Heian Period." *Harvard Journal of Asiatic Studies* 27 (1967): 103–67.

McLaughlin, Levi. "Did Aum Change Everything?" *Japanese Journal of Religious Studies* 39, no. 1 (2012): 51–75.

———. "Sōka Gakkai in Japan." Ph.D. diss., Princeton University, 2009.

Meeks, Lori. "Buddhist Renunciation and the Female Life Cycle: Understanding Nunhood in Heian and Kamakura Japan." *Harvard Journal of Asiatic Studies* 70, no. 1 (2010): 1–59.

———. "The Disappearing Medium: Reassessing the Place of *Miko* in the Religious Landscape of Premodern Japan." *History of Religions* 50, no. 3 (2011): 208–60.

———. *Hokkeji and the Reemergence of Female Monastic Orders in Premodern Japan*. Honolulu: University of Hawai'i Press, 2010.

———. "Reconfiguring Ritual Authority: The Ordination of Aristocratic Women in Premodern Japan." *Japanese Journal of Religious Studies* 33, no. 1 (2006): 51–74.

Mikoshiba, Daisuke. "Empress Kōmyō's Buddhist Faith: Her Role in the Founding of the State Temple and Convent System." In *Engendering Faith: Women and Buddhism in Premodern Japan*, edited by Barbara Ruch, 21–40. Ann Arbor: University of Michigan Center for Japanese Studies, 2002.

Miller, Laura. "Tantalizing Tarot and Cute Cartomancy in Japan." *Japanese Studies* 31, no. 1 (2011): 73–91.

Mitamura, Engyo. *Goten jochū*. Tokyo: Seiabō, 1982.

Miyake, Hitoshi. "Kingendai no sangaku shūkyō to shugendō: shinbutsu bunrirei to shintō shirei e no taiō o chūshin ni." *Meiji shōtoku kinen gakkai kiyō* 43 (2006): 42–61.

Miyanaga, Kuniko. "Social Reproduction and Transcendence: An Analysis of the Sekai Mahikari Bunmei Kyōdan, a Heterodox Religious Movement in Contemporary Japan." Ph.D. diss., University of British Columbia, 1983.

Miyazaki, Fumiko. "Female Pilgrims and Mt. Fuji: Changing Perspectives on the Exclusion of Women." *Monumenta Nipponica* 60, no. 3 (2005): 339–91.

Mori, Barbara. "The Traditional Arts as Leisure Activities for Contemporary Women." In *Re-imagining Japanese Women*, edited by Anne Imamura, 117–34. Berkeley: University of California Press, 1996.

Morimoto, Kazuhiko. *Senzo saishi to ie no kakuritsu: handanka kara ikka ichiji e.* Kyoto: Minerva Shobō, 2006.

Morrell, Robert. "Mirror for Women: Mujō Ichien's *Tsuma kagami*." *Monumenta Nipponica* 35, no. 1 (1980): 45–74.

Morris, Ivan, trans. *The Pillow Book of Sei Shōnagon*. New York: Columbia University Press, 1967.

Nakamura, Kyōkō Motomochi, ed. and trans. *Miraculous Stories from the Japanese Buddhist Tradition: The Nihon Ryōiki of the Monk Kyōkai*. Cambridge: Harvard University Press, 1973.

Nattier, Jan. "Gender and Hierarchy in the *Lotus Sūtra*." In *Readings of the Lotus Sūtra*, edited by Stephen Teiser and Jacqueline Stone, 83–106. New York: Columbia University Press, 2009.

Nishida, Kahoru. "Miko." In *Minkan ni ikiru shūkyōsha*, edited by Takano Toshihiko, 51–90. Tokyo: Yoshikawa Kōbunkan, 2000.

Nishiguchi, Junko. "Murakumo Nichi'ei." In *Asahi Nihon rekishi jinbutsu jiten*, edited by Asahi Shinbunsha, 1677. Tokyo: Asahi Shinbunsha, 1994.

———. *Onna no chikara: kodai no josei to Bukkyō*. Tokyo: Heibonsha, 1987.

Nishimoto, Toyohiro. "Buta to Nihonjin." In *Hito to dōbutsu no nihon shi*, vol. 1, *Dōbutsu no kōkogaku*, edited by Nishimoto Toyohiro, 215–25. Tokyo: Yoshikawa Kōbunkan, 2008.

Nitta, Mitsuko. "Nihon no shūkyō to mizuko kuyō." In *Mizuko kuyō: gendai shakai no fuan to iyashi*, edited by Takahashi Saburō, 173–206. Kyoto: Kōrosha, 1999.

Nomura, Ikuyo. *Bukkyō to onna no seishinshi*. Tokyo: Yoshikawa Kōbunkan, 2004.

Obara, Hitoshi. "The Rebirth of Women into Paradise: Women in Fujiwara no Munetada's Diary *Chūyūki* (1087–1138)." In *Engendering Faith: Women and Buddhism in Premodern Japan*, edited by Barbara Ruch, 441–62. Ann Arbor: University of Michigan Center for Japanese Studies, 2002.

Odaira, Mika. *Josei shinshoku no kindai*. Tokyo: Perikansha, 2009.

Oguri, Junko. *Nihon no kindai shakai to Tenrikyō*. Tokyo: Hyōronsha, 1969.

Ōhashi, Hidetoshi. "Okinawa shamanizumu no rekishi: yuta kin'atsu no shosō to haikei." *Tōhoku daigaku bungakubu kenkyū nenpō* 32 (1982): 106–41.

Okuda, Akiko. Introduction to *Women and Religion in Japan*, edited by Okuda Akiko and Okano Haruko, 9–16. Wiesbaden: Harrassowitz, 1998.

Ooms, Emily Groszos. *Women and Millenarian Protest in Meiji Japan: Deguchi Nao and Ōmotokyō*. Ithaca: East Asia Program, Cornell University, 1993.

Ōsumi, Kazuo. "Historical Notes on Women and the Japanization of Buddhism." In *Engendering Faith: Women and Buddhism in Premodern Japan*, edited by Barbara Ruch, xxvii–xlii. Ann Arbor: University of Michigan Center for Japanese Studies, 2002.

Parker, Helen. "Women, Christianity, and Internationalism in Early Twentieth-Century Japan: Tsuda Ume, Caroline Macdonald and the Founding of the Young Women's Christian Association in Japan." In *Japanese Women Emerging from Subservience, 1868–1945*, edited by Hiroko Tomida and Gordon Daniels, 178–91. Folkestone: Global Oriental, 2005.

Perkins, Dorothy. *Encyclopedia of China: The Essential Reference to China, Its History and Culture*. New York: Roundtable Press, 2000.

Philippi, Donald, trans. *Kojiki*. Tokyo: University of Tokyo Press, 1989.

Piggott, Joan. *The Emergence of Japanese Kingship*. Stanford: Stanford University Press, 1997.

Robertson, Jennifer. "The Shingaku Woman: Straight from the Heart." In *Recreating Japanese Women, 1600–1945*, edited by Gail Lee Bernstein, 88–107. Berkeley: University of California Press, 1992.

Rowe, Mark. *Bonds of the Dead: Temples, Burial, and the Transformation of Contemporary Japanese Buddhism*. Chicago: University of Chicago Press, 2011.

———. "Grave Changes: Scattering Ashes in Contemporary Japan." *Japanese Journal of Religious Studies* 30, nos. 1–2 (2003): 85–118.

Ruch, Barbara. "Woman to Woman: *Kumano bikuni* Proselytizers in Medieval and Early Modern Japan." In *Engendering Faith: Women and Buddhism in Premodern Japan*, edited by Barbara Ruch, 537–89. Ann Arbor: University of Michigan Center for Japanese Studies, 2002.

Ruppert, Brian. *Jewel in the Ashes: Buddha Relics and Power in Early Medieval Japan*. Cambridge: Harvard University Asia Center, 2000.

Sakurai, Yoshihide. "Gendai Nihon shakai to supirichuariti būmu." In *Karuto to supiritchuariti: gendai Nihon ni okeru "sukui" to "iyashi" no yukue*, edited by Sakurai Yoshihide, 245–75. Kyoto: Minerva Shobō, 2009.

———. *Rei to kane: supiricharu bijinesu no kōzō*. Tokyo: Shinchōsha, 2009.

Sansom, George. "Early Japanese Law and Administration." Pt. 2. *Transactions of the Asiatic Society of Japan*, 2nd ser., 11 (1934): 117–49.

Sawada, Janine. *Confucian Values and Popular Zen: Sekimon Shingaku in Eighteenth Century Japan*. Honolulu: University of Hawai'i Press, 1993.

———. "Sexual Relations as Religious Practice in the Late Tokugawa Period: Fujidō." *Journal of Japanese Studies* 32, no. 2 (2006): 341–66.

Seiwert, Hubert. *Popular Religious Movements and Heterodox Sects in Chinese History*. Leiden: Brill, 2003.

Sekiguchi, Hiroko. "The Patriarchal Family Paradigm in Eighth-Century Japan." In *Women and Confucian Cultures in Premodern China, Korea, and Japan*, edited by Dorothy Ko, JaHyun Kim Haboush, and Joan Piggott, 27–46. Berkeley: University of California Press, 2003.

Sekiguchi, Sumiko. "Confucian Morals and the Making of a 'Good Wife and Wise Mother': From 'Between Husband and Wife There Is Distinction' to 'As Husbands and Wives Be Harmonious.'" *Social Science Japan Journal* 13, no. 1 (2010): 95–113.

———. "Gender in the Meiji Renovation: Confucian 'Lessons for Women' and the Making of Modern Japan." *Social Science Japan Journal* 11, no. 2 (2008): 201–21.

Shibahara, Takeo. "Through Americanized Japanese Woman's Eyes: Tsuda Umeko and the Women's Movement in Japan in the 1910s." *Journal of Asia Pacific Studies* 1, no. 2 (2010): 225–34.

Shimazono, Susumu. *From Salvation to Spirituality: Popular Religious Movements in Modern Japan*. Melbourne: Transpacific Press, 2004.

———. *Supirichuariti no kōryū: shinreisei bunka to sono shūhen*. Tokyo: Iwanami Shoten, 2007.

Shitara, Hiromi. "Jōmonjin no dōbutsukan." In *Hito to dōbutsu no nihon shi*, vol. 1, *Dōbutsu no kōkogaku*, edited by Nishimoto Toyohiro, 10–34. Tokyo: Yoshikawa Kōbunkan, 2008.

Sievers, Sharon. *Flowers in Salt: The Beginnings of Feminist Consciousness in Modern Japan*. Stanford: Stanford University Press, 1983.

Skord, Virginia. *Tales of Tears and Laughter: Short Fiction of Medieval Japan*. Honolulu: University of Hawai'i Press, 1991.

Smith, Bardwell. *Narratives of Sorrow and Dignity: Japanese Women, Pregnancy Loss, and Modern Rituals of Grieving*. New York: Oxford University Press, 2013.

Smith, Robert. "Wedding and Funeral Ritual: Analysing a Moving Target." In *Ceremony and Ritual in Japan: Religious Practices in an Industrialized Society*, edited by Jan van Bremen and Dolores P. Martinez, 25–37. London: Routledge, 1995.

Sonoda, Kōyū. "Early Buddha Worship." In *The Cambridge History of Japan*, vol. 1, *Ancient Japan*, edited by Delmer Brown, 359–414. Cambridge: Cambridge University Press, 1993.

Stanley, Amy. *Selling Women: Prostitution, and the Household in Early Modern Japan*. Berkeley: University of California Press, 2012.

Starling, Jessica. "A Family of Clerics: Temple Wives, Tradition and Change in Contemporary Jōdo Shinshū Temples." Ph.D. diss., University of Virginia, 2012.

Stevenson, Miwa, trans. "The Founding of the Monastery Gangōji and a List of Its Treasures." In *Religions of Japan in Practice*, edited by George Tanabe, 299–315. Princeton: Princeton University Press, 1999.

Sugano, Noriko. "State Indoctrination of Filial Piety in Tokugawa Japan: Sons and Daughters in the *Official Records of Filial Piety.*" In *Women and Confucian Cultures in Premodern China, Korea, and Japan*, edited by Dorothy Ko, JaHyun Kim Haboush, and Joan Piggott, 170–89. Berkeley: University of California Press, 2003.

Suzuki, Kentarō. "Divination in Contemporary Japan." *Japanese Journal of Religious Studies* 22, nos. 3–4 (1995): 249–66.

Tabata, Yasuko. "Female Attendants and Wives of the Medieval Warrior Class." In *Gender and Japanese History*, vol. 2, edited by Wakita Haruko, Anne Bouchy, and Ueno Chizuko, 313–47. Osaka: Osaka University Press, 1999.

Teeuwen, Mark. "The Creation of a *honji suijaku* Deity: Amaterasu as the Judge of the Dead." In *Buddhas and* kami *in Japan*: Honji suijaku *as a Combinatory Paradigm*, edited by Mark Teeuwen and Fabio Rambelli, 115–44. New York: RoutledgeCurzon, 2003.

Tenrikyō Church Headquarters, ed. *A Short History of Tenrikyō*. Tenri City: Headquarters of Tenrikyō Church, 1958.

Tensho-Kotai-Jingu-Kyo. *Prophet of Tabuse*. Tabuse: Tensho Kotai Jingu Kyo, 1954.

Toby, Ronald. "Why Leave Nara? Kammu and the Transfer of the Capital." *Monumenta Nipponica* 40, no. 3 (1985): 331–47.

Tocco, Martha. "Norms and Texts for Women's Education in Tokugawa Japan." In *Women and Confucian Cultures in Premodern China, Korea, and Japan*, edited by Dorothy Ko, JaHyun Kim Haboush, and Joan Piggott, 193–218. Berkeley: University of California Press, 2003.

Tonomura, Hitomi. "Coercive Sex in the Medieval Japanese Court: Lady Nijō's Memoir." *Monumenta Nipponica* 61, no. 3 (2006): 283–338.

———. "Re-envisioning Women in the Post-Kamakura Age." In *The Origins of Japan's Medieval World: Courtiers, Clerics, Warriors, and Peasants in the Fourteenth Century*, edited by Jeffrey Mass, 138–69. Stanford: Stanford University Press, 1997.

Toshitani, Nobuyoshi. "The Reform of Japanese Family Law and Changes in the Family System." *U.S.-Japan Women's Journal*, English supplement, 6 (1994): 66–82.

Tsuda, Ume. *The Attic Letters: Ume Tsuda's Correspondence to Her American Mother*. Edited by Furuki Yoshiko. New York: Weatherhill, 1991.

———. *Woman's Life in Japan*. Philadelphia: Board of Foreign Missions, Reformed Church in the United States, n.d.

Tucker, Mary Evelyn. "Kaibara Ekken." In *Sources of Japanese Tradition*, vol. 2, *1600–1868*, compiled by William Theodore de Bary, Carol Gluck, and Arthur E. Tiedemann, 222–35. New York: Columbia University Press, 2006.

Uchino, Kumiko. "The Status Elevation Process of Sōtō Sect Nuns in Modern Japan." *Japanese Journal of Religious Studies* 10, nos. 2–3 (1983): 177–94.

Ueno, Chizuko. "In the Feminine Guise: A Trap of Reverse Orientalism." *U.S.-Japan Women's Journal*, English supplement, 13 (1997): 3–25.

Uno, Kathleen. "The Death of 'Good Wife, Wise Mother.' " In *Postwar Japan as History*, edited by Andrew Gordon, 293–322. Berkeley: University of California Press, 1993.

———. "Womanhood, War and Empire: Transmutations of 'Good Wife, Wise Mother' before 1931." In *Gendering Modern Japanese History*, edited by Barbara Molony and Kathleen Uno, 493–519. Cambridge: Harvard University Asia Center, 2005.

Ury, Marian, trans. *Tales of Times Now Past: Sixty-Two Stories from a Medieval Japanese Collection*. Ann Arbor: Center for Japanese Studies, 1979.

Ushiyama, Yoshiyuki. "Buddhist Convents in Medieval Japan." In *Engendering Faith: Women and Buddhism in Premodern Japan*, edited by Barbara Ruch, 131–64. Ann Arbor: University of Michigan Center for Japanese Studies, 2002.

Usui, Atsuko. "Women's 'Experience' in New Religious Movements: The Case of Shinnyoen." *Japanese Journal of Religious Studies* 30, nos. 3–4 (2003): 217–41.

Vaporis, Constantine. *Breaking Barriers: Travel and the State in Early Modern Japan*. Cambridge: Council on East Asian Studies, Harvard University, 1994.

Wakita, Haruko. "The Medieval Household and Gender Roles within the Imperial Family, Nobility, Merchants, and Commoners." In *Women and Class in Japanese History*, edited by Tonomura Hitomi, Anne Walthall, and Wakita Haruko, 81–98. Ann Arbor: Center for Japanese Studies, University of Michigan, 1999.

Walthall, Anne. "The Life Cycle of Farm Women in Tokugawa Japan." In *Recreating Japanese Women, 1600–1945*, edited by Gail Lee Bernstein, 42–70. Berkeley: University of California Press, 1991.

———. "Preparation for Marriage through Service in Households of the Great: The Late Tokugawa Period." *Annual Report of the Institute for International Studies* (Meijigakuin University) 11 (2008): 105–15.

———. *The Weak Body of a Useless Woman: Matsuo Taseko and the Meiji Restoration*. Chicago: University of Chicago Press, 1998.

Ward, Haruko. "Jesuits, Too: Jesuits, Women Catechists and Jezebels in Christian-Century Japan." In *The Jesuits II: Cultures, Sciences, and the Arts, 1540–1773*, edited by John W. O'Malley, Gauvin Alexander Bailey, Stephen J. Harris, and T. Frank Kennedy, 638–57. Toronto: University of Toronto Press, 2006.

———. *Women Religious Leaders in Japan's Christian Century, 1549–1650*. Burlington, VT: Ashgate, 2009.

Watson, Burton, trans. *The Lotus Sutra*. New York: Columbia University Press, 1993.

Welter, Barbara. "The Cult of True Womanhood: 1820–1860." *American Quarterly* 18, no. 2.1 (1966): 151–74.

Whelan, Christal. "Religious Responses to Globalization in Japan: The Case of the God Light Association." Ph.D. diss., Boston University, 2007.

Whelan, Christal. "Shifting Paradigms and Mediating Media: Redefining a New Religion as 'Rational' in Contemporary Society." *Nova Religio* 10, no. 3 (2006): 54–72.

Williams, Duncan Ryūken. "Funerary Zen: Sōtō Zen Death Management in Tokugawa Japan." In *Death and the Afterlife in Japanese Buddhism*, edited by Jacqueline I. Stone and Mariko Namba Walter, 207–46. Honolulu: University of Hawai'i Press, 2008.

Winkler, Christian. *The Quest for Japan's New Constitution: An Analysis of Visions and Constitutional Reform Proposals, 1980–2009.* London: Routledge, 2011.

Wöhr, Ulrike. *Frauen und die neuen Religionen: Die Religionsbegründerinnen Nakayama Miki und Deguchi Nao.* Vienna: Universität Wien Institut für Japanologie, 1989.

Wright, Diana. "The Power of Religion/the Religion of Power: Religious Activities as *Upaya* for Women of the Edo Period—The Case of Mantokuji." Ph.D. diss., University of Toronto, 1996.

Yamamoto, Sharon. "Visual and Material Culture at Hōkyōji Imperial Convent: The Significance of 'Women's Art' in Early Modern Japan." Ph.D. diss., University of California at Berkeley, 2010.

Yamashita, Akiko. "Tenrin-o and Henjo-nanshi: Two Women Founders of New Religions." *Japanese Religions* 25, no. 1 (2002): 89–103.

Yang, Sunyoung. "Kantō daishinsai to baishō undō: Nihon Kirisutokyō fujin kyōfūkai no katsudō o chūshin ni." *Kokuritsu josei kyōiku kaikan kenkyū kiyō* 9 (2005): 95–105.

Yasutake, Rumi. "Transnational Women's Activism: The Woman's Christian Temperance Union in Japan and Beyond, 1858–1920." Ph.D. diss., University of California, Los Angeles, 1998.

Yoshida, Atsuhiko. "The Beginning of the Cult of Mother Earth in Europe and in Japan." In *Women and Religion*, 341–57. Tenri City: Tenri Jihosha, 2003.

Yoshida, Kazuhiko. "The Enlightenment of the Dragon King's Daughter in the *Lotus Sutra.*" In *Engendering Faith: Women and Buddhism in Premodern Japan*, edited by Barbara Ruch, 297–324. Ann Arbor: University of Michigan Center for Japanese Studies, 2002.

Yoshie, Akiko. "Tamayori saikō: *Imo no chikara* hihan." In *Miko to joshin*, edited by Ōsumi Kazuo and Nishiguchi Junko, 51–90. Tokyo: Heibonsha, 1989.

———. "When Antiquity Meets the Modern: Representing Female Rulers in the Making of Japanese History." Paper presented at the Conference of the International Federation for Research in Women's History: Women's History Revisited—Historiographical Reflections on Women and Gender in a Global Context, Sydney, Australia, 9 July 2005. http://www.historians.ie/women/Akiko.pdf.

Yoshikawa, Shinji. "Ladies-in-Waiting in the Heian Period." In *Gender and Japanese History*, vol. 2, edited by Wakita Haruko, Anne Bouchy, and Ueno Chizuko, 283–311. Osaka: Osaka University Press, 1999.

Young, Richard. "Magic and Morality in Modern Japanese Exorcistic Technologies: A Study of Mahikari." *Japanese Journal of Religious Studies* 17, no. 1 (1990): 29–49.

Young, Serinity, ed. *An Anthology of Sacred Texts by and about Women.* New York: Crossroad, 1993.

Yusa, Michiko. "Women in Shinto: Images Remembered." In *Women and Religion,* edited by Arvind Sharma, 93–119. Albany: State University of New York Press, 1994.

FOR FURTHER READING

The following primary sources in translation can be paired with each chapter. Additional resources can be found on the companion website: http://nyupress.org/ambros.

CHAPTER 1. THE PREHISTORICAL JAPANESE ARCHIPELAGO
Aston, William George, trans. *Nihongi: Chronicles of Japan from the Earliest Times to A.D. 697*. Rutland, VT: Charles Tuttle, 1972. Pages 1:32–33 contain the story of Tsukiyomi slaying the food goddess Ukemochi.

de Bary, William Theodore, et al. "Japan in the Chinese Dynastic Histories." In *Sources of Japanese Tradition*, vol. 1, *From Earliest Times to 1600*, compiled by William Theodore de Bary, Donald Keene, George Tanabe, and Paul Varley, 5–13. New York: Columbia University Press, 2001.

Philippi, Donald, trans. *Kojiki*. Tokyo: University of Tokyo Press, 1989. Page 87 contains the story of Susanoo slaying the food goddess Ōgetsuhime.

CHAPTER 2. ANCIENT JAPANESE MYTHOLOGY
Bock, Felicia, trans. "*Engi-shiki*, Book V: Bureau of the Consecrated Imperial Princess." In *Engishiki: Procedures of the Engi Era, Books I–V*, 151–54. Tokyo: Sophia University, 1970.

———. "Introduction to the Translation: *Engi-shiki*, Book V: Bureau of the Consecrated Imperial Princess." In *Engishiki: Procedures of the Engi Era, Books I–V*, 51–56. Tokyo: Sophia University, 1970. Introduction to the chapter on the office of the high priestess at the Ise Shrines.

de Bary, William Theodore, et al. "The Earliest Japanese Chronicles" and "Legends Concerning Shinto Deities." In *Sources of Japanese Tradition*, vol. 1, *From Earliest Times to 1600*, compiled by William Theodore de Bary, Donald Keene, George Tanabe, and Paul Varley, 13–31. New York: Columbia University Press, 2001.

Philippi, Donald, trans. "Grand Shrine of Ise: When the High Priestess Assumes Her Office." In *Norito: A Translation of the Ancient Ritual Prayers*, 66. Princeton: Princeton University Press, 1990.

CHAPTER 3. THE INTRODUCTION OF BUDDHISM
Nakamura, Kyōkō Motomochi, ed. and trans. *Miraculous Stories from the Japanese Buddhist Tradition: The Nihon Ryōiki of the Monk Kyōkai*. Cambridge: Harvard University Press, 1973. See stories 1.13, 1.35, 2.4, 2.8, 2.11, 2.12, 2.14, 2.27, 2.28, 2.30, 2.41, 2.42, 3.11, and 3.34.

Stevenson, Miwa, trans. "The Founding of the Monastery Gangōji and a List of Its Treasures." In *Religions of Japan in Practice*, edited by George Tanabe, 299–315. Princeton: Princeton University Press, 1999.

Young, Serinity, ed. *An Anthology of Sacred Texts by and about Women*. New York: Crossroad, 1993. Pages 317–23 in the Buddhism chapter contain key passages from the Devadatta and Avalokiteśvara chapters of the *Lotus Sutra*, the encounter between the goddess and Śāriputra in the *Vimalakīrti Sutra*, and the prophecy of Queen Śrīmālā's Buddhahood in the *Śrīmālā Sutra*.

CHAPTER 4. THE HEIAN PERIOD

Bock, Felicia, trans. "*Engi-shiki*, Book VI: Procedures for the Saiin-shi, Office of the Princess Consecrated to the Kamo Shrines." In *Engishiki: Procedures of the Engi Era, Books VI–X*, 9–14. Tokyo: Sophia University, 1972.

———. "Introduction to Book VI: The Princess Consecrated to the Kamo Shrines." In *Engishiki: Procedures of the Engi Era, Books VI–X*, 1–8. Tokyo: Sophia University, 1972.

Bowring, Richard, trans. *The Diary of Lady Murasaki*. New York: Penguin, 1996. A description of an exorcism is found on pages 7–13.

Deal, William. "Women and Japanese Buddhism: Tales of Birth in the Pure Land." In *Religions of Japan in Practice*, edited by George Tanabe, 176–84. Princeton: Princeton University Press, 1999.

Dykstra, Yoshiko. *Miraculous Tales of the Lotus Sutra from Ancient Japan*. Honolulu: University of Hawai'i Press, 1983. See 3:98–100 and 3:117–24.

Nakamura, Kyōko Motomochi, trans. *Miraculous Stories from the Japanese Buddhist Tradition: The Nihon Ryōiki of the Monk Kyōkai*. Cambridge: Harvard University Press, 1973. See 2.33 for a story on sexual violence against a woman perpetrated by a male demon.

Seidensticker, Edward, trans. "Heartvine." In *The Tale of Genji*, 174–80. New York: Knopf, 1992.

Tyler, Royall, trans. *Japanese Tales*. New York: Pantheon, 1987. For early examples of the demonization of women in the *Konjaku monogatari*, see "The Grisly Box" and "The Bridge."

Ury, Marian, trans. *Tales of Times Now Past: Sixty-Two Stories from a Medieval Japanese Collection*. Berkeley: University of California Press, 1979. For early examples of the demonization of women in the *Konjaku monogatari*, see "How a Monk of Dōjōji in the Province of Kii Copied the *Lotus Sutra* and Brought Salvation to Serpents," "How a Woman Who Was Bearing a Child Went to South Yamashina, Encountered an *Oni*, and Escaped," and "How the Hunter's Mother Became an *Oni* and Tried to Devour Her Children."

CHAPTER 5. THE MEDIEVAL PERIOD

de Bary, William Theodore, et al. "Women's Education." In *Sources of Japanese Tradition*, vol. 1, *From Earliest Times to 1600*, compiled by William Theodore de Bary, Donald Keene, George Tanabe, and Paul Varley, 399–412. New York: Columbia University Press, 2001.

Elisonas, Jurgis. "The Evangelic Furnace: Japan's First Encounter with the West." In *Sources of Japanese Tradition*, vol. 2, *1600–2000*, pt. 1, *1600–1868*, compiled by William Theodore de Bary, Carol Gluck, and Arthur E. Tiedemann, 127–57. New York: Columbia University Press, 2006. See especially "A Jesuit Priest's Observations of Women" and an excerpt from *Myōtei mondō* in "Fabian Fucan Pro and Contra."

Kleine, Christoph, and Livia Kohn, trans. "The Nun Toran." In "Daoist Immortality and Buddhist Holiness: A Study and Translation of the Honchō shinsen-den." *Japanese Religion* 24, no. 2 (1999): 154–55.

Strong, John, ed. "Women and the Sangha: Nichiren on Chanting and Menstruation." In *The Experience of Buddhism: Sources and Interpretations*, 332–34. Belmont, CA: Wadsworth, 2008.

Takemi, Momoko, trans. "Bussetsu Mokuren shōkyō ketsubon kyō." In "Menstruation Sutra Belief in Japan." *Japanese Journal of Religious Studies* 10, nos. 2–3 (1983): 230–32.

Tyler, Royall, trans. *The Miracles of the Kasuga Deity*. New York: Columbia University Press, 1990. See stories 4.4, 4.5, 6.3, 10.1, and 15.5.

Ury, Marian, trans. "Section 18:3: (The Nun Toran)." In "*Genkō shakusho*: Japan's First Comprehensive History of Buddhism," 312–13. Ph.D. diss., University of California at Berkeley, 1970.

CHAPTER 6. THE EDO PERIOD

Goodwin, Janet, et al. "Solitary Thoughts: A Translation of Tadano Makuzu's *Hitori Kangae* (1)." *Monumenta Nipponica* 56, no. 1 (2001): 21–38.

Hardacre, Helen. "The New Religions: Tenrikyō." In *Sources of Japanese Tradition*, vol. 2, *1600–2000*, pt. 2, *1868–2000*, compiled by William Theodore de Bary, Carol Gluck, and Arthur E. Tiedemann, 421–31. New York: Columbia University Press, 2006.

Kaneko, Sachiko, and Robert Morrell, trans. "Tokeiji: Kamakura's 'Divorce Temple' in Edo Popular Verse." In *Religions of Japan in Practice*, edited by George Tanabe, 523–50. Princeton: Princeton University Press, 1999.

Reader, Ian, Esben Andreasen, and Finn Stefánsson, eds. "From the *Ofudesaki* of Nakayama Miki" and "The Shrine of Tsukihi." In *Japanese Religions: Past and Present*, 128–31. Honolulu: University of Hawai'i Press, 1993.

Tucker, Mary Evelyn. "The Great Learning for Women (*Onna Daigaku*)." In *Sources of Japanese Tradition*, vol. 2, *1600–2000*, pt. 1, *1600–1868*, compiled by William Theodore de Bary, Carol Gluck, and Arthur E. Tiedemann, 229–35. New York: Columbia University Press, 2006.

CHAPTER 7. IMPERIAL JAPAN

Craig, Albert. "Enlightenment Thinkers of the Meirokusha: On Marriage." In *Sources of Japanese Tradition*, vol. 2, *1600–2000*, pt. 2, *1868–2000*, compiled by William Theodore de Bary, Carol Gluck, and Arthur E. Tiedemann, 42–49. New York: Columbia University Press, 2006.

Furuki, Yoshiko, Akiko Ueda, and Mary Althaus, eds. *Tsuda Umeko Monjo: The Writings of Umeko Tsuda*. Tokyo: Tsudajuku Daigaku, 1984. See especially pages 33–38, 49–64, 69–92, and 503–6.

Hardacre, Helen. "The New Religions: Ōmoto." In *Sources of Japanese Tradition*, vol. 2, *1600–2000*, pt. 2, *1868–2000*, compiled by William Theodore de Bary, Carol Gluck, and Arthur E. Tiedemann, 431–38. New York: Columbia University Press, 2006.

Jaffe, Richard, trans. "A Refutation of Clerical Marriage." In *Religions of Japan in Practice*, edited by George Tanabe, 78–86. Princeton: Princeton University Press, 1999.

Rubinger, Richard. "The Education of Women in the Meiji Period." In *Sources of Japanese Tradition*, vol. 2, *1600–2000*, pt. 2, *1868–2000*, compiled by William Theodore de Bary, Carol Gluck, and Arthur E. Tiedemann, 115–16. New York: Columbia University Press, 2006.

———. "Imperial Rescript on Education." In *Sources of Japanese Tradition*, vol. 2, *1600–2000*, pt. 2, *1868–2000*, compiled by William Theodore de Bary, Carol Gluck, and Arthur E. Tiedemann, 779–81. New York: Columbia University Press, 2006.

CHAPTER 8. THE POSTWAR PERIOD

Davis, Winston. "A Single Woman's Experience of Possession and Healing in Mahikari." In *Religion in the Japanese Experience: Sources and Interpretations*, edited by H. Byron Earhart, 288–90. Belmont, CA: Wadsworth, 1997.

Hardacre, Helen. *Lay Buddhism in Contemporary Japan: Reiyūkai Kyōdan*. Princeton: Princeton University Press, 1984. For Reiyūkai women's first-person testimonials, see "Text 38, 1:42–47" (pages 189–93) and "Text 116, 2:72–75" (pages 212–15).

King, Sallie, trans. "Awakening Stories of Zen Buddhist Women." In *Buddhism in Practice*, edited by Donald Lopez, 513–24. Princeton: Princeton University Press, 1995.

LaFleur, William, trans. "Buddhism and Abortion: 'The Way to Memorialize One's *Mizuko*.'" In *Religions of Japan in Practice*, edited by George Tanabe, 193–96. Princeton: Princeton University Press, 1999.

Pratt, Cherish. "The Shinto Wedding Ceremony: A Modern *Norito*." In *Religions of Japan in Practice*, edited by George Tanabe, 135–38. Princeton: Princeton University Press, 1999.

Reader, Ian, Esben Andreasen, and Finn Stefánsson, eds. "How Does Mahikari, the Divine Spiritual Radiation, Change Our Daily Lives?" In *Japanese Religions: Past and Present*, 151–52. Honolulu: University of Hawai'i Press, 1993.

CHAPTER 9. THE LOST DECADES

de Bary, Brett. "Postwar Japanese Feminism." In *Sources of Japanese Tradition*, vol. 2, *1600–2000*, pt. 2, *1868–2000*, compiled by William Theodore de Bary, Carol Gluck, and Arthur E. Tiedemann, 488–504. New York: Columbia University Press, 2006.

GLA. GLA: Discover Your Soul—The Power to Live into the Future. http://www.gla -intl.com/. GLA website in English.

Kawahashi, Noriko. "Feminist Buddhism as Praxis: Women in Traditional Buddhism." *Japanese Journal of Religious Studies* 30, nos. 3–4 (2003): 291–313.

Naito, Yuko. "Psychic Knowledge to a Degree." *Japan Times*, 19 February 2000. http:// www.japantimes.co.jp/community/2000/02/10/general/psychic-knowledge-to-a -degree/#.UthBVP3Mz6o.

Noracom Doubutsu Uranai Premium. http://world.doubutsu-uranai.com/. Animal divination website in English.

Shinnyo. http://www.shinnyoen.org/. Shinnyoen website in English.

INDEX

abortion, 149–52, 168–69
abstinence keepers, 18, 20, 64–65.
  See also pollution
adopted heirs, 59, 105, 124
adultery, 24–25, 57
Agatainukai Tachibana no Michiyo, 48
Amaterasu (sun deity), 1, 23; Ame no
  Uzume and, 108; children of, 31–32;
  creation of, 29; Ise Shrines of, 14–15,
  17, 26, 35–38; Izanami/Izanagi and,
  26, 30; Susanoo and, 7–8, 30–36, 38
Amaterasu Ōmikami, 109, 143
Ame no Uzume, 33–34, 108
Amitābha Buddha, 66, 68–71, 84. *See also*
  Pure Land Buddhism
ancestor veneration, 74, 144–45, 167
Asian financial crisis (1990s), 154
Aum Shinrikyō, 154, 162, 167, 168
Avalokiteśvara, 68, 70, 87, 110

Ban Zhao, 24
Benevolent King's Sutra, 65
Bidatsu, Emperor, 40, 43
Biography of the Goddess Miyabi, 108
Blood Pool Sutra, 85–89, 174–75
Book of Rites, 24, 107. *See also*
  Confucianism
Buddhism, 5, 22–23, 40–55; femi-
  nist movement and, 159–60; Five
  Obstructions of, 53–55, 66, 84–85;
  God Light Association and, 165; kami
  worship and, 44, 115, 123–24; linguis-
  tic taboos of, 37–38, 64–65; *mizuko*
  memorial rites in, 150–52; nuns of,

40–45, 47; popular spread of, 51–54;
  prelates of, 46; reform movements of,
  82–83, 121–25, 137–40; relic veneration in, 41–42, 74, 83; royal patronage
  of, 45–51, 62, 65–66, 71, 73; soteriol-
  ogy of, 47–48, 66–70, 83–88, 175,
  190n20. *See also specific sects*
burial associations, 157, 174
burial customs, 9–10, 13, 19, 29, 32, 68,
  86, 157, 173

chastity, 25, 57, 103–104; Christian vows
  of, 94, 95; Confucian view of, 19, 81,
  102, 105; mutual, 116; patrilineal
  households and, 72, 77
childbirth rituals, 9–10, 62, 74, 113,
  149–52
China, 9, 11–12, 18–19; Buddhism in,
  22–23, 43, 80, 82; concubinage in, 87;
  convents in, 82; Japanese war with,
  118; marriage in, 58, 103; shaman-
  ism in, 13, 94; women's education in,
  102–103
Chingen, 67–68
Christianity, 118, 128, 150; feminist
  movement and, 159; God Light
  Association and, 165; introduction
  of, 79, 94–96; legalization of, 115;
  wedding ceremonies of, 156–57;
  women's organizations of, 119,
  124–25
Chūai, Emperor, 16
Civil Code (1898), 117–18, 128–29, 173
Como, Michael, 29, 34

ABOUT THE AUTHOR

Barbara R. Ambros is Associate Professor in the Department of Religious Studies at the University of North Carolina at Chapel Hill. She is the author of *Bones of Contention: Animals and Religion in Contemporary Japan* and *Emplacing a Pilgrimage: The Ōyama Cult and Regional Religion in Early Modern Japan*.